"Can Acts teach us about modern church life? Andy Chambers says, 'Yes indeed,' and shows us how its portrait can enliven the church. It is a book worth reading with ideas worth implementing."

Darrell Bock, Research Professor of New Testament Studies, Professor of Spiritual Development and Culture, Dallas Theological Seminary

"Today pastors spend a great deal of time scanning the shelves of Amazon or brick-and-mortar bookstores for the next church-growth or missional 'magic bullet,' longing for help in building their communities of faith. Yet a rich repository of insights on church life, health, and mission lies, often untapped, in the pages of the Book of Books itself. As Andy Chambers demonstrates, in the summary narratives of Acts Luke—theologian, historian, and churchman—teaches us how the first followers of Jesus lived life together as the church in the first century and, consequently, how Christian community can be lived out today. In Chambers's *Exemplary Life* you can find help for building the modern church on an ancient and rock-solid foundation."

George H. Guthrie, Benjamin W. Perry Professor of Bible, Union University

"Far too many approaches to the book of Acts treat it merely as authoritative church history. Andy Chambers firmly believes that the book of Acts is deeply relevant to the church and to the Christian life in our contemporary age. His thorough study of Acts will be of great benefit to the church, and I warmly welcome the publication of this book."

R. Albert Mohler Jr., President, The Southern Baptist Theological Seminary

"Andy Chambers puts forward a persuasive thesis that a major purpose of Acts was to portray the ideal church. This has often been maintained for the 'summaries' of church life in chapters 1–5, but Chambers shows how the same characteristics of the earliest Jerusalem churches are consistently shown in both Jewish and Gentiles churches throughout Acts. Academics will find his research on the Lukan summaries particularly informative. Pastors seeking help in rejuvenating their churches will find quite useful his full summaries of the main traits of life in the churches of Acts."

John Polhill, Senior Professor of New Testament Interpretation, The Southern Baptist Theological Seminary

"There are a lot of great exegetical books on the Acts of the Apostles and plenty of books on contemporary church life that utilize Acts. However, far too few books bridge the gap between scholarship and the needs of the church today. Andy Chambers in his book *Exemplary Life* seeks to close that gap by showing how Luke embedded a vision for exemplary church life within his narrative. He demonstrates how Luke was deeply concerned to show Christ's followers a portrait of what life together could be like and how they could shape their own churches after the apostolic pattern. This volume helps us hear Luke's distinctive voice on the church alongside other Bible authors. I highly recommend it."

Thom Rainer, president and CEO, LifeWay Christian Resources

"Andy Chambers argues that the three 'summary narratives' that describe the life of the early church in Acts are more than mere summary. Against earlier approaches that have tended to create and enforce a distance between text and life, Chambers invites us to a view of these passages through the lens of narrative technique in a rhetorical strategy that closes that distance. The summaries describe *and* recommend. Chambers has done readers of Acts a great service. His work provides a strong and welcome encouragement and guidance for theologically mindful and energetic contemporary expressions of church life today."

Brian Rapske, Professor of New Testament Studies at ACTS Seminaries/Trinity Western University

"Andy Chambers believes we have underemphasized Luke's voice in our efforts to think biblically about church life in the twenty-first century. He reminds us that Luke was more than a church historian when he wrote the book of Acts. Luke partnered with Paul in the ministry of planting and strengthening churches. Chambers argues that Acts is about going and *gathering* as well as going and *telling*, because Luke shows gospel preaching resulting in local churches. Luke's missiology cannot be separated from his ecclesiology. In a day of tremendous upheaval and debate over what church life should look like, we need a book that brings Luke's voice back into the conversation. Chambers's volume does just that."

Ed Stetzer, author, *Subversive Kingdom*, www.edstetzer.com

"Andy Chambers's *Exemplary Life* aims to help churches recoup from Acts a first-century fervor and model for church life today. The book is well researched, insists on the historicity of Acts, and makes use of current literary approaches to Acts. The book's 20 points of application are fundamentally practical and helpful. To those churches that are already practicing these essentials, I would exclaim, 'Press on!' To those churches that are not doing these things, I would ask, 'Why not?' This book is worth your while."

Terry L. Wilder, Professor of New Testament, Chair of the Biblical Studies Division, Southwestern Baptist Theological Seminary

"Andy Chambers profoundly furthers the recovery of theological interpretation within evangelicalism. Surpassing problematic modernist, historicist readings of Scripture, he treats the book of Acts as the work of a theologian, even while remaining fully conversant with the best scholarship. In lucid language, Chambers provides a compelling argument that Luke's rhetorical strategy is to illuminate a model for the church's life before God and the world. I highly recommend this volume for pastors and academics, as well as their students."

Malcolm B. Yarnell III, Professor of Systematic Theology and Director of the Center for Theological Research, Southwestern Baptist Theological Seminary

"There are a host of books about the book of Acts that fail to capture the essence of 'why' the church (and its mission) is important to New Testament disciples. In many works, there exists too much proof-texting for preconceived systems about contemporary church life. The missing ingredient is the historical perspective that demonstrates an exemplary church in Acts that is the fertile soil for proclaiming the gospel and making disciples in every culture, race, and nation. Dr. Chambers's twenty characteristics of the exemplary church are a unique contribution to the theology of the church and provide a measurement for a local church's fulfillment of purpose. *Exemplary Life* is a must read for the genuine church statesman/woman who wants to be engaged in God's movement for these times."

John L. Yeats, Executive Director of the Missouri Baptist Convention Recording Secretary of the Southern Baptist Convention

EXEMPLARY LIFE

EXEMPLARY LIFE

A Theology of Church Life in Acts

ANDY CHAMBERS

ACADEMIC

Nashville, Tennessee

CONTENTS

Bible Translation Abbreviations

CEV . . . . . . Contemporary English
Version
ESV . . . . . . English Standard
Version
GNT . . . . . . Good News Translation
HCSB . . . . . Holman Christian
Standard Bible
KJV . . . . . . King James Version
LXX . . . . . . Septuagint
MSG . . . . . . The Message
NAB . . . . . . New American Bible
NASB . . . . . New American
Standard Bible

NCV . . . . . . New Century Version
NIV . . . . . . New International
Version
NJB . . . . . . New Jerusalem Bible
NKJV . . . . . New King James
Version
NLT . . . . . . New Living Translation
NRSV . . . . . New Revised Standard
Version
RSV . . . . . . Revised Standard
Version

Bible Book Abbreviations

Gen . . . . Genesis
Exod . . . . Exodus
Lev . . . . Leviticus
Num . . . . Numbers
Deut . . . . Deuteronomy
Josh . . . . Joshua
Judg . . . . Judges
Ruth . . . . Ruth
1 Sam . . . . 1 Samuel
2 Sam . . . . 2 Samuel
1 Kgs . . . . 1 Kings
2 Kgs . . . . 2 Kings
1 Chr. . . . . 1 Chronicles
2 Chr. . . . . 2 Chronicles
Ezra . . . . Ezra
Neh. . . . . Nehemiah
Esth . . . . Esther
Job . . . . Job
Ps(s) . . . . Psalms
Prov . . . . Proverbs

Eccl . . . . Ecclesiastes
Song . . . . Song of Songs
Isa. . . . . Isaiah
Jer. . . . . Jeremiah
Lam . . . . Lamentations
Ezek . . . . Ezekiel
Dan. . . . . Daniel
Hos . . . . Hosea
Joel . . . . Joel
Amos . . . . Amos
Obad. . . . . Obadiah
Jonah . . . . Jonah
Mic. . . . . Micah
Nah. . . . . Nahum
Hab. . . . . Habakkuk
Zeph . . . . Zephaniah
Hag. . . . . Haggai
Zech . . . . Zechariah
Mal . . . . Malachi

Matt . . . . Matthew	2 Tim . . . . 2 Timothy
Mark. . . . . Mark	Titus . . . . Titus
Luke . . . . Luke	Phlm. . . . . Philemon
John . . . . John	Heb. . . . . Hebrews
Acts . . . . Acts	Jas. . . . . James
Rom . . . . Romans	1 Pet . . . . 1 Peter
1 Cor. . . . . 1 Corinthians	2 Pet . . . . 2 Peter
2 Cor. . . . . 2 Corinthians	1 John. . . . . 1 John
Gal . . . . Galatians	2 John. . . . . 2 John
Eph. . . . . Ephesians	3 John. . . . . 3 John
Phil. . . . . Philippians	Jude . . . . Jude
Col . . . . Colossians	Rev . . . . Revelation
1 Thess . . . . 1 Thessalonians	OT . . . . Old Testament
2 Thess . . . . 2 Thessalonians	NT . . . . New Testament
1 Tim . . . . 1 Timothy	

PUBLICATION ABBREVIATIONS

AB . . . . Anchor Bible
ABD . . . . . . *The Anchor Bible Dictionary*, ed. David Noel Freedman, 6 vols.
(New York: Doubleday, 1992)
AJP. . . . . . . *American Journal of Philology*
ANF . . . . . . *Ante-Nicene Fathers*
ANTC. . . . . Abingdon New Testament Commentaries
BAGD. . . . . Walter Bauer, William F. Arndt, Friedrich W. Gingrich, and
Frederick W. Danker, *A Greek-English Lexicon of the New
Testament and Other Early Christian Literature*, 2nd ed.
(Chicago: University of Chicago, 1979)
BDF . . . . . . Friedrich Blass, Albert Debrunner, and Robert W. Funk,
*A Greek Grammar of the New Testament and Other Early
Christian Literature* (Chicago: University of Chicago Press,
1961)
BECNT . . . Baker Exegetical Commentary on the New Testament
BSac . . . . . . *Bibliotheca sacra*
BBR . . . . . . *Bulletin for Biblical Research*
Bib . . . . *Biblica*
BJRL. . . . . . *Bulletin of the John Rylands Library*
BTB . . . . . . *Biblical Theology Bulletin*
BTCB . . . . . Brazos Theological Commentary on the Bible

BZ. . . . . . . *Biblische Zeitschrift*
CBC . . . . . . Cornerstone Biblical Commentary
CBQ . . . . . . *Catholic Biblical Quarterly*
CP . . . . *Classical Philology*
CQ . . . . *Classical Quarterly*
ColT . . . . . . *Collectanea theologica*
CTR . . . . . . *Criswell Theological Review*
DJG . . . . . . *Dictionary of Jesus and the Gospels*, ed. Joel Green and Scot
　　　　　　McKnight (Downers Grove, IL: InterVarsity, 1992)
DLNT . . . . . *Dictionary of the Later New Testament and Its Developments*,
　　　　　　ed. Ralph P. Martin and Peter H. Davids (Downers Grove, IL:
　　　　　　InterVarsity Press, 1997)
DNTB . . . . . *Dictionary of New Testament Background*, ed. Craig A. Evans
　　　　　　and Stephen E. Porter (Downers Grove, IL: InterVarsity, 2000)
DPL . . . . . . *Dictionary of Paul and His Letters*, ed. Gerald F. Hawthorne
　　　　　　and Ralph P. Martin (Downers Grove, IL: InterVarsity, 1993)
DRev. . . . . . *Downside Review*
EBC . . . . . . Expositor's Bible Commentary
ETL. . . . . . . *Ephemerides theologicae lovanienses*
EvJ . . . . *Evangelical Journal*
EvQ . . . . . . *Evangelical Quarterly*
ExpTim . . . . *Expository Times*
GRBS . . . . . *Greek, Roman, and Byzantine Studies*
HNTC. . . . . Harper's New Testament Commentaries
Hor. . . . . . . *Horizons*
HTR . . . . . . *Harvard Theological Review*
HUCA. . . . . *Hebrew Union College Annual*
ICC. . . . . . . International Critical Commentary
Int. . . . . *Interpretation*
JAAR. . . . . . *Journal of the American Academy of Religion*
JBL. . . . . . . *Journal of Biblical Literature*
JETS. . . . . . *Journal of the Evangelical Theological Society*
JHS. . . . . . . *Journal of Hellenic Studies*
JRS . . . . *Journal of Roman Studies*
JRT. . . . . . . *Journal of Religious Thought*
JSJ . . . . *Journal for the Study of Judaism*
JSNT. . . . . . *Journal for the Study of the New Testament*
JSNTSup . . Journal for the Study of the New Testament Supplement Series
JSOT. . . . . . *Journal for the Study of the Old Testament*
JTS . . . . *Journal of Theological Studies*
LSJ . . . . Henry George Liddell and Robert S. Scott, *A Greek-English
　　　　　　Lexicon*, ed. Henry Stuart Jones (Oxford: Clarendon, 1968)
LTQ . . . . . . *Lexington Theological Quarterly*
NAC . . . . . . New American Commentary

NBD³ . . . . . *New Bible Dictionary*, ed. D. R. W. Wood, 3rd ed. (Downers Grove, IL: InterVarsity, 1996)

NCBC. . . . . New Century Bible Commentary

NIB . . . . . . *The New Interpreter's Bible*, ed. Leander E. Keck, 12 vols. (Nashville: Abingdon, 1994–2004)

NICNT . . . . New International Commentary on the New Testament

NIDNTT . . . *New International Dictionary of New Testament Theology*, ed. Colin Brown, 4 vols. (Grand Rapids: Zondervan, 1975–85)

NovT. . . . . . *Novum Testamentum*

NTS. . . . . . . *New Testament Studies*

OCD . . . . . . *The Oxford Classical Dictionary*, ed. Simon Hornblower and Antony Spawforth, 3rd ed. (New York: Oxford University Press, 1996)

PIBA. . . . . . Proceedings of the Irish Biblical Association

PNTC . . . . . Pillar New Testament Commentary

PRSt . . . . . . *Perspectives in Religious Studies*

RCT . . . . . . *Revista catalana de teología*

ResQ. . . . . . *Restoration Quarterly*

RevExp . . . . *Review and Expositor*

SBLSP . . . . *Society of Biblical Literature Seminar Papers*

SBLSymS. . Society of Biblical Literature Symposium Series

ScrB . . . . . . *Scripture Bulletin*

SE. . . . . *Studia evangelica*

SHBC. . . . . Smyth and Helwys Bible Commentary

SK. . . . . *Skrif en kerk*

SNTSMS . . Society for New Testament Studies Monograph Series

SNTSU. . . . Studien zum Neuen Testament und seiner Umwelt

SP. . . . . Sacra pagina

ST . . . . *Studia theologica*

STDJ. . . . . . *Studies on the Texts of the Desert of Judah*

SwJT. . . . . . *Southwestern Journal of Theology*

TBT. . . . . . . *The Bible Today*

TDNT . . . . . *Theological Dictionary of the New Testament*, ed. Gerhard Kittel and Gerhard Friederich, trans. Geoffrey W. Bromiley, 10 vols. (Grand Rapids: Eerdmans, 1964–76)

Them. . . . . . *Themelios*

TNTC . . . . . Tyndale New Testament Commentaries

TS . . . . *Theological Studies*

TynBul . . . . *Tyndale Bulletin*

TZ. . . . . *Theologische Zeitschrift*

WUNT . . . . Wissenschaftliche Untersuchungen zum Neuen Testament

WW. . . . . . . *Word and World*

ZNW . . . . . . *Zeitschrift für die neutestamentliche Wissenschaft*

ZTK . . . . . . *Zeitschrift für Theologie und Kirche*

FOREWORD

E ver since my time as a doctoral student at Southwestern Baptist
Theological Seminary, Luke's portrait of church life in Acts has
refused to let me go. Lorin Cranford's Ph.D. seminar on New
Testament interpretation taught me to view Acts not only as a theologically
oriented history of the first thirty years of the Christian movement but also
as great literature. Luke's faith and writing were shaped by the gospel
accounts and the story of Israel in the Old Testament. However, he also
utilized his training in Greco-Roman history writing and rhetoric to great
effect in his narrative, especially in his descriptions of church life. One
reason we miss many of Luke's rhetorical clues on this subject is that
Acts was meant to be read orally in public church meetings (1 Tim 4:13).
The rhetorical clues Luke embedded in his narrative would not have been
missed by careful "hearers" of his story. In this book I set out to explain
how Luke exploited a simple narrative technique called "summarization"
to shape a rhetorically powerful portrait of church life in Acts 2:42–47;
4:32–35; and 5:12–16, commonly referred to as the summary narratives.

Luke set forth his portraits of church life for believers and church leaders who needed guidance for shaping their own churches.

The church in late modern times is faced with significant challenges. Many are asking what aspects of church life are more tied to modernity and the whole Enlightenment project than to the Bible. How can we be faithful to Scripture as we carry out the church's mission in the twenty-first century?[1] I believe Luke's voice in Acts has been underemphasized and needs to be reasserted in this conversation. Though primarily exegetical in orientation, I have endeavored in this volume to offer a theology of church life in Acts that can be of service to the church today.

This work has been a labor of love for me, and I am grateful to many friends who helped me along the way. I wish first to express gratitude to my president at Missouri Baptist University, Alton Lacey, who provided me with a sabbatical leave in 2008 to begin this project. I am a busy administrator and professor who really did not need something else to do. He saw, however, how this book was tugging on me and, with a generosity that is typical of him, encouraged me to pursue writing it.

I am grateful to many who made this book better than it would have been without their help. The following friends, colleagues, and partners in ministry read and commented on portions of the book: Chris Conley, Lorin Cranford, Matt Easter, Karen Glaser, Allen Glosson, Doug Hume, Bob Johnston, Charles Kimball, Duane Manuel, Steve Phillips, Michael Shattuck, and Marie Tudor. Several of them read the entire manuscript and offered extensive feedback on each chapter. I also wish to thank my editors at B&H Publishing Group: first Terry Wilder (now at Southwestern Seminary), who initially offered me a contract, and Chris Cowan, who shepherded it through to completion. I also want to thank Mark Given and Brad Chance, who allowed me to present two chapters at the Central States Regional Meeting of the Society of Biblical Literature in 2008 and 2009. I wish to thank my staff in Student Development at Missouri Baptist University, especially my administrative assistant, Krista Huse. They offered me tremendous support and good-natured prodding when I was weary.

I am grateful to my precious children—Amanda, Bethany, Eric, and Michael. I appreciate your pushing and encouraging me and also your patience with me while I wrote.

---

[1] I sought to address this issue some time ago in an article. See Andy Chambers, "The Promise and Peril of Postmodernism for Ministry Today," *Intégrité* (Fall 2003): 53–69.

Most of all, I am grateful to my wife and closest friend Diana. We have been married for twenty-six years as of this writing and have been through many trials and triumphs together. I would not have completed this book without your support and encouragement. You are the best friend a man could have, and this book is affectionately dedicated to you.

Andy Chambers
Senior Vice President for Student Development
Professor of Bible
Missouri Baptist University, St. Louis

INTRODUCTION

WHY WE NEED LUKE'S THEOLOGY OF CHURCH LIFE NOW

Peter's Pentecost message about the resurrected Christ burst upon Jerusalem like a bolt of lightning, piercing his hearers to the heart. They asked, "What must we do?" Peter told them to repent and be baptized in the name of Jesus Christ for the forgiveness of sins, and they too would receive the gift of the Holy Spirit. Luke tells us that those who accepted Peter's message were baptized, and about three thousand were added to their number that day. The result was the first church in the history of the world, and for a while the only church (see Luke 24:48–53; Acts 1:8–15; 2:1–41).

The way Luke tells the story of the birth of the church, the sense of expectation was palpable. Just days earlier, these believers watched the risen Jesus taken up before they returned to Jerusalem to wait for His promise of power. About 120 people met together constantly to pray and

1

to wait. Then Pentecost Day arrived. A sound like a violent wind from heaven interrupted their gathering and filled the house. They saw what looked like tongues of fire separate and rest on each person. The Holy Spirit filled them, and they began to speak in other tongues. Jews from many nations were in Jerusalem. They were stunned to hear these people declaring the wonders of God in their own languages, and they wondered what it meant. Peter had an answer. He boldly declared that God's promise through the prophet Joel, that He would pour out His Spirit on all people (Acts 2:16–17), was being fulfilled in their midst. Three thousand people believed and were baptized and added to their number. Power had indeed come.

The enthusiasm of Pentecost did not end that day. Immediately after the three thousand were added, Luke provided his first of three portraits of daily life in the new community of believers in Acts 2:42–47:

> *And they devoted themselves to the apostles' teaching, to fellowship, to the breaking of bread, and to prayers. Then fear came over everyone, and many wonders and signs were being performed through the apostles. Now all the believers were together and had everything in common. So they sold their possessions and property and distributed the proceeds to all, as anyone had a need. And every day they devoted themselves [to meeting] together in the temple complex, and broke bread from house to house. They ate their food with gladness and simplicity of heart, praising God and having favor with all the people. And every day the Lord added to them those who were being saved.*[1]

Despite immediate opposition from the Jewish authorities, who threw Peter and John in jail, the church quickly grew to about five thousand. Although the Sanhedrin threatened Peter and John, they could not silence them so the apostles were released. When the church heard their story, they cried out to God their prayers for boldness. God answered by shaking the place where they met. They were all filled with the Holy Spirit and spoke God's word boldly (see Acts 4:1–31). After God answered the believers' prayer, Luke painted a second portrait of church life in 4:32–35:

---

[1] Unless indicated, all Scripture quotations are from the Holman Christian Standard Bible (Nashville: Holman Bible Publishers, 2009).

Now the multitude of those who believed were of one heart and soul, and no one said that any of his possessions was his own, but instead they held everything in common. And with great power the apostles were giving testimony to the resurrection of the Lord Jesus, and great grace was on all of them. For there was not a needy person among them, because all those who owned lands or houses sold them, brought the proceeds of the things that were sold, and laid them at the apostles' feet. This was then distributed to each person as anyone had a need.

The church was not perfect, and Luke did not ignore this fact. People like Barnabas gave freely, but not everyone had integrity in their giving. Ananias and Sapphira lied about their gift, and their duplicity cost them their lives. Great fear came upon everyone who heard about what happened to them (see Acts 4:36–5:11). Immediately after this occurrence, Luke supplied a third portrait of church life in 5:12–16:

Many signs and wonders were being done among the people through the hands of the apostles. By common consent they would all meet in Solomon's Colonnade. None of the rest dared to join them, but the people praised them highly. Believers were added to the Lord in increasing numbers—crowds of both men and women. As a result, they would carry the sick out into the streets and lay them on beds and pallets so that when Peter came by, at least his shadow might fall on some of them. In addition, a multitude came together from the towns surrounding Jerusalem, bringing sick people and those who were tormented by unclean spirits, and they were all healed.

Why This Book?

My purpose for writing this book grows out of a deep love for the local church. I long to see churches thriving with the life of Christ, bringing glory to God and blessing to their communities. The early chapters of Acts surveyed above paint a portrait of church life so compelling that countless Christians have turned to them for guidance as to what their churches could be. I believe Luke wanted to provoke such a response from readers. Throughout Acts as Luke describes the beginnings of the Christian movement, he does not simply show the gospel spreading from city to city. He shows gospel preaching resulting in local churches, beginning in Jerusalem. Sometimes we hear only of the church's original meeting place in a particular city, like Lydia's home in Philippi (Acts 16:40). Other times we hear that the gospel has spread across entire cities. Teaching and preaching in Acts occurred "in various homes" in Jerusalem, "from house to house," and even in a rented "lecture hall" in Ephesus (5:42; 19:9; 20:20). Yet everywhere a church was planted Acts tells readers something about life in the newly formed community of believers.

Good questions need to be asked of biblical texts in order to get at their respective author's concerns. Through the years many excellent questions have been asked of Acts that have resulted in numerous scholarly studies and fruitful insights into Luke's message.[2] However, insufficient attention has been paid to Luke's vision for church life. The question needs to be asked of Acts, "What did Luke think life in the gathered church should look like?" My book will answer this question.

Luke had definite convictions about life in the community of faith that he skillfully wove into the fabric of his narrative. However, when recent commentary introductions consider the purpose and major themes of Acts, they often overlook or give insufficient attention to Luke's concern for church life. The desire to write a theologically oriented history of the beginnings of the Christian movement usually tops lists of Luke's purposes for writing Acts. Another popular argument is that Luke wrote to evangelize Gentiles in an effort to bring educated pagans to Christ. Less widely accepted theories include a political defense for the church or for Paul before Roman authorities. Still others argue that Luke wrote to counter false teachers like the Gnostics or the Judaizers.[3] Somewhere in dis-

---

[2] Helpful overviews of recent scholarship on Acts can be found in: Mark Allan Powell, *What Are They Saying About Acts?* (New York: Paulist Press, 1991); Peter Anthony, "What Are They Saying About Luke-Acts?" *ScrB* 40, no. 1 (Jan. 2010): 10–21; Charles H. Talbert, "Luke-Acts," in *The New Testament and Its Modern Interpreters*, ed. Eldon Jay Epp and George W. MacRae (Philadelphia: Fortress, 1989), 297–320; I. Howard Marshall, "Acts in Current Study," *ExpTim* 115 (2003): 49–52; Steve Walton, "Acts: Many Questions, Many Answers," in *The Face of New Testament Studies: A Survey of Recent Research*, ed. Scot McKnight and Grant R. Osborne (Grand Rapids: Baker Academic, 2004), 229–50.

[3] For surveys of proposals for the purpose of Acts see: Joseph A. Fitzmyer, *The Acts of the Apostles*, AB (New York: Doubleday, 1998), 55–60; W. Ward Gasque, *A History of the Interpretation of the Acts of the Apostles*, rev. ed. (Peabody, MA: Hendrickson, 1989), 346–57; I. Howard Marshall, *The Acts of the Apostles*, New Testament Guides (Sheffield, UK: Sheffield Academic Press, 2001), 31–46; David Peterson, "Luke's Theological Enterprise: Integration and Intent," in *Witness to the Gospel:*

cussions of the purpose of Acts a concern to edify believers and churches is usually noted, but most do not identify church life as a major theme.[4] Interpreters with an eye on contemporary church concerns tend to focus on missional aspects of Acts. They read Acts as a call to believers to "go and *tell*" in fulfillment of Christ's promise in Acts 1:8 that His disciples would be His witnesses to the ends of the earth. Acts can be no less than that. Yet, Luke was deeply concerned with "going and *gathering*" too, with the kind and quality of churches being planted in the growing Christian movement.[5] Luke's missiology cannot be separated from his ecclesiology.

Luke's Theology of Church Life in the Summary Narratives

I propose that forging a vision for what life could be like in the gathered church, while certainly not his only priority and perhaps not his highest, was clearly one of Luke's major concerns in writing Acts. Luke's starting point and core texts for his theology of church life are his well-known descriptions of ideal life in the Jerusalem church in Acts 2:42–47; 4:32–35; and 5:12–16, commonly referred to as the summary narratives.[6] Luke does not state his purpose for these three paragraphs explicitly. From a historical perspective, they simply provide a snapshot of life in the newly formed Jerusalem congregation. From a rhetorical perspective, however, I believe Luke deliberately chose positive aspects of church life for inclusion in the summary narratives. He did this in order to present his portraits of church life as a positive example for readers to study and emulate in their own churches.[7] For Luke, the summary narratives describe what life could be like in an exemplary church.

The Theology of Acts, ed. I. Howard Marshall and David Peterson (Grand Rapids: Eerdmans, 1998), 521–44.

[4] Themes like the salvation of God, the role of the Holy Spirit, the legitimacy of the Gentile mission, the triumph of the gospel over barriers to its spread, and reassurance for believers struggling in the face of resistance are among the many offered as emphases Luke wanted readers to embrace.

[5] I am in debt to Stephen Chapman of Duke Divinity School for calling my attention to this concern in Acts. Several years ago Stephen challenged me to see how "mission" in Acts is commonly understood as "going forth," and it is. Yet, for Luke there is also an emphasis on going and "gathering."

[6] They tend to be referred to as "summary narratives" when the writer using the term focuses on Acts 2:42–47; 4:32–35; and 5:12–16. The word *summaries* is commonly used to reference texts of a summary-like quality in Acts and in the Synoptic Gospels, especially Mark. "Summarization" refers to the narrative technique of switching from scenic or episodic narration into summary mode.

[7] This was the thesis of my dissertation under Lorin Cranford; Andy Chambers, "An Evaluation of Characteristic Activity in a Model Church as Set Forth by the Summary Narratives of Acts," Ph.D. diss. (Fort Worth, TX: Southwestern Baptist Theological Seminary, 1994).

The summary narratives have long been recognized for the way they emphasize positive aspects of life in the Jerusalem church.[8] Yet, few commentary introductions mention the summary narratives in discussions of major themes in Acts. They tend to be referenced only in sections on literary forms, along with prologues, speeches, episodes, and the like, without reference to their contribution to the theology of Acts as a whole. What is missed is how the literary shape of the summary narratives and their relationship to the rest of Acts set them apart within Acts and highlight their theology of church life for readers. I believe that presenting an exemplary pattern for church life was high on Luke's theological agenda and that he started with the summary narratives to make his case. I will argue that Acts 2:42–47; 4:32–35; and 5:12–16 function precisely this way in Acts. To make my case I plan to show how summarization could be used in an ancient author's narrative/rhetorical strategy generally and how Luke employed summarization to suit his own rhetorical purposes.

The historical-critical methodologies that dominated twentieth-century New Testament research, especially source, form, and redaction criticism, tended to separate the summary narratives from their literary context within Acts. As a result, interpreters often missed their contribution to the overall theological vision of Acts. This development was unfortunate, because it eclipsed the role of the summary narratives in articulating a theology of church life for readers of Acts. As a consequence, Luke's voice through the summary narratives has been overshadowed in contemporary conversations about the formation of biblically faithful churches. I do not suggest that Luke's voice is not heard at all today. His rhetorical appeal for the special function of these texts comes through even in English translations of the Bible, as evidenced by the tendency of modern authors to navigate toward specific verses in them when discussing current church concerns.[9] Yet their contribution as a whole to the theology of Acts, especially as a resource for discussions of New Testament ecclesiology,

---

[8] See, for example, H. Alan Brehm, "The Significance of the Summaries for Interpreting Acts," *SwJT* 33, no. 1 (Fall 1990): 29–40; Robrecht Michiels, "The Model of Church in the First Christian Community of Jerusalem: Ideal and Reality," *Louvain Studies* 10 (1985): 303–23.

[9] For examples of contemporary authors who reference portions of the summary narratives in their prescriptions for church life, see Soong-Chan Rah, *The Next Evangelicalism: Freeing the Church from Western Cultural Captivity* (Downers Grove, IL: InterVarsity, 2009), 106–7; Mark Liederbach and Alvin L. Reid, *The Convergent Church: Missional Worshipers in an Emerging Culture* (Grand Rapids: Kregel, 2009), 286; and Frank Viola, *Reimagining Church: Pursuing the Dream of Organic Christianity* (Colorado Springs: David C. Cook, 2008), 84–86, 102–3.

is still being missed.[10] We shortchange our efforts to develop a Scripture shaped vision for church life when we do not give adequate attention to the extensive descriptions and reflections of the church's earliest historian. My hope is that this book will help to correct this imbalance.

Overview

Chapter 1 will survey modern critical approaches to Acts and situate the study of the summary narratives within the larger context of Acts scholarship. I will seek to show how twentieth-century critical approaches to Acts contributed to the separation of the summary narratives from their literary context and led interpreters to underemphasize or even overlook Luke's theology of church life revealed in them. The chapter concludes by commending the value of the narrative and rhetorical perspective for reconnecting the summary narratives to the rest of Acts and for understanding Luke's didactic purpose in them. Chapter 2 will apply the tools of narrative and rhetorical criticism to the summary narratives. I will argue that Luke utilized summarization as a narrative technique, modified to suit his own rhetorical purposes, to set forth his positive descriptions of life in the Jerusalem church as exemplary portraits of church life for readers. Chapters 3 through 5 will offer a close reading of the summary narratives with an eye toward what Luke wanted to teach readers about life together in the local church.

Chapter 6 will show how Luke reinforced his message in the summary narratives with his descriptions of church life in the emerging Gentile mission movement. I will emphasize the almost constant repetition of themes from the summary narratives in Luke's descriptions of the Gentile churches in Acts and the significance of this phenomenon. Luke wanted to make doubly clear for readers what he believed should characterize life in exemplary churches. He especially wanted Gentile readers and churches to look to his portraits of the Jewish church in Jerusalem as a pattern for shaping their own churches. Chapter 7 will pull together the many themes of the summary narratives and their echoes in the Gentile churches to articulate a theology of church life in Acts.

Chapter 8 will propose several directions for applications of this study to contemporary discussions over church practice. I want to make it clear at the outset that I do not expect my recommendations to end debates and

---

[10] For an exception, see Dennis E. Johnson, *The Message of Acts in the History of Redemption* (Phillipsburg, NJ: P&R, 1997), 9, 70–83.

reveal one model as the right one. I don't think I have that answer! My goal is more modest. I want to see Luke's theology of church life reasserted in the conversation. Acts has much to say about the formation of biblically faithful churches, and Luke's voice needs to be heard anew. Before we can do this, we need to see how Luke's theology of church life was lost, which is the burden of chapter 1.

CHAPTER ONE

HOW WE LOST LUKE'S
THEOLOGY OF CHURCH LIFE

Research into the summary narratives in the twentieth century followed traditional lines of application of source, form, and redaction criticism to the book of Acts. These interpretive methods have their roots in the historical-critical method, which developed in the nineteenth century as a product of the Enlightenment. To understand how Luke's theology of church life in Acts was lost, we need to grasp how the historical-critical method cast its shadow over the way Acts is read.

ACTS AND THE RISE OF THE
HISTORICAL-CRITICAL METHOD

The Enlightenment brought about three profound shifts in the way people approached historical knowledge and documents like Acts that purport to tell about the past. First, a methodological skepticism led people away from accepting the authority of the church on the nature of Scripture toward treating the Bible like any other human document.[1] In one sense, reading the Bible as a historical document affirms that God revealed Himself in history and that the early church produced written documents in order to preserve the knowledge of God's deeds in the world. Asking questions of a historical nature about things like authorship, date, occasion, genre, and purpose affirms that God's self-disclosure did not occur in a historical vacuum. I. Howard Marshall correctly observes that anyone who tries to "understand the New Testament or defend its historicity against skeptics by any kind of reasonable argument is already practicing the historical method."[2] The difference between a historical perspective and that of the Enlightenment, however, is that the latter argued that purely historical questions should be asked about Scripture without reference to doctrine or any dogmatic position of the church on the nature and authority of Scripture.[3]

Second, the rise of the scientific method led to the naive assumption that a dispassionate objectivity in every area of knowledge is possible. This led to the belief that history writing was a science that could recreate the past in a purely unbiased way.[4] Of course, the Bible's historical documents are anything but unbiased. The Gospels and Acts were written by passionately devoted followers of the resurrected Jesus. They were committed, without apology, to persuading readers to follow Jesus too. As Daniel Marguerat points out, "Luke does not display a historian's intellectual autonomy; his reading of history is a believer's reading."[5] From the perspective of nineteenth-century scientific historiography, this perceived lack of objectivity in the New Testament raised serious doubts about the reliability of biblical accounts of history like the kind seen in Acts.

Third, the scientific method also demanded that claims about truth and knowledge be verifiable through empirical testing and that explanations for all extraordinary phenomena be sought strictly in terms of causes and effects observable in nature. Thus, the fact that the Bible reports a

---

[1] F. F. Bruce, "The History of New Testament Study," in *New Testament Interpretation: Essays on Principles and Methods*, ed. I. Howard Marshall (Grand Rapids: Eerdmans, 1977), 37.

[2] I. Howard Marshall, "Historical Criticism," in Marshall, *New Testament Interpretation*, 131.

[3] David S. Dockery, *Christian Scripture: An Evangelical Perspective on Inspiration, Authority, and Interpretation* (Nashville: Broadman and Holman, 1995), 134–36.

[4] E. Earle Ellis, "Historical-Literary Criticism—After 200 Years: Origins, Aberrations, Contributions, Limitations," in *The Proceedings of the Conference on Biblical Inerrancy* (Nashville: Broadman, 1987), 412–13.

[5] Daniel Marguerat, *The First Christian Historian: Writing the Acts of the Apostles*, trans. Ken McKinney, Gregory J. Laughery, and Richard Bauckham, SNTSMS 121 (New York: Cambridge University Press, 2002), 21.

miracle no longer warranted the conclusion that the laws of nature had been suspended and a miracle had actually occurred. A rational explanation was now to be preferred. This created a tremendous crisis for people who wanted to remain intellectually relevant in society and hold on to the divine inspiration and authority of the Bible, because Scripture, especially the book of Acts, is driven throughout by the miraculous.[6] As a result of these shifts, the historical reliability of the Bible came under a withering assault in the universities of Europe in the nineteenth century. The methodology for interpreting the Bible that arose out of this new mindset is called the historical-critical method.

Acts in the Shadow of F. C. Baur

F. C. Baur and the Tübingen school in Germany that he represents epitomized the application of the historical-critical method to the text of Acts. Baur contributed an important insight when he recognized that the New Testament itself is part of church history. By that he meant that the history of doctrine did not begin when the last book of the Bible was written. The New Testament introduces us to people of different cultural and religious backgrounds all striving, sometimes against each other (see Acts 15:1–2; Gal 2:11–14), to come to grips with the meaning of Jesus Christ.[7] Early in his career Baur adopted the dialectical philosophy of Friedrich Hegel as his lens for understanding the conflict he saw in the New Testament. Hegel viewed the movement of history in terms of a thesis, an antithesis, and a resulting synthesis. An idea or thesis emerges in history and grows in influence until it provokes an opposing point of view or antithesis. At some point the conflict between the opposing viewpoints resolves itself in a new reality or synthesis.

For Baur, the Hegelian thesis was the emergence of a thoroughly Jewish Christianity represented by Peter and the church in Jerusalem.

---

[6] Luke began Acts with a reference to Jesus presenting Himself alive "by many convincing proofs" after His suffering (Acts 1:3), and he showed God regularly verifying the preaching of the apostles and Stephen with miraculous signs and wonders (2:43; 5:12; 6:8). Also see 2:19,22,43; 4:30; 5:12; 6:8; 7:36; 8:6,13; 14:3; 15:12; 19:11–12; 28:6–9 for examples of Luke's emphasis on miracles characterizing God's activity in Acts.

[7] Stephen Neill and Tom Wright, *The Interpretation of the New Testament from 1861–1986* (New York: Oxford University Press, 1988), 20. At least three distinct groups and perspectives are represented among the early converts in Acts. The first two came out of Judaism, ethnically Jewish followers of Christ and converts to Judaism who later converted to Christ. Acts 6:1 calls these disciples Hebraic Jews and Hellenistic Jews respectively. The third group, Gentile converts, came to Christ out of Roman society at large and not through Judaism (see 11:20–21).

As the gospel moved beyond the borders of Judaism, a culturally Gentile Christianity emerged, an antithesis that was represented by Paul and the church in Antioch. The earliest decades of Christian history, as Baur saw them, were marked by conflict between these two factions. The application of Hegel's dialectic so magnified the discord between Jewish and Gentile Christianity that Baur only accepted as authentic those New Testament books that evidenced the strife between them, like Galatians and 1 Corinthians. The book of Acts, on the other hand, has a more conciliatory tone. Acts displays a united church, as the summary narratives show (see Acts 2:44; 4:32). Acts also shows the Jewish and Gentile factions resolving their differences (15:1–35) and the emergence of a synthesis in the form of an "early catholicism." Baur believed that this synthesis did not emerge until at least the mid to late second century AD. Therefore, in Baur's view, Acts could not have been written any earlier than the middle of the second century and so was of little historical value to him. This does not mean Baur did not study Acts from a historical perspective. Rather, he sought, with the historical-critical method he helped develop, to go behind the text of Acts (which for him represented the situation of the late second-century church) in order to get at the actual history of the first-century church.[8]

Baur left a permanent mark on subsequent Acts scholarship among those who followed his presuppositions. Nearly a century later, Rudolf Bultmann would argue in his *Theology of the New Testament* that the New Testament contains two strata, the first embodying the early church's *kerygma* (or preaching) and the second representing an early catholic falling away from the truth. For Bultmann, Luke's writings belonged to the early catholic distortion of the gospel message. He did not see them as normative for the church's faith as he thought Paul's letters and John's Gospel should be.[9]

---

[8] Helpful analyses of Baur's presuppositions and methodology can be found in William Baird, *From Deism to Tübingen, Volume 1: History of New Testament Research* (Minneapolis: Augsburg Fortress, 1992), 258–96; Gerald Bray, *Biblical Interpretation: Past and Present* (Downers Grove, IL: InterVarsity, 1996), 321–29, 564–68; W. Ward Gasque, *A History of the Interpretation of the Acts of the Apostles*, rev. ed. (Peabody, MA: Hendrickson, 1989), 21–54; Edgar Krentz, *The Historical-Critical Method* (Philadelphia: Fortress, 1975), 25–28; and Neill and Wright, *Interpretation of the New Testament from 1861–1986*, 19–28. Also see Mary E. Andrews, "Tendenz Versus Interpretation: F. C. Baur's Criticisms of Luke," *JBL* 58 (1939): 263–76, for an analysis of how Baur applied his methodology to the Gospel of Luke.

[9] See the discussion in Charles H. Talbert, *Reading Luke-Acts in the Mediterranean Milieu* (Leiden: Brill Academic Publishers, 2003), 10.

Not everyone was persuaded by Baur's conclusions. J. B. Lightfoot of Cambridge University challenged Baur's late date for Acts. Lightfoot published commentaries on several New Testament books that are still in print today. He also wrote extensively on postapostolic literature, especially the late first- and early second-century letters of Clement of Rome and Ignatius of Antioch. Lightfoot demonstrated convincingly that 1 Clement and the seven letters of Ignatius were genuine and written near the turn of the first century. Their writings do not reveal the disunity between Peter and Paul and between Jewish and Gentile Christianity that Baur was convinced dominated the first-century church. Lightfoot's response significantly discredited Baur's position on the late date of Acts and its lack of reliability as a historical resource for knowledge of early Christianity.[10] Lightfoot desired to write a commentary on Acts but was not able, and we are poorer for it. However, he did publish several extensive critiques of Baur's conclusions.[11]

With regard to the summary narratives, an affirmation and a basic criticism of Baur can be made. He correctly observed the conciliatory nature of Acts. Luke portrays the Gentile and Jewish wings of the church resolving their differences (see especially Acts 15 in re the Jerusalem Council). I would go farther than Baur and argue that Luke does more. Luke commends their faith and churches to each other. He especially commends his portraits of exemplary church life drawn from the Jewish mother church in Jerusalem to his Gentile readers in churches scattered throughout the Empire, and he shows Gentile churches adopting many of the practices of the Jerusalem church. Baur's observation of the tendency of Acts toward conciliation is an enduring contribution. However, he wrongly assumed that the display of unity in Acts between factions in the church demands that we believe Luke misrepresented the facts as he knew them. Baur's radically historicist approach unnecessarily pits historical and theological concerns in Acts against each other. This led to the assumption that the

---

[10] Bray, *Biblical Interpretation*, 344. The author of Acts, Luke, according to the earliest witnesses in church history, was a contemporary of Paul, because he traveled with Paul during part of his missionary journeys as evidenced by the famous "we" passages (Acts 16:10–17; 20:5–21:26; 27:1–28:16). Depending on Luke's age when he was with Paul in Rome during the early 60s Acts could have been written up to several decades after that time.

[11] See J. B. Lightfoot, "Acts of the Apostles," in *Smith's Dictionary of the Bible*, ed. H. B. Hackett (Boston: Houghton Mifflin, 1892), 1:25–43; and J. B. Lightfoot, "Discoveries Illustrating the Acts of the Apostles," in *Essays on the Work Entitled Supernatural Religion* (London: Macmillan, 1889), 291–302. For a critique of Baur from an American perspective, see A. T. Robertson, "Acts of the Apostles," in *The International Standard Bible Encyclopedia*, ed. James Orr (Chicago: Howard-Severance Company, 1915), 1:39–48.

more theologically-oriented Luke was, the less reliable a historian he had to be—or worse, the more willing he was to write falsehoods in order to advance his own theological agenda.

The longer view of reading Acts through church history reveals a more basic principle animating reflection on tendencies in Acts and in Scripture generally. It is that Christianity is at heart a historical religion. This is reinforced from the call of Abraham and the formation and preservation of Israel to the ministry of Jesus and beyond. The Bible continually speaks of a God who reigns over and intervenes in history to accomplish His purposes. The death and resurrection of Jesus are presented as historical events on which the faith itself was said to hang (1 Cor 15:12–19) and which a person must believe happened if they want to be saved (Rom 10:9). Reading Acts in view of the Bible's habit of presenting Christianity as a historical faith should lead one to resist pitting theological concerns against the historical concerns in the study of Acts.[12] Baur is a case study on how presuppositions can affect the direction and even the outcome of research and how interpreters can be swayed by the influence of their own presuppositions.

The Summary Narratives in the Shadow of Historical Criticism

The tendency of the Tübingen school to separate the actual history of the early church from what they saw as the theological tendencies of Acts profoundly impacted the interpretation of the summary narratives in the twentieth century, as they were read through the lenses of source, form, and redaction criticism.[13] These tools continued the historical-critical quest to go behind what were seen as the theologically biased and therefore historically unreliable statements of Acts to the supposedly real history of the early church.

Source and Form Criticism. Source and form criticism developed first as tools for analyzing the Synoptic Gospels and then were applied to Acts. Source criticism sought to identify the sources used by the writers of the

---

[12] I. Howard Marshall's classic statement on the positive relationship between history and theology in Acts is of tremendous value on this point. See I. Howard Marshall, *Luke: Historian and Theologian* (Grand Rapids: Zondervan, 1989), 21–52; and I. Howard Marshall, *The Acts of the Apostles*, New Testament Guides (Sheffield, UK: Sheffield Academic Press, 2001), 83–101. Also see V. Philips Long, "The Art of Biblical History," in *Foundations of Contemporary Interpretation*, ed. Moisés Silva (Grand Rapids: Zondervan, 1996), 338–45.

[13] Joseph B. Tyson, "The Legacy of F. C. Baur and Recent Studies of Acts," *Forum* 4, no. 1 (Spring 2001): 125–44.

Gospels and Acts.[14] Form criticism treated these sources as the end stage of a process of handing down traditions of the teachings and deeds of Jesus until they were codified in recognizable literary forms. Form critics saw in these forms evidence of the sources utilized by the authors of the Gospels and Acts in their compositions.[15]

Martin Dibelius in 1923 pioneered the application of form criticism of the Gospels to Acts in his *Aufsätze zur Apostelgeschichte* (*Studies in the Acts of the Apostles*) through a method he called "style criticism."[16] He made a distinction between the style of Luke's sources (like the episodes and speeches) and the editorial summaries that tie the episodes together. Dibelius argued that Luke's sources were older and therefore closer to the actual historical circumstances of the early church. He believed that Luke creatively composed the summaries as generalizations that made individual scenes appear as particular instances of typical circumstances. Dibelius identified Acts 1:13–14; 2:42,43–47; 4:4,32–35; 5:12–16,42; 6:7; 9:31; and 12:24 as examples of Luke's generalizing tendency.[17] These texts summarize in an ideal way the ongoing life and growth of the Jerusalem church, but because Dibelius saw them as later Lukan contributions, he believed they were deliberate departures from the older tradition and therefore historically suspect.[18]

Henry J. Cadbury based his form-critical analysis of the summaries in Acts on his study of summarization in the Synoptic Gospels.[19] He believed that the summaries in Mark were the latest addition to his Gospel, which he distilled from the episodes in order to provide generalizations and fill

---

[14] Perhaps the earliest source analysis of the summary narratives can be found in Johannes Jüngst, *Die Quellen der Apostelgeschichte* (Gotha: Friedrich Andreas Perthes, 1895), 51–56. Helpful surveys of the development and utilization of source criticism can be found in Daniel J. Harrington, *Interpreting the New Testament: A Practical Guide* (Wilmington, DE: Michael Glazier, 1979), 56–69; and Christopher Tuckett, *Reading the New Testament: Methods of Interpretation* (Philadelphia: Fortress, 1987), 78–94.

[15] Helpful surveys of the development and use of form criticism can be found in Craig L. Blomberg, "Form Criticism," in *DJG*, 243–50; and Stephen H. Travis, "Form Criticism," in Marshall, *New Testament Interpretation*, 153–64.

[16] See the chapter in Martin Dibelius, "Stilkritisches zur Apostelgeschichte," in *Aufsätze zur Apostelgeschichte*, ed. Heinrich Greeven (Göttingen: Vandenhoecht & Ruprecht, 1951), 9–28. References are to the English translation, *Studies in the Acts of the Apostles*, trans. Mary Ling (New York: Charles Scribner's Sons, 1956), 1–25.

[17] Dibelius, *Studies in the Acts of the Apostles*, 9.

[18] Ibid., 125–29.

[19] Henry J. Cadbury, "The Summaries in Acts," in *The Beginnings of Christianity*, ed. F. J. Foakes-Jackson and Kirsopp Lake, vol. 5, *Additional Notes to the Commentary*, ed. Kirsopp Lake and Henry J. Cadbury (London: MacMillan, 1933), 392–402.

voids between detached scenes. He also argued that Luke utilized Mark's summaries in his Gospel as evidenced by his tendency to repeat and multiply them, while still adhering closely to their content.[20] In Acts, Cadbury argued that the summaries were derived from a date later than the episodes they joined and, like the Synoptics, were designed to fill voids between detached scenes with generalizations that indicated "single events of the type described were multiplied at other times and places."[21] Cadbury adopted a more moderate posture than Dibelius regarding the historical reliability of Acts, stating that Luke was limited by the accuracy or inaccuracy of his sources.[22]

Joachim Jeremias, Lucien Cerfaux, and Pierre Benoit turned their attention to analyzing the internal development of the summary narratives in an effort to distinguish between sources and Luke's contribution to their composition. All three held that the disjointed construction of the summaries showed some parts came from earlier sources and others from the author or a later editor, but they came to different conclusions about which parts were early and which were late.[23] The lack of a consensus between them illustrates how efforts to separate Luke's sources for the summary narratives from his own contribution really are speculative at best.[24] In their quest for the history behind texts, form critics ended up isolating those texts from their literary and theological contexts in the final canonical form of the book. Form criticism does raise an important question about whether the summary narratives should be considered a distinct literary form within Acts (a tendency of form-criticism) or a narrative technique used by Luke in his rhetorical strategy in Acts (the tendency of narrative and rhetorical criticism). I will say more on this in chapter 2.

---

[20] Cadbury, "Summaries in Acts," 393–94. See also Henry J. Cadbury, *The Style and Literary Method of Luke* (Cambridge, MA: Harvard University Press, 1920), 108–15.

[21] Henry J. Cadbury, "Acts of the Apostles," in *Interpreter's Dictionary of the Bible*, ed. George A. Buttrick (Nashville: Abingdon, 1962), 1:33. Also see Cadbury, *The Making of Luke-Acts* (New York: Macmillan, 1927), 58–59.

[22] Cadbury, *Making of Luke-Acts*, 360–68; Cadbury, "Summaries in Acts," 402.

[23] Joachim Jeremias, "Untersuchungen zum Quellenproblem der Apostelgeschichte," *ZNW* 36 (1937): 206–8; Lucien Cerfaux, "La Composition de la première partie du Livre des Actes," *ETL* 13 (1936): 673; Cerfaux, "La première communauté chrétienne à Jérusalem," *ETL* 16 (1939): 5–31; Pierre Benoit, "Remarques sur les 'Sommaires' des Actes II, IV, et V," in *Exégèse et Théologie* (Paris: Les Editions du Cerf, 1961), 2:183.

[24] This is the conclusion of two recent assessments of source theories for Acts: Perry Kea, "Source Theories for the Acts of the Apostles," *Forum* 4, no. 1 (Spring 2001): 7–26; Henry Wansbrough, "The Book of Acts and History," *DRev* 113 (1995): 96–103.

Redaction Criticism. Redaction critics saw the writers of the Gospels and Acts as theologians in their own right, who modified their sources to achieve their own theological goals in their writings. In their view, source and form criticism's emphasis on seeking the history behind the Bible led interpreters to dissect and atomize individual texts to the point where they overlooked the theology of the book's final redactor (or editor). They believed his theology could be identified in the editorial seams that connect the sources he used in his composition.[25]

In 1956 Ernst Haenchen applied redaction criticism in his commentary on Acts. He spent considerable energy analyzing Luke's theological tendencies in the summary narratives. He also argued that Luke inserted them in order to separate Peter's speeches in chapters 2 and 3 by a "representation of the life of the community." Rather than emphasize their disjointed construction, which form criticism tended toward, Haenchen sought to identify a basic order in the progression of subjects in the summaries.[26] Heinrich Zimmermann in 1961 also sought to identify possible strategies in the way the summaries were constructed by Luke to advance his theological agenda.[27]

In 1963 Hans Conzelmann argued for Lukan authorship of the summaries. However, he attributed their apparent lack of organization to Luke's understanding of history, saying, "Luke does not think in terms of causal connections, but rather finds the meaning of the whole in individual parts."[28] For Conzelmann, Luke's portrait of church life in the summary narratives, especially the sharing of property, is idealized and should not be taken as historical. He also did not think Luke intended to present them as normative for the church in his time. Rather, Luke is associating

---

[25] For surveys of the development of redaction criticism, see D. A. Carson, "Redaction Criticism: On the Legitimacy and Illegitimacy of a Literary Tool," in *Scripture and Truth*, ed. D. A. Carson and John D. Woodbridge (Grand Rapids: Zondervan, 1983), 119–42; Grant R. Osborne, "Redaction Criticism," in *DJG*, 662–69; and Robert H. Stein, *Gospels and Tradition: Studies on the Redaction of the Synoptic Gospels* (Grand Rapids: Baker, 1991).

[26] In Acts 2:42–47 Haenchen ordered the topics as follows: religious activity in the congregation (2:42), religious awe (2:43), religiously inspired social activity (2:44–45), temple attendance, ritual meals, and the favorable impression they made on the Jewish people (2:46–47). See Ernst Haenchen, *The Acts of the Apostles*, trans. R. McL. Wilson (Philadelphia: Westminster Press, 1971), 195–96.

[27] In each summary narrative Zimmerman identified a theme statement, followed by a description of elements of church life, and concluded by restating and expanding the initial theme. Heinrich Zimmermann, "Die Sammelberichte der Apostelgeschichte," *BZ* 5 (1961): 71–82. Also see J. Lach, "Katechese über die Kirche von Jerusalem in der Apostelgeschichte (2,42–47; 4,32–35; 5,12–16)," *ColT* 52, no. Supplement (1982): 141–53.

[28] Hans Conzelmann, *Acts of the Apostles*, trans. James Limburg, A. Thomas Kraabel, and Donald H. Juel, Hermeneia (Philadelphia: Fortress, 1987), xliii.

the earliest days of the church with Greek utopian ideals in the minds of his readers.[29] Conzelmann reiterated his position on the historicity of the summary narratives in his 1979 book on New Testament interpretation, coauthored with Andreas Lindemann:

> *As sources, the summaries in Acts (see 2:42–47; 4:32–35; 5:12–16) have as little immediate value as the speeches. They do not permit a glance into the actual conditions of the early church; rather they present the ideal picture of the church desired by the author. . . . The picture of the church that is drawn in the summaries is not historically authentic but represents an idealization of the early period of the kind frequently observed in classical historiography ("golden era").*[30]

Conzelmann assumed that Luke made up his ideal portrait of the church, because he thought Luke wanted readers to have one. The mere existence of an idealized utopian tradition in Greek literature was evidence enough to conclude that Luke must have done the same thing with his ideal portraits. Conzelmann does not appear to have even entertained the possibility that Luke had access to accurate information about the Jerusalem church through eyewitnesses he could have interviewed. Jews from all over the Roman Empire were in Jerusalem on the day of Pentecost. Paul said that most of the eyewitnesses to the resurrected Jesus were still living when he wrote 1 Corinthians. Surely they and others who experienced church life in Jerusalem in the early days were still alive and available for Luke to consult.[31] Instead, for Conzelmann, Luke's decision to present an ideal portrait of the Jerusalem church excluded the possibility that his statements were rooted in what actually happened.

---

[29] Ibid., 24.

[30] The quote is from the English translation. Hans Conzelmann and Andreas Lindemann, *Interpreting the New Testament: An Introduction to the Principles and Methods of N.T. Exegesis*, trans. Siegfried S. Schatzmann (Peabody, MA: Hendrickson, 1988), 243. Also see Paul S. Minear, *Images of the Church in the New Testament* (Philadelphia: Westminster Press, 1960), 141; and Gerd Lüdemann, *The Acts of the Apostles: What Really Happened in the Earliest Days of the Church?* (Amherst, NY: Prometheus, 2005), 58–59.

[31] See Luke 1:2; Acts 2:9–11; 1 Cor 15:6. On the plausibility of credible eyewitnesses being available for Luke to consult, see Richard Bauckham, *Jesus and the Eyewitnesses: The Gospels as Eyewitness Testimony* (Grand Rapids: Eerdmans, 2006), 114–53, 330–46, and chapter 10, "Christianity in the Making: Oral Mystery or Eyewitness History," in Ben Witherington III, *What's in the Word? Rethinking the Socio-Rhetorical Character of the New Testament* (Waco, TX: Baylor University Press, 2009), 121–42.

The Loss of Luke's Theology of Church Life

At this point a few observations can be made about the impact of the historical-critical method on the interpretation of the summary narratives. A general consensus exists on two points. First, scholars have continued to agree with Dibelius's basic literary insight that the summary narratives do appear to generalize on specific events in order to show them as typical occurrences in the early church. Second, regardless of where an interpreter stands on the historicity of the summary narratives, Conzelmann's view that Luke wanted readers to have a portrait of ideal church life when he wrote the summary narratives is generally agreed upon too.

However, F. C. Baur and the historical-critical method have cast a shadow over the modern study of Acts and the summary narratives with two unfortunate results. First, a basic presupposition has persisted that the theological tendency of Acts means that Luke's purpose did not include accurately relating the facts of early church history. Scholars of this mind-set have emphasized the wideness of the gap they believe exists between the final canonical form of Acts and the history behind it. Thus, they spent all their energy trying to get behind the text to the kernel of history referred to by them. The canonical form of Acts lost its "pride of place" among historical critics looking for primary source evidence for reconstruction of the history of the earliest churches.[32] Ironically, the supposed history obtained by historical critics bears a striking resemblance to the anti-supernatural bias of nineteenth-century Enlightenment scholarship led by Baur and the Tübingen school.[33] Because the summary narratives do have the appearance of editorial seams that link episodes together, under the historical-critical paradigm they were seen as the latest parts of Acts to be written. To form and redaction critics, therefore, they represented Luke's

---

[32] Richard Walsh, "Reconstructing the New Testament Churches: The Place of Acts," in *With Steadfast Purpose: Essays on Acts in Honor of Henry Jackson Flanders*, ed. Naymond H. Keathley (Waco, TX: Baylor University Press, 1990), 324–25.

[33] Although the focus of this book is not on establishing the historical reliability of Acts, another trajectory in modern Acts scholarship was virtually ignored by adherents of the historical-critical method. Scholars like J. B. Lightfoot, William Ramsay, Eduard Meyer, and others near the end of the nineteenth century rejected Baur and the Tübingen school's radically negative assessment of Acts. Their heirs include scholars like F. F. Bruce, Colin Hemer, Everett Harrison, I. Howard Marshall, Richard Longenecker, Darrell L. Bock, and others in the twentieth century and today who, while not monolithic in their conclusions, nevertheless see Acts as historically reliable. See the discussion in Gasque, *History of the Interpretation*, 136–63, 258–83; and the brief but illuminating comparative study by Andrew Southwell, "German and British Approaches to Acts Research: A Comparative Study of F. C. Baur, Ernst Troeltsch, and William Ramsay," Th.M. thesis (St. Louis, MO: Covenant Theological Seminary, 1994), 55–63.

theological bias and were dismissed as sources of reliable information on the Jerusalem church.

Second, so much effort has gone into analyzing the sources and composition of the summary narratives that scholars have neglected their literary context and theological role in the final canonical form of Acts. The contribution of Maria Anicia Co illustrates this tendency. Co completed her lengthy two-volume dissertation at Louvain University in 1990 (420 pages!) and published an article on the composition of the summary narratives in 1992. Her extensive analysis of the linguistic interrelationships between the summary narratives concludes that they are from Luke's hand.[34] Co put an end to speculation about which parts are Lukan and which are from his sources. However, Co also epitomizes the tendency of historical-critical scholarship to drill so deeply into the composition of the summary narratives that little energy is left to consider broader concerns, such as what they contribute to Luke's theological vision as a whole.[35]

Interpretive methodologies and their presuppositions inevitably impact exegesis and theology. Form criticism's focus on the history behind the summary narratives and redaction criticism's tendency to isolate Luke's theology in them from the rest of Acts distracted interpreters from considering their role in the final canonical form of Acts. Because the summary narratives focus on church life, the result has been an underemphasis on church life in the study of the theology of Acts.

A survey of forty mainly English-language commentaries on Acts written over the last fifty or so years illustrates this imbalance. Under

---

[34] Maria Anicia Co, "The Major Summaries in Acts," *ETL* 68 (1992): 49–81; Co, *The Composite Summaries in Acts 2–5: A Study of Luke's Use of Summary as a Narrative Technique* (Louvain, Belgium: Louvain University, 1990).

[35] A few scholars have attempted to move in this direction. Wilhelm Ott, *Gebet und Heil: Die Bedeutung der Gebetsparänese in der lukanischen Theologie* (München: n.p., 1965), 125–29, saw two summaries standing side by side in Acts 2:41–47. Acts 2:41–42 describes the conclusion to Pentecost and the daily life of new converts. Acts 2:43–47 describes the life of the entire church. Acts 4:32–5:16 forms a greater summary which parallels and explains further the material in 2:42–47. Sijbolt J. Noorda, "Scene and Summary: A Proposal for Reading Acts 4,32–5,16," in *Les Actes des Apôtres: traditions, redaction et théologie*, ed. Jacob Kremer (Louvain, Belgium: University Press, 1979), 475–83, sought to read Acts 2–5 from a narrative perspective as the alternation between scene and summary, in order to maintain close contact between the episodes and speeches of Acts 2–5 and the summaries that connect them. Stephan J. Joubert, "Die gesigpunt van die verteller en die funksie van die Jerusalemgemeente binne die 'opsommings' in Handelinge," *SK* 10 (1989): 21–35, argued that, rather than give a comprehensive account of the Jerusalem church, Luke's aim was to present the church as the visible fulfillment of Christ's promise in Acts 1:8. Though none of these studies declare their intention to move beyond the constraints of form and redaction criticism, their sensitivity to potential literary connections with surrounding material clearly moves the discussion forward.

discussions of major themes in introductory sections, only nine commentaries (23%) identify the church or church life as important enough to be treated as a distinct theme.[36] Under discussions of literary features, seven commentaries (18%) single out summarization for comment in separate sections.[37] Four commentaries (10%) bring specific verses from the summary narratives into their discussions of the church.[38] However, only three commentaries (8%) mention the summary narratives, or at least a significant portion of them, in their discussions of church life.[39] None of the forty commentaries surveyed identified Acts 2:42–47; 4:32–35; and 5:12–16 specifically as core texts for articulating Luke's theology of church life.[40]

Even otherwise outstanding New Testament theologies published in recent years tend to overlook Luke's emphasis on church life in the summary narratives when they discuss the doctrine of the church in Acts.[41]

---

[36] Seven treat church life in separate discussions. See William Neil, *The Acts of the Apostles*, NCBC (Grand Rapids: Eerdmans, 1973), 45–52; I. Howard Marshall, *Acts*, TNTC (Grand Rapids: Eerdmans, 1980), 32–34; F. F. Bruce, *The Acts of the Apostles: The Greek Text with Introduction and Commentary* (Grand Rapids: Eerdmans, 1990), 61–63; Luke Timothy Johnson, *The Acts of the Apostles*, SP (Collegeville, MN: Michael Glazier, 1992), 15; Beverly Roberts Gaventa, *The Acts of the Apostles*, ANTC (Nashville: Abingdon, 2003), 39–44; William J. Larkin, *Acts*, CBC (Carol Stream, IL: Tyndale House, 2006), 370–71; David Peterson, *The Acts of the Apostles*, PNTC (Grand Rapids: Eerdmans, 2009), 92–97. Justo L. González, *Acts: The Gospel of the Spirit* (Maryknoll, NY: Orbis Books, 2001), 7; and Everett F. Harrison, *Acts: The Expanding Church* (Chicago: Moody, 1975), 13, identify church life as an important theme in their introductory remarks.

[37] Haenchen, *Acts*, 154–55, 193–96; Conzelmann, *Acts*, xliii; Joseph A. Fitzmyer, *The Acts of the Apostles: A New Translation with Introduction and Commentary*, AB (New York: Doubleday, 1998), 97; Ben Witherington III, *The Acts of the Apostles: A Socio-Rhetorical Commentary* (Grand Rapids: Eerdmans, 1998), 46, 99–102, 157–59; Peterson, *Acts*, 42; J. Bradley Chance, *Acts*, SHBC (Macon, GA: Smyth & Helwys, 2007), 90; and Richard I. Pervo, *Acts*, Hermeneia (Minneapolis: Fortress, 2009), 8–9, 89, give considerable attention to summaries as a literary feature of Acts either in separate sections or as an excursus in their comments on Acts 2:42–47. John Polhill, *Acts*, NAC (Nashville: Broadman, 1992), 48; Johnson, *Acts*, 9; also see Luke Timothy Johnson, "Luke-Acts," in *ABD*, 4:409; Robert W. Wall, "The Acts of the Apostles," in *NIB*, 10:15; and Darrell L. Bock, *Acts*, BECNT (Grand Rapids: Baker Academic, 2007), 13, 149, mention them briefly and indicate their literary qualities.

[38] Neil, *Acts*, 51; Marshall, *Acts*, 32; Bruce, *Acts of the Apostles: The Greek Text*, 62; Gaventa, *Acts*, 41. Gaventa makes Acts 2:42–47 a focal text in her discussion of the church.

[39] Johnson, *Acts*, 15 (Acts 2:42–47; 4:32–37); Larkin, *Acts*, 370 (2:42–47; 4:32–37; 5:12–16), and Peterson, *Acts*, 92–93 (2:42–47).

[40] By "specifically" I mean with these particular verses as boundaries. Opinions vary widely as to which verses should form their proper boundaries. In chapter 2 I will argue that Acts 2:42–47; 4:32–35; and 5:12–16 contain the boundaries Luke intended for readers/hearers to recognize.

[41] References to individual verses within the summary narratives abound, but the summary narratives as a whole are not identified as a resource for understanding Luke's ecclesiology. See Donald Guthrie, *New Testament Theology* (Downers Grove, IL: InterVarsity, 1981), 731–42; George Eldon Ladd, *A Theology of the New Testament* (Grand Rapids: Eerdmans, 1974), 342–56; I. Howard Marshall, *New Testament Theology: Many Witnesses, One Gospel* (Downers Grove, IL: InterVarsity, 2004), 155–206; Frank Thielmann, *Theology of the New Testament: A Canonical and Synthetic Approach* (Grand Rapids: Zondervan, 2005), 111–50.

Books focused more narrowly on the doctrine of the church in the Bible do the same.[42] Church life, especially life in the Jerusalem church and church life as a general theological emphasis in Acts, has been emphasized much less than I believe Luke intended it to be.

I want to be careful not to overstate my contention here. Church life in Acts has been underemphasized, not ignored. However, an approach to the summary narratives is needed that will address their relationship to the whole text of Acts. To do this, the helpful perspective of more recent literary approaches will be utilized, especially narrative and rhetorical criticism. These two methodologies developed along somewhat different trajectories, but their emergence is part of a larger literary turn in New Testament studies.

THE LITERARY TURN IN NEW TESTAMENT STUDIES

After more than a century of domination by the historical-critical method, scholars began to seek a way beyond its atomizing tendencies toward a greater appreciation of the literary dimensions of Scripture. This development was needed, because every part of Scripture is in some sense literature, making interaction with literary theory unavoidable in interpretation.[43] For many this turn represented a retreat from the quest for sources behind texts and, unfortunately, away from an interest in the historical world behind the sources. Their focus turned to the final form of the biblical books and the recognition that biblical narratives also create their own narrative worlds through the stories they tell.[44] The literary turn has been compared to shifting from viewing the Bible as a window to seeing it as

---

[42] Edmund P. Clowney, *The Church* (Downers Grove, IL: InterVarsity, 1995), 60, 77, 81, 102, 204, mentions Acts 2:42 four times, Acts 2:47 twice, and Acts 5:15 once. In his chapter on the church in Acts, Kevin Giles, *What on Earth Is the Church? An Exploration in New Testament Theology* (Downers Grove, IL: InterVarsity, 1995), 76–79, gives attention to the "communal dimension" of the gift of the Holy Spirit on Pentecost that resulted in the "Community of the New Age." His main texts are various verses from Acts 2:42–47 and 4:32–37. Graham H. Twelftree's *People of the Spirit: Exploring Luke's View of the Church* (Grand Rapids: Baker, 2009) mentions significant portions of the summary narratives at various points (100, 130, 179, 195).

[43] Grant R. Osborne, "Literary Theory and Biblical Interpretation," in *Words and the Word: Explorations in Biblical and Literary Theory*, ed. David G. Firth and Jamie A. Grant (Downers Grove, IL: InterVarsity, 2008), 48.

[44] William A. Beardslee, *Literary Criticism of the New Testament* (Philadelphia: Fortress, 1969), 20–23.

a mirror.[45] Rather than looking through biblical narrative, as through a window, at events referred to by it, interpreters began to focus on the inner workings of the biblical text, like looking at a mirror, and the narrative world it depicts as a source of meaning in itself.[46]

The Influence of Literary Criticism

In America, the heritage of church-state separation tended to separate English faculties, where literary studies were pursued, from New Testament faculties in divinity schools, which remained mired in the historical-critical paradigm.[47] However, several developments in modern literary criticism became influential in biblical studies in the later decades of the twentieth century. English critics were turning their attention to the formal features of narrative texts and to developing methodologies for analyzing the connections between these features and the meaning they communicate. Literary critics were abandoning such historical questions as the pursuit of an author's intended meaning in favor of seeing texts as entities independent from their authors and capable of creating their own meaning as they encounter readers. Called literary formalism and New Criticism early on, the discipline of narratology represents the full flowering of this text-centered methodology.[48]

Narratology. The definitions of narratology are as diverse as the perspectives of the scholars who employ the word, and the discipline is constantly in flux.[49] I am especially interested in the earlier efforts of narrative theorists toward developing a systematic approach to the interpretation of narrative.[50] Narratology studies the nature, form, and function of narrative

---

[45] S. Scott Bartchy, "Narrative Criticism," in *DLNT*, 788.

[46] Murray Krieger, *A Window to Criticism: Shakespeare's Sonnets and Modern Poetics* (Princeton, NJ: Princeton University Press, 1964), 3–4.

[47] Lorin L. Cranford, "Modern New Testament Interpretation," in *Biblical Hermeneutics: A Comprehensive Guide to Interpreting Scripture*, ed. Bruce Corley, Steve Lemke, and Grant Lovejoy (Nashville: Broadman & Holman, 1996), 126.

[48] Anthony C. Thiselton, *Hermeneutics: An Introduction* (Grand Rapids: Eerdmans, 2009), 24–25. On the influence of formalism on the development of NT narrative criticism, see Brook W. R. Pearson, "New Testament Literary Criticism," in *Handbook to Exegesis of the New Testament*, ed. Stanley E. Porter (Leiden: Brill Academic, 2002), 248–51.

[49] For a survey of the development and varieties of narratologies in contemporary scholarship, see "Introduction," in *Narratology: An Introduction*, ed. Susana Onega and José Angel García Landa (New York: Longman Group, 1996), 1–41, particularly their survey of the transition from New Criticism to narratology (21–29). Also helpful is Gerald Prince, "Surveying Narratology," in *What Is Narratology? Questions and Answers Regarding the Status of a Theory*, ed. Tom Kindt and Hans-Harald Müller (Berlin: Walter de Gruyter, 2003), 1–16.

[50] Paul Cobley, "Narratology," in *The Johns Hopkins Guide to Literary Theory and Criticism,*

texts with a threefold goal of (1) examining the formal aspects that various narratives have in common with each other (i.e., all narratives have a narrator, characters, a setting, plot, point of view, and an implied worldview, etc.); (2) accounting for what makes them different from each other; and, (3) understanding how the various parts of a narrative function together to convey meaning to readers.[51] It is important to avoid the same error that historical critics made of reducing interpretation to a mere science of the mechanics of narratives. On the other hand, most narrative texts do have in common basic attributes that impact the reading process and can be recognized and comprehended across languages, cultures, even generations, no matter the genre.[52] Narratology provides helpful tools for examining these attributes, which Bible scholars have taken advantage of through the discipline of narrative criticism.[53]

Narrative Criticism. Narrative criticism focuses on the formal features of narrative discourse and how they work together to convey meaning. David Rhoads and Donald Michie originally developed narrative criticism as an application of the principles of narratology to reading the Gospel of Mark as narrative.[54] Studies of the other Gospel narratives and of Acts soon followed.[55]

---

ed. Michael Groden, Martin Kreiswirth, and Imre Szeman (Baltimore: Johns Hopkins University Press, 2005), 677.

[51] My definition expands on the definition of narratology in Gerald Prince, *A Dictionary of Narratology* (Lincoln: University of Nebraska Press, 1987), 65.

[52] C. Joachim Classen, "Rhetoric and Literary Criticism: Their Nature and Their Functions in Antiquity," *Mnemosyne* 48 (1995): 515.

[53] Probably the most influential introductions to narratology and narrative theory among Bible scholars are: Seymour B. Chatman, *Story and Discourse: Narrative Structure in Fiction and Film* (Ithaca, NY: Cornell University Press, 1978); Mieke Bal, *Narratology: Introduction to the Theory of Narrative* (Toronto: University of Toronto Press, 1997); Gerard Genette, *Narrative Discourse: An Essay in Method*, trans. Jane E. Lewin (Ithaca, NY: Cornell University Press, 1980); Gerald Prince, *Narratology: The Form and Functioning of Narrative* (Berlin: Walter de Gruyter, 1982); and Shlomith Rimmon-Kenan, *Narrative Fiction: Contemporary Poetics* (New York: Methuen, 1983).

[54] See the preface in David M. Rhoads and Donald Michie, *Mark as Story: An Introduction to the Narrative of a Gospel* (Philadelphia: Fortress, 1982), xv; David M. Rhoads, "Narrative Criticism and the Gospel of Mark," *JAAR* 50 (1982): 411–34; and David M. Rhoads, "Narrative Criticism: Practices and Prospects," in *Characterization in the Gospels: Reconceiving Narrative Criticism*, ed. David M. Rhoads and Kari Syreeni (Sheffield, England: Sheffield Academic Press, 1999), 264–85. Their joint effort arose out of an invitation by Rhoads to Michie, his colleague from the English department at Carthage College, to visit his NT introduction class to show how one would read one of the Gospels as literature. The endnotes in *Mark as Story* read like a Who's Who among narrative theorists. The term first appeared in print in George W. Coats, "On Narrative Criticism," *Semeia* 3 (1975): 137–41.

[55] See R. Alan Culpepper, *Anatomy of the Fourth Gospel: A Study in Literary Design* (Philadelphia: Fortress Press, 1983); Jack D. Kingsbury, *Matthew as Story* (Philadelphia: Fortress, 1988); Robert C. Tannehill, *The Narrative Unity of Luke-Acts: A Literary Interpretation, Volume 1: The Gospel According to Luke* (Minneapolis: Fortress, 1986) and *Volume 2: The Acts of the Apostles* (Minneapolis:

Although narratology and narrative criticism are closely related, they differ at an important point. Both seek to understand narrative texts, but narratology is more concerned with developing theories of how narratives work, while narrative criticism uses the theories of narratologists in the work of exegesis. Meir Sternberg's magisterial *The Poetics of Biblical Narrative* develops what he calls a "discourse-oriented analysis" of a narrative text as a pattern of meaning. He asks questions about the rules governing the relationship between the biblical author and his readers, such as: Is this text prose or verse, parable or chronicle, fiction or history? What image of the world does the narrator project for readers? What is the role played by the characters, by the varying settings, and by the movement of time in the narrative? How does the work hang together? How do the individual parts of the narrative relate to the whole?[56]

Sternberg's last two questions are of particular importance for our study of summarization in Acts. We have seen that most modern commentators on Acts agree that Luke makes his narrative hang together with numerous brief summaries that connect major episodes. Building on the insights of narrative criticism, I want to argue that, through their subject matter, Luke also skillfully emphasizes important aspects of the unfolding drama of the church for readers, all the while remaining in the narrative mode. Luke's narrator is the key to his literary accomplishment and to the persuasive effect he seeks to have on readers, which is a primary concern of rhetorical-criticism.

Fortress, 1990); and William S. Kurz, *Reading Luke-Acts: Dynamics of Biblical Narrative* (Louisville, KY: Westminster/John Knox, 1993). By 1992 Mark Powell could list seventy-four scholarly articles and monographs dealing with Luke and Acts from a literary perspective. Mark Allan Powell, *The Bible and Modern Literary Criticism: A Critical Assessment and Annotated Bibliography*, Bibliographies and Indexes in Religious Studies (New York: Greenwood Press, 1992), 308–24.

[56] Meir Sternberg, *The Poetics of Biblical Narrative: Ideological Literature and the Drama of Reading* (Bloomington: Indiana University Press, 1985), 15. Sternberg's volume is technical but worth the effort. His literary approach is what would be called synchronic, in that while he does not disregard the historical context out of which the Bible emerged, his focus is on the final form as a compositional unity. Consequently, Sternberg's expositional model rejects many of the diachronic assumptions of higher criticism. On his method, see Bernard M. Levinson, "The Right Chorale: From the Poetics to the Hermeneutics of the Hebrew Bible," in *"Not in Heaven": Coherence and Complexity in Biblical Narrative*, ed. Jason P. Rosenblatt and Joseph C. Sitterson (Bloomington: Indiana University Press, 1991), 129–32. Other helpful introductions under the general label of narrative criticism include: Robert Alter, *The Art of Biblical Narrative* (New York: Basic Books, 1981); John A. Beck, *God as Storyteller: Seeking Meaning in Biblical Narrative* (St. Louis, MO: Chalice Press, 2008); Bartchy, "Narrative Criticism"; James L. Resseguie, *Narrative Criticism of the New Testament* (Grand Rapids: Baker Academic, 2005).

Rhetorical Criticism. Narrative criticism and rhetorical criticism have been linked as two sides of the same coin in the interpretive task.[57] Whereas narrative criticism considers how the formal features of narrative discourse work together to convey meaning, rhetorical criticism focuses on the persuasive effect an author sought to have on readers through his discourse.[58] Contemporary approaches to the rhetorical analysis of the New Testament are diverse and flourishing, ranging from more traditional historical methods to modern and even postmodern approaches.[59] The historical approach, exemplified in the work of George A. Kennedy, compares biblical texts to other ancient texts or to commonly accepted guidelines in ancient rhetorical handbooks in order to understand the kinds of techniques and patterns of persuasion Bible authors might have employed in their writings.[60] More recent approaches, exemplified by Vernon K. Robbins's socio-rhetorical perspective, deliberately combine traditional tools with multiple contemporary methodologies arising out of modern language theory and hermeneutics.[61]

When rhetoric is mentioned, public speaking usually comes to mind. Luke was educated in an oral culture that valued skillful argumentation and the ability to persuade through speech making. Rhetorical-critical analysis of Acts has focused on the speeches of Acts, rather than narrative sections.[62] However, an education that included rhetoric would surely have impacted not just a student's thinking and speaking, but his writing as

---

[57] Dennis L. Stamps, "Rhetorical and Narratological Criticism," in Porter, *Handbook to Exegesis of the New Testament*, 220–21.

[58] Michael McGuire, "The Rhetoric of Narrative: A Hermeneutic, Critical Theory," in *Narrative Thought and Narrative Language*, ed. Bruce K. Britton and Anthony D. Pellegrini (Hillsdale, NJ: Lawrence Erblaum Associates, 1989), 221.

[59] By 2006 Duane Watson could count twenty-nine recent studies of Luke-Acts, sixty-seven of Luke, and an astonishing seventy-two studies of Acts that are informed by rhetorical criticism. See Duane F. Watson, *The Rhetoric of the New Testament: A Bibliographic Survey* (Blandford Forum, UK: Deo Publishing, 2006), 105–16. For an outstanding survey of the field of NT rhetorical criticism, see the appendix "Rhetorical Criticism: A New Direction," in Blake Shipp, *Paul the Reluctant Witness: Power and Weakness in Luke's Portrayal* (Eugene, OR: Cascade Books, 2005), 121–58.

[60] George A. Kennedy, *New Testament Interpretation through Rhetorical Criticism* (Chapel Hill: University of North Carolina Press, 1984). See Blake Shipp, "George Kennedy's Influence on Rhetorical Interpretation of the Acts of the Apostles," in *Words Well Spoken: George Kennedy's Rhetoric of the New Testament*, ed. C. Clifton Black and Duane F. Watson, Studies in Rhetoric and Religion (Waco, TX: Baylor University Press, 2008), 107–23.

[61] See Vernon K. Robbins, *Exploring the Texture of Texts: A Guide to Socio-Rhetorical Interpretation* (Valley Forge, PA: Trinity Press International, 1996); and Vernon K. Robbins, *The Tapestry of Early Christian Discourse: Rhetoric, Society, and Ideology* (London: Routledge, 1996).

[62] On the speeches of Acts see Simon J. Kistemaker, "The Speeches in Acts," *CTR* 5, no. 1 (1990): 31–41; Marion L. Soards, *The Speeches in Acts: Their Content, Context, and Concerns* (Louisville, KY: Westminster John Knox, 1994); and Bruce W. Winter, "Official Proceedings and the

well. Luke's education most likely included training in the *progymnasmata*, which were collections of speaking and writing exercises for students of rhetoric.[63] Several manuals of progymnasmata survive, including that of Aelius Theon, who was quite possibly a first-century contemporary of Luke.[64] Theon believed that the practice of the exercises was valuable not just for students who wished to become orators, but also for those "who wish to practice the art of the poets or historians."[65] He also said that the student who learns to express himself well and in a variety of ways in a narrative or a fable "will also compose a history well."[66] To be sure, Luke's narrative style in Acts and his message are also deeply influenced by the Old Testament history of God's people.[67] Yet, Luke also seems to be aware of the kind of narrative conventions one would expect to see in the writings of someone who cut his teeth on the rhetorical manuals and the historians that were part of the standard curriculum of his day.[68] Therefore, as we study the narrative style of the summaries, it will be helpful to ask how Luke uses his narrator to call for a particular response from readers and what situation might have called for Luke to address his readers the

---

Forensic Speeches in Acts 24–26," in *The Book of Acts in Its Ancient Literary Setting*, ed. Bruce W. Winter and Andrew D. Clarke (Grand Rapids: Eerdmans, 1993), 305–36.

[63] J. David Fleming, "The Very Idea of a Progymnasmata," *Rhetoric Review* 22, no. 2 (2003): 109–14; Ian H. Henderson, "Quintilian and the Progymnasmata," *Antike und Abendland* 37 (1991): 82–99.

[64] See Malcolm Heath, "Theon and the History of the Progymnasmata," *GRBS* 43 (2002–2003): 9–19, for a discussion of evidence for and against a first-century date for Theon's progymnasmata.

[65] Aelius Theon, *Progymnasmata* 70. Theon instructed students to begin with Herodotus, because of his stylistic simplicity. Then, he encouraged them to go on to Theopompus, Xenophon, Philistus, Ephorus, and Thucydides. See the excellent study of the relevance of the progymnasmata for training in history writing in Craig A. Gibson, "Learning Greek History in the Ancient Classroom: The Evidence of the Treatises on Progymnasmata," *CP* 99, no. 2 (2004): 103–29, esp. 116.

[66] Aelius Theon, *Progymnasmata* 60.3–4. Theon believed that the best narratives shared the qualities of clarity, conciseness, and plausibility or persuasiveness (79.20–22). Mikeal Parsons contributed an outstanding analysis of Luke's potential awareness of and formation as a writer by progymnasmatic theorists like Theon. See Mikeal C. Parsons, "Luke and the Progymnasmata: A Preliminary Investigation into the Preliminary Exercises," in *Contextualizing Acts: Lukan Narrative and Greco-Roman Discourse*, ed. Todd C. Penner and Caroline Vander Stichele, SBLSymS 18 (Atlanta: Society of Biblical Literature, 2003), 43–63, esp. 51–56. Also see Todd Penner, "Reconfiguring the Rhetorical Study of Acts: Reflections on the Method in and Learning of a Progymnastic Poetics," *PRSt* 30 (2003): 425–39.

[67] H. Douglas Buckwalter, "Luke as Writer of Sacred History," *EvJ* 14, no. 2 (1996): 86–99; Jacob Jervell, "The Future of the Past: Luke's Vision of Salvation History and Its Bearing on His Writing of History," in *History, Literature, and Society in the Book of Acts*, ed. Ben Witherington III (New York: Cambridge University Press, 1996), 104–26; Joseph B. Tyson, "From History to Rhetoric and Back: Assessing New Trends in Acts Studies," in Penner and Stichele, *Contextualizing Acts*, 38–39.

[68] Philip E. Satterthwaite, "Acts against the Background of Classical Rhetoric," in Winter and Clarke, *The Book of Acts in Its Ancient Literary Setting*, 378–79.

way he does. Narrative and rhetorical criticism are well suited for inquiry
into these questions.

A WORD ABOUT METHOD

Before I turn to specific rhetorical features of summarization in chapter 2, a few words about method are in order. First, although narrative
criticism has its critics, I believe the qualified use of contemporary narrative theory can greatly aid the exegesis and interpretation of biblical narratives.[69] It would be naive to reject the insights of narrative criticism simply
because it arose as a response to an exhausted historical criticism that is
still unwilling to abandon its negative assessment of Acts as history. We
should study the literary dimensions of Acts, not because it is currently
fashionable to do so, but because Acts is great literature. If a contemporary
literary term or category helps interpreters see more clearly what is actually present in the text, its qualified use can promote greater accuracy in
exegesis.[70]

Second, although I borrow freely from modern literary categories, my
approach could arguably still be categorized as historical with regard to
authorial intention and historical concerns. I have argued for a more text-
focused approach that seeks to understand the way the narrator of Acts
interacted with the story he was telling in order to achieve certain effects
on readers. Nevertheless, I believe Luke had specific intentions in mind
with his narrative and that seeking to understand them is still a worthy goal

---

[69] Martin Hengel's concern about the dangers of imposing "our modern categories taken over from
other fields on ancient texts that are innocent of them" is timely, but perhaps overstated. See Martin
Hengel, "Tasks of New Testament Scholarship," *BBR* 6 (1996): 84–85; and Pheme Perkins, "Crisis
in Jerusalem: Narrative Criticism in New Testament Studies," *TS* 50 (1989): 312–23. The primary
difference between ancient and modern narrative theory is that modern theory has had more time to
develop and be refined. For an example of the use of contemporary theory for interpreting ancient
historians, see Simon Hornblower, "Narratology and Narrative Techniques in Thucydides," in *Greek
Historiography*, ed. Simon Hornblower (Oxford: Clarendon Press, 1996), 131–66.

[70] It should be kept in mind that contemporary narrative theory has focused more on fiction.
Though fiction and history have in common the fact that they are different varieties of narrative,
there are important differences. Helpful perspectives on the differences and similarities between historical and fictional narratives can be found in the chapter "Fictional Narrative, Factual Narrative"
in Gerard Genette, *Fiction and Diction*, trans. Catherine Porter (Ithaca, NY: Cornell University
Press, 1993), 54–84; Martin Löschnigg, "Narratological Categories and the (Non-) Distinction
Between Factual and Fictional Narratives," *Groupe de Recherches Anglo-Américaines de Tours* 21
(1999): 31–48; Gregory J. Laughery, "Ricoeur on History, Fiction, and Biblical Hermeneutics," in
Behind the Text: History and Biblical Interpretation, ed. Craig Bartholomew, C. Stephen Evans, Mary
Healy, and Murray Rae, *Scripture and Hermeneutics* (Grand Rapids: Zondervan, 2003), 338–73;
and William Nelson, *Fact or Fiction: The Dilemma of the Renaissance Storyteller* (Cambridge, MA:
Harvard University Press, 1973), 38–55.

in interpretation.[71] I will not bracket out historical concerns either, because I do not share the assumption of the historical-critical method that a theological tendency in Acts of necessity implies an intentional fictionalization of history. Nor do I share the assumption of many narrative critics that a literary approach to Acts requires one to bracket out historical concerns.[72] I want to understand both the historical situation of the early church and *how* Luke tells his story in order to guide readers toward aspects of the early church's story he wants to emphasize.

Third, my approach is confessionally rooted in the Christian faith and aimed at strengthening the church. It is important to acknowledge the role of faith in interpretation. I resist the demand for a strictly nonconfessional approach to the Bible as a document of religious history, which often dominates university religion departments.[73] Much can be learned from diverse perspectives, including those who do not share the Christian worldview. However, Christians need not leave their faith in Christ and their confidence in the trustworthiness of Scripture at the door when they wrestle with Acts from a literary perspective. Reading Acts historically, theologically, and as literature conflicts with reading Acts as Scripture only if we decide in advance that it will.

SUMMARY

The introduction proposed the thesis that Luke intended his descriptions of life in the Jerusalem church in the summary narratives as exemplary portraits for readers. Chapter 1 demonstrated that the summary narratives were overshadowed in twentieth-century scholarship on Acts

---

[71] Robert H. Stein, "The Benefits of an Author-Oriented Approach to Hermeneutics," *JETS* 44 (2001): 451–66; Kevin J. Vanhoozer, *Is There a Meaning in This Text? The Bible, the Reader, and the Morality of Literary Knowledge* (Grand Rapids: Zondervan, 1998). In this sense my approach could technically not be referred to as literary at all in the sense that modern literary critics mean when they set literary concerns over against historical concerns like authorial intention. See Stanley E. Porter, "Literary Approaches to the New Testament: From Formalism to Deconstruction and Back," in *Approaches to New Testament Study*, ed. Stanley E. Porter and David Tombs, JSNTSup 120 (Sheffield, England: Sheffield Academic Press, 1995), 86, 94–95; Timothy Wiarda, *Interpreting Gospel Narratives: Scenes, People, and Theology* (Nashville: B&H Academic, 2010), 5–6.

[72] Joel B. Green, "Narrative and New Testament Interpretation: Reflections on the State of the Art," *LTQ* 39, no. 3 (2004): 159–61; Osborne, "Literary Theory and Biblical Interpretation," 36–37.

[73] Markus Bockmuehl, *Seeing the Word: Refocusing New Testament Study* (Grand Rapids: Baker Academic, 2006), 55–56; Duane F. Watson, "Why We Need Socio-Rhetorical Criticism and What It Might Look Like," in *Rhetorical Criticism and the Bible*, ed. Stanley E. Porter and Dennis L. Stamps (New York: Sheffield Academic Press, 2002), 133, 136–38; and Francis B. Watson, "Bible, Theology and the University: A Response to Philip Davies," *JSOT* 71 (1996): 3–16.

by the historical-critical method, which undermined confidence in their historical reliability and cut them off from their surrounding context in Acts. Thus, their contribution to the overall theological vision of Acts, especially Luke's theology of church life, has not been emphasized sufficiently. Chapter 2 will demonstrate that the summary narratives are at the heart of Luke's vision for life together in the local church.

CHAPTER TWO

THE RHETORIC OF
SUMMARIZATION AND EXEMPLARY
CHURCH LIFE IN ACTS

hapter 1 argued that Luke's theology of church life has been underemphasized in the study of Acts. The historical-critical method, applied to the summary narratives, contributed to this imbalance by undermining confidence in their historical reliability and by separating them from their literary and theological context in Acts. These two tendencies in interpretation led to an underappreciation of their role in the emphasis on church life that runs throughout Acts. In spite of the imbalance in scholarship, Christian readers instinctively turn to these passages when they look for resources in Scripture for thinking about the faithful formation of churches. Why do the summary narratives have this persuasive power that invites people to listen, learn, and be guided by their vision for church life?

Ben Witherington's commentary on Acts appeals to a rhetorical perspective to justify his claim that Luke sought to do something unique through the summary narratives. He notes the prologues, the speeches, the "summaries," and Luke's own travelogue as examples of "where Luke's use of rhetoric becomes most apparent."[1] Witherington identifies repeated elements in 2:43–47 and 4:32–37 as "possible rhetorical indicators for Luke that these behaviors should be normative for the church."[2] I agree with his instincts. However, a more formal analysis of summarization in Acts is needed to explain how Luke imbued the summary narratives with a persuasive power that sets forth their content for readers. Chapter 2 will demonstrate how Luke used the narrative technique of summarization, modified to suit his own rhetorical purposes in the summary narratives, to present his portraits of the church in Jerusalem in an exemplary fashion. Luke emphasized their content deliberately through his narrative style in order to persuade readers to adopt his vision for church life as they sought to lead their own congregations toward God's best for them.

THREE DIMENSIONS OF BIBLICAL HISTORY

In order to get at the rhetorical function of summarization in Acts, a framework must be established for interpreting historical biblical narratives. The place to begin is by considering how narratives like Acts function in three dimensions: as history, as literature, and as theology.[3] Considered abstractly as three principles, they might appear to conflict with each other in terms of their goals and the different forms of communication each employs. However, they function together in historical works like Acts, which tells the history of the early church in a rhetorically sophisticated

---

[1] Ben Witherington III, *The Acts of the Apostles: A Socio-Rhetorical Commentary* (Grand Rapids: Eerdmans, 1998), 46.

[2] Ibid., 99–100. Also see the "Editor's Addendum" by Witherington in W. J. McCoy, "In the Shadow of Thucydides," in *History, Literature, and Society in the Book of Acts*, ed. Ben Witherington III (New York: Cambridge University Press, 1996), 23–32.

[3] Meir Sternberg, *The Poetics of Biblical Narrative: Ideological Literature and the Drama of Reading* (Bloomington: Indiana University Press, 1985), 41–42. See James Barr, *The Bible in the Modern World* (Philadelphia: Trinity Press International, 1987), 61–63, who referred to the referential, poetic (aesthetic), and intentional (mind of the writer) processes of Bible study. See also Robert Scholes, James Phelan, and Robert Kellogg, *The Nature of Narrative* (New York: Oxford University Press, 2006), 86–88; and Amos N. Wilder, *The Bible and the Literary Critic* (Minneapolis: Fortress, 1991), 134. Robert W. Wall structures the introduction to his commentary on Acts around these three dimensions: (1) Acts as Conversation: Reading Acts as History; (2) Acts as Composition: Reading Acts as Literature; (3) Acts as Confession: Reading Acts as Theology. See Robert W. Wall, "The Acts of the Apostles," in *NIB*, 5–26.

way, in order to persuade readers to adopt a specific theological perspective on what happened.

The Historiographical Dimension

While an actual historical event and its representation in a narrative text are not the same thing, real events lie behind the historical books of the Bible.[4] The relationship between events and their depiction, or representation, in literature is described by the Greek word *mimesis*, which means "imitation."[5] How did ancient historians perceive their role in representing the past in their historical works? Historians utilized a variety of sources to construct their narrative.[6] Primary sources included the historian's personal experiences if he was a contemporary of his subject,[7] documents written preferably by eyewitnesses,[8] or interviews with eyewitnesses wherever possible.[9] Historians abridged, expanded, and omitted material, combined sources, shaped their narratives, and made minor improvements in detail.[10] They even arranged material topically on occasion, rather than chronologically, though this practice was seen as confusing to readers.[11] Nevertheless, a general ethos existed among historians that the truth about the past be discovered and faithfully told.[12] Historical narratives that falsified the past were like "a living creature which has

---

[4] John A. Beck, *God as Storyteller: Seeking Meaning in Biblical Narrative* (St. Louis, MO: Chalice Press, 2008), 21.

[5] D. A. Russell, *Criticism in Antiquity* (Berkeley: University of California Press, 1981), 99. See James A. Arieti and John M. Crossett, *Longinus: On the Sublime* (Lewiston, NY: Edwin Mellen, 1985), 79–82; and George A. Kennedy, *Quintilian* (New York: Twayne Publishers, 1969), 113–17, for surveys of the development of the idea of *mimesis* in classicism.

[6] Dionysius of Halicarnassus, *Ant. rom.* 1.1.1; 1.7.1–2. For information on abbreviations of classical works, see Patrick H. Alexander et al., eds., *The SBL Handbook of Style* (Peabody, MA: Hendrickson, 1999).

[7] Personal experience was seen as the most valuable source in ancient historiography (Herodotus, *Hist.* 2.99), which made personal means and the opportunity for travel prerequisites for being considered a competent historian (Appian, 12; Lucian, *How to Write History* 47). Also see Thucydides, *Hist.* 1.1.20–22.

[8] Polybius, 28.4.8; 38.4.8; Arrian, *Anab.* 1.1–3.

[9] Polybius, 4.2.2; Dionysius of Halicarnassus, *Ant. rom.* 1.7.3; id. *Thuc.* 5,8; Herodotus, *Hist.* 2.123.1. See Luke 1:2–3; Lucian, *How to Write History* 47; and Josephus, *Ant.* 1.17.

[10] David E. Aune, *The New Testament in Its Literary Environment* (Philadelphia: Westminster Press, 1987), 82. According to the early church historian Eusebius, sticking to the general sense of sources was more important for secular historians than transcribing them verbatim (*Praep. ev.* 4.7.1).

[11] Dionysius of Halicarnassus, *Pomp.* 3.

[12] Herodian, 1.3; Arrian, *Anab.* 1.1–3; Dionysius of Halicarnassus, *Ant. rom.* 11.1.5; Quintilian, *Inst.* 10.1.34; Lucian, *How to Write History* 7–9, 39–41, 51. Matthew Fox, "Dionysius, Lucian, and the Prejudice against Rhetoric in History," *JRS* 91 (2001): 76–93.

lost its eyesight."[13] Flamboyance and overdramatization were considered weaknesses. For example, Lucian admonished writers to avoid tasteless displays of their own word power and indulgence of their own interests at the expense of history.[14] Whether or not a particular historian succeeded at representing the past faithfully was the subject of much debate among ancient historians and literary critics.[15] Yet, the very existence of such a debate shows that many ancient historians believed that the truth about the past should be told in their historical accounts.

Opinions vary widely among contemporary scholars as to how pervasive this ethos was. Some believe that the rhetorical shaping of events by historians implies that they had a persuasive agenda, but not necessarily a concern for factual truthfulness.[16] Readers of Acts as Scripture need to be mindful of the doctrine of Scripture when it comes to assessing the relationship between the narrative of Acts and the real world behind it. If some ancient historians did not consider factual truthfulness to be of greater importance than their personal agenda, it does not automatically mean that Luke mimicked their approach and worldview or that God could not have overseen the writing process so as to keep Luke from error.[17]

The Narrative Dimension

The narrative dimension addresses the discourse of a historical work, or how a historian told his story of the past. All narratives—whether history, fiction, or epic—have the story and the discourse as their two basic components.[18] When studying the discourse of ancient historical works, the interpreter looks for narrative techniques employed by the writer as rhetorical markers that guide readers to understand its meaning.

On the surface, the narrative dimension simply acknowledges that historians sought to do more than merely relate facts. They desired to write in

---

[13] Polybius, 1.14. Also Thucydides, *Hist.* 1.20.1.

[14] Lucian, *How to Write History* 57; Seneca, *Epistles* 59.4–5.

[15] Herodian, 1.1; Thucydides, *Hist.* 1.1.21–22; Cassius Dio, *Roman History* 1.2; Cicero, *Brut.* 42; idem., *De or.* 2.51–55; Plutarch, *Adol. poet. aud.* 2.

[16] For surveys of opinions, see Gareth L. Schmeling, "The Spectrum of Narrative: Authority of the Author," in *Ancient Fiction and Early Christian Narrative*, ed. Ronald F. Hock, J. Bradley Chance, and Judith Perkins (Atlanta: Scholars Press, 1998), 26–27; and Cynthia Damon, "Rhetoric and Historiography," in *A Companion to Roman Rhetoric*, ed. William Dominik and Jon Hall (Oxford: Blackwell, 2007), 439–50.

[17] Henri Blocher, "Biblical Narrative and Historical Reference," in *Issues in Faith and History*, ed. Nigel M. de S. Cameron (Edinburgh: Rutherford House, 1989), 102–22.

[18] Seymour B. Chatman, *Story and Discourse: Narrative Structure in Fiction and Film* (Ithaca, NY: Cornell University Press, 1978), 23.

a manner that would please and move readers too.[19] Cicero criticized historians who merely compiled annals that lacked attractiveness.[20] Lucian, whose concern for historical accuracy was noted above, also encouraged historians to make their final compositions beautiful, enhancing them with "charms of expression, figure, and rhythm."[21] Quintilian believed that historians should be trained in rhetoric and be able to maintain balance in their writing style, neither stating facts dryly nor adorning them with far-fetched descriptions that amounted to poetic license.[22]

At a deeper level, however, this principle recognizes that historians wanted to persuade readers to embrace their perspective on the events they wrote about. Narrative and rhetorical criticism call for close readings of texts in order to understand how an author sought to shape the response of readers through his discourse.[23] The *narrator* plays a crucial role in the persuasive process because narrators are central to the rhetoric of the story they tell. Every narrative, regardless of genre, is in some way filtered through the narrator's voice and point of view. This gives him tremendous influence over the way readers experience his story.[24]

In historical biblical narratives, narrators tended to be more covert in comparison to Greco-Roman historians. Although this is true of the narrators of the Gospels and Acts, they still demonstrate varying degrees of presence. For example, when Luke speaks to Theophilus in his prologues, he is (in the language of narratology) an "intrusive" narrator, but less so than Herodotus in his prologue. Luke also calls himself a "servant of the word" (see Luke 1:2). The apostle John, near the end of his Gospel, identifies himself through his narrator as a reliable eyewitness to the events he wrote about (John 20:31; 21:24). Though their presence is perceptible, Matthew and Mark could hardly be called "intrusive" narrators. Thus, we have in the New Testament narrators who present themselves as omniscient, authoritative, and utterly reliable. Yet, humanly speaking, they go

---

[19] 2 Maccabees 2:25. Also see 2 Maccabees 2:22–32; 15:38–39; Horace, *Ars Poetica* 343–44.

[20] Cicero, *De or.* 2.51–55. See id., *De or.* 30–32; and id., *Opt. gen.* 15.

[21] Lucian, *How to Write History* 34, 48–49.

[22] Quintilian, *Institutio oratoria* 2.4.3–4.

[23] David M. Rhoads, "Narrative Criticism: Practices and Prospects," in *Characterization in the Gospels: Reconceiving Narrative Criticism*, ed. David M. Rhoads and Kari Syreeni (Sheffield, England: Sheffield Academic Press, 1999), 273.

[24] John A. Darr, "Narrator as Character: Mapping a Reader-Oriented Approach to Narration in Luke-Acts," *Semeia* 63 (1993): 54. On the role of narrators in biblical narrative, see Tremper Longman III, *Literary Approaches to Biblical Interpretation* (Grand Rapids: Zondervan, 1987), 85–87, 105–6; Mark Allan Powell, *What Is Narrative Criticism?* (Minneapolis: Fortress, 1990), 25–27; Steven M. Sheeley, "The Narrator in the Gospels: Developing a Model," *PRSt* 16 (1989): 213–23.

out of their way to keep themselves out of the limelight, perhaps following the anonymous Old Testament historians, or simply the attitude of early followers of Jesus like John the Baptist who said that Jesus must increase, while he must decrease (John 3:30).[25] Occasionally, a biblical author did enter his appearance through his narrator to provide descriptions of settings, summaries, reports of a character's thoughts, evaluations of a character's motives, or commentary.[26] His intrusions allowed him to comment more directly on an event's significance. Biblical narrators presented themselves as omniscient and reliable, and they strove to lead readers to accept their evaluation of the events narrated as absolutely trustworthy.[27]

The narrator has a counterpart in the text called the *narratee*—the encoded "you" addressed by the narrator. The narratee is always presupposed by the story because the narrator speaks to someone. However, the narrator usually does not name him.[28] The goal of an author is to mediate his story through his narrator directly to his narratee and, indirectly, to readers. As he did this, the author also sought to communicate his worldview to readers, which is the domain of the theological principle.

The Theological Dimension

The theological dimension concerns the worldview operating within historical biblical narratives. Little attention was paid among ancient historians to the development of a theological perspective.[29] However, they did seek to link historical events to each other in a coherent narrative that

---

[25] Armin D. Baum, "The Anonymity of the New Testament History Books: A Stylistic Device in the Context of Greco-Roman and Ancient Near Eastern Literature," *NovT* 50 (2008): 120–42, esp. 137–42.

[26] Chatman, *Story and Discourse*, 219–26.

[27] Gerald Prince, *A Dictionary of Narratology* (Lincoln: University of Nebraska Press, 1987), 39. Literary critics speak of reliable versus unreliable narrators who are imbued by an author with varying degrees of knowledge of surrounding events and characters. In biblical categories, we speak of the narrator as reliable and omniscient, because his voice is that of God speaking and revealing His perfect perspective. See Sternberg, *Poetics of Biblical Narrative*, 12.

[28] An exception in the Bible is Theophilus, who is the narratee addressed by the narrator of Luke-Acts in Luke 1:3 and Acts 1:1. For more on the role of the narratee, see R. Robert Creech, "The Most Excellent Narratee: The Significance of Theophilus in Luke-Acts," in *With Steadfast Purpose: Essays on Acts in Honor of Henry Jackson Flanders, Jr.*, ed. Naymond H. Keathley (Waco, TX: Baylor University Press, 1990), 107–26; and Gerald Prince, "Introduction to the Study of the Narratee," in Onega and Landa, *Narratology*, 190–202.

[29] Dionysius of Halicarnassus frequently mentioned religious aspects of events like causation by the gods and their reactions (*Ant. rom.* 1.1.2; 2.17.1; 2.68.2; 3.35.6; 5.56.1). However, he did not attempt to motivate readers religiously. On the role of religion in Herodotus, see John Gould, "Herodotus and Religion," in *Greek Historiography*, ed. Simon Hornblower (Oxford: Clarendon Press, 1996), 91–105; and Thomas Harrison, "'Prophecy in Reverse'? Herodotus and the Origins of History," in *Herodotus and His World*, ed. Peter Derow and Robert Parker (Oxford: Oxford University Press, 2003), 237–56.

would explain their meaning and importance for readers. Conversely, the biblical historian's worldview thoroughly shaped his interpretation of the past for readers. Of historical biblical narratives, the theological principle asks how the worldview operating within a narrative functions as a grid for the interpretation of the events recounted there. We see this principle operating in the Old Testament which regularly explained Israel's history in light of the theological framework provided by the law and the covenants. God's blessing resulted from obedience, and His discipline resulted from Israel's disobedience to His commands and a rejection of her special relationship to God as His holy people.[30]

NARRATIVE CRITICISM MOVING TOWARD BIBLICAL THEOLOGY

How can interpreters get at the theological emphases set forth by authors for readers of biblical narratives? The challenge here is that narratives like Acts are not like New Testament letters. Paul's letters have a theological and pastoral character to them wherein he addresses readers directly in a didactic manner. Acts tells a story. Much theology is set forth in the speeches of various characters, but on the level of the narrator Luke does not regularly intrude into the story to offer commentary. For the most part he lets the story speak for itself and expresses his worldview through his narrative.[31] This does not mean he operated within a theological vacuum. A set of values and beliefs clearly guided him as he wrote, which narrative and rhetorical criticism help us discern.

Implied Authors and Implied Readers

Narrative critics use the concept of an implied author and an implied reader to refer to the act of communicating the worldview operating within a narrative. The *implied author* is the writer called for by a text. In the implied author we see the concerns, values, and theological perspective of the real author as he reveals them to readers in his narrative.[32] In biblical

---

[30] See Deut 28; Judg 6:1–10; 10:6–16; 2 Kgs 17:7–23; 21:1–15; 2 Chr 7:13–14; Jer 22:8–9 for examples.

[31] William S. Campbell, "The Narrator as 'He,' 'Me,' and 'We': Grammatical Person in Ancient Histories and in the Acts of the Apostles," *JBL* 129 (2010): 405; Mark Allan Powell, "Toward a Narrative-Critical Understanding of Luke," *Int* 48 (1994): 344.

[32] Grant R. Osborne, *The Hermeneutical Spiral: A Comprehensive Introduction to Biblical Interpretation* (Downers Grove, IL: InterVarsity, 1991), 155.

interpretation the concept of an implied author is helpful for works like Acts that were written anonymously. Our knowledge of Luke is limited primarily to the "we" sections of Acts, the few details we know about him from Paul's letters (e.g., Col 4:14; Phlm 24), and a few traditions preserved by the early church. Yet, his voice is always present in the text, even if it is hidden behind his representation of the words and deeds of characters. Luke's worldview comes through more directly, however, when his narrator enters his appearance in the story.

The concept of the *implied reader* parallels the implied author. In biblical interpretation, it is important to learn as much as possible about a work's intended readers. However, when they are not identified, we must ask who is implicitly addressed by the work.[33] We are told very little about whether Luke has a particular audience in mind, beyond Theophilus (Luke 1:4; Acts 1:1). However, through a close reading of Acts, we can look for clues that tell us much about what Luke believes is important for readers to understand and embrace. We are not speaking first here of particular historical readers like the churches Paul addresses in his letters. What is in view is the reader presupposed by the discourse itself.[34] The implied reader is the cumulative picture, derived from clues within the narrative, of the presuppositions, values, competencies, and beliefs that the author required readers to know in order to understand the story correctly.[35] To seek the implied reader is to ask what kind of reader is called for by the text. The question can be asked of a whole book. However, it would also be appropriate to ask it of specific texts within a general work like Acts that covers many topics and themes. Whether the focus is on an entire narrative text or some part of it, faithful interpretation requires readers to approach it as the implied reader in order to grasp the worldview of the implied author.[36]

---

[33] See Richard Bauckham, "For Whom Were the Gospels Written?" in *The Gospel for All Christians*, ed. Richard Bauckham (Grand Rapids: Eerdmans, 1998), 9–48; and Grant R. Osborne, "Literary Theory and Biblical Interpretation," in *Words and the Word: Explorations in Biblical and Literary Theory*, ed. David G. Firth and Jamie A. Grant (Downers Grove, IL: InterVarsity, 2008), 41. It makes sense to see Acts as having been written for a general audience. Nevertheless, the concept of an implied reader is useful for considering specific texts and the kind(s) of reader(s) Luke might have had in mind with them.

[34] Chatman, *Story and Discourse*, 148.

[35] Terence J. Keegan, *Interpreting the Bible: A Popular Introduction to Biblical Hermeneutics* (Mahwah, NJ: Paulist Press, 1985), 105–6; Wayne C. Booth, *The Rhetoric of Fiction* (Chicago: University of Chicago Press, 1961), 138; and Jonathan Culler, *Structuralist Poetics: Structuralism, Linguistics, and the Study of Literature* (Ithaca, NY: Cornell University Press, 1975), 123–24.

[36] Edgar V. McKnight, *The Bible and the Reader: An Introduction to Literary Criticism* (Philadelphia: Fortress, 1985), 103; Peter J. Rabinowitz, *Before Reading: Narrative Conventions and*

An additional benefit of seeking the identity of the implied reader is that it limits the subjectivity of actual readers by calling attention to the reader called for by the text.[37] We will return to this idea later in chapter 2 when the implied reader of the summary narratives is considered.

Narrative Techniques that Guide the Implied Reader

How was the author of a biblical narrative able to communicate his theological vision and influence readers to accept it? His narrator was crucial to this effort. The narrator can mark a story with a realism that renders characters, dialogue, and emotion with an immediacy that invites readers into the action. Yet, a narrator retains the freedom to analyze, comment, assign meaning to events, and ultimately judge what is happening in the story.[38] The narrator can speak to his narratee about these things above the heads of characters as he communicates the worldview governing his story. Biblical narrators do not present the worldview of the Bible in tightly worded propositions like the Ten Commandments and the Beatitudes or in a systematic statement of faith like the Apostles' and Nicene creeds. It has to be assembled as the drama unfolds in the deeds and recorded speech of characters, as well as in the commentary and asides he provides for readers. It is there nonetheless, and it impacts readers during the act of reading or hearing the story.[39]

The author of a historical biblical narrative guided readers by employing a variety of narrative techniques and compositional patterns in order to shape their response. He might have adapted techniques and patterns to his own rhetorical agenda that were common in the literary environment of his day.[40] Some examples of commonly used techniques and patterns follow:[41]

---

the *Politics of Reading* (Ithaca, NY: Cornell University Press, 1987), 43; and Scholes, Phelan, and Kellogg, *Nature of Narrative*, 83.

[37] Mark Allan Powell, "Narrative Criticism," in *Hearing the New Testament: Strategies for Interpretation*, ed. Joel B. Green (Grand Rapids: Eerdmans, 2010), 243; Leland Ryken, *Windows to the World: Literature in Christian Perspective* (Grand Rapids: Zondervan, 1985), 108.

[38] Robert Alter, *The Pleasures of Reading in an Ideological Age* (New York: Simon and Schuster, 1989), 185.

[39] David M. Rhoads and Donald Michie, *Mark as Story: An Introduction to the Narrative of a Gospel* (Philadelphia: Fortress, 1982), 39.

[40] Duane F. Watson, "The Influence of George Kennedy on Rhetorical Criticism of the New Testament," in C. C. Black and D. F. Watson, *Words Well Spoken: George Kennedy's Rhetoric of the New Testament* (Waco, TX: Baylor University Press, 2008), 44. See Simon Hornblower, "Narratology and Narrative Techniques in Thucydides," in *Greek Historiography*, ed. Simon Hornblower (Oxford: Clarendon Press, 1996) for a discussion of narrative patterns and techniques in Thucydides.

[41] This list is an abridgement and modification of the list of narrative patterns developed by David Bauer, with several additional patterns added. See David R. Bauer, *The Structure of Matthew's Gospel: A Study in Literary Design* (Sheffield: Almond Press, 1988), 13–20; Helmut Bonheim, *The*

Aside	halting of narrative time while the narrator makes a comment to his narratee
Causation	ordering events narrated in terms of causes and effects
Chiasm	a-b-b'-a' pattern in narrative discourse
Climax	movement of events from lesser to greater intensity
Comparison	juxtaposition of similar elements in a narrative
Contrast	juxtaposition of dissimilar elements in a narrative
Defocalization	expansion of focus in a narrative from specifics toward generalities
Description	giving the narratee details about some aspect of the story
Digression	temporary turn away from the story to deal with an item of lesser importance
Focalization	narrowing of focus toward narration that emphasizes specifics and details
Foreshadowing	inclusion of material at one point that prepares readers for what is to come
Inclusion	repetition of features at each end of a narrative unit that binds it together
Intercalation	insertion of one literary unit inside another
Interchange	a-b-a'-b' pattern in narrative discourse
Narration	recounting of events in an orderly process through means of a narrator
Pivot	change in the direction of a narrative
Purpose Statement	statement by the narrator of the purpose for a narrative
Repetition	recurrence of similar elements in a narrative
Summarization	interscenic compression of specific events into generalized statements

Every ancient work of narrative art is the sum of a vast number of selective and combinational decisions that result in observable patterns of

---

Narrative Modes: Techniques of the Short Story (Cambridge: D. S. Brewer, 1982), 18–36; Irving L. Jensen, *Independent Bible Study* (Chicago: Moody, 1963), 39–42; Walter L. Liefeld, *New Testament Exposition: From Text to Sermon* (Grand Rapids: Zondervan, 1984), 60–72; Bonnie J. F. Meyer and G. Elizabeth Rice, "The Interaction of Reader Strategies and the Organization of Text," *Text* 2 (1982): 155–92; Eugene A. Nida et al., *Style and Discourse: With Special Reference to the Text of the Greek New Testament* (Cape Town, South Africa: Bible Society, 1983), 22–45; Osborne, *Hermeneutical Spiral*, 35–40; Sternberg, *Poetics of Biblical Narrative*, 120–21; James L. Resseguie, *Narrative Criticism of the New Testament* (Grand Rapids: Baker Academic, 2005), 41–78, for more development of these and other compositional patterns.

discourse.[42] Some patterns are the result of the author's unconscious habits of composition developed through years of training in the progymnasmata.[43] This must be taken into account when making judgments about how much significance to attach to each pattern detected. Nevertheless, many are deliberate compositional choices that serve as rhetorical markers on an intentionally designed map through the narrative. Careful observation of these indicators can help interpreters discern both how the biblical author constructed his narrative and the persuasive effect he sought to have on readers.[44]

For example, the repetition of key words and themes can reinforce a plot. Inclusions at each end of a narrative unit can indicate an author's main emphasis in the unit. The use of comparison and contrast can reinforce or polarize aspects of events and character actions. Even more explicit in their guidance are direct intrusions by the narrator into his story to speak to his narratee and, beyond the narratee, to readers. To do this the narrator has to stop the time of the story and turn to readers in order to comment on an item of relevance. The purpose statement, the digression, and the aside are the most intrusive of these interruptions.

Somewhere between unconscious habits of composition and deliberate intrusions by the narrator, summaries lie as an indirect means of guiding the implied reader. The following discussion evaluates the function of summarization as a narrative technique in a writer's rhetorical strategy for guiding readers toward important aspects of his discourse.

Summarization as a Narrative Technique in a Rhetorical Strategy

Summaries compress the occurrence of many events or multiple occurrences of a single event into concise generalizations. They usually appear as unfocused narrative bridges between episodes. Time within a narrative continues to pass when a narrator summarizes, meaning that summaries remain part of the narrative even though the narrator has entered his

---

[42] Sternberg, *Poetics of Biblical Narrative*, 66.

[43] On Luke's rhetorical training, see Craig A. Gibson, "Learning Greek History in the Ancient Classroom: The Evidence of the Treatises on Progymnasmata," *CP* 99, no. 2 (2004), 103–29; Mikeal C. Parsons, "Luke and the *Progymnasmata*: A Preliminary Investigation into the Preliminary Exercises," in *Contextualizing Acts: Lukan Narrative and Greco-Roman Discourse*, ed. Todd C. Penner and Caroline Vander Stichele, SBLSymS 18 (Atlanta: Society of Biblical Literature, 2003), 43–64; Todd Penner, "Reconfiguring the Rhetorical Study of Acts: Reflections on the Method in and Learning of a Progymnastic Poetics," *PRSt* 30 (2003): 431–39.

[44] Dennis L. Stamps, "Rhetorical and Narratological Criticism," in *Handbook to Exegesis of the New Testament,* ed. S. E. Porter (Leiden: Brill Academic, 2002), 230.

appearance through them to address his narratee. This feature makes summarization a powerful but subtle means of guiding readers toward emphases the author wanted readers to note.

Summarization functions as a narrative technique. There are four
things an author can accomplish through his narrator with summarization.

First, summarization tells readers things happened as opposed to
showing them happening.[45] Plato spoke of two basic types of narration
as diegetic (*diegesis* or narrative telling) and mimetic (*mimesis* or repre-
sentational showing) and said that any story or poem employs either telling or showing or a mixture of both.[46] Aristotle refined Plato's distinction
between *diegesis* and *mimesis* by fleshing out what happens when an epic-
poet steps forward through his narrator as a commentator on his story.[47]

Showing and telling are two imprecise ends of a spectrum along
which a narrator mediates a story to readers in terms of his intrusiveness
in the discourse.[48] When a narrator shows events happening, he places
them directly in front of readers, while his voice remains hidden behind
the action.[49] When he tells, his voice intrudes into the narrative while he
speaks to readers directly. Through summarization the narrator can remind
readers that he is there as a reliable guide to what is happening. When
Luke summarizes in Acts, his narrator is less overt than when his narrator
speaks to readers directly through the use of a prologue, a narrative aside,
or as one of the characters in the "we" sections of Acts.[50]

---

[45] Resseguie, *Narrative Criticism*, 126–30; Powell, *What Is Narrative Criticism?* 52–53.

[46] Plato, *Resp.* 392–94. For an overview of this distinction in the *Republic* and in classicism, see
Gerald F. Else, "Imitation in the Fifth Century," *CP* 53 (1958): 73–90; Stephen Halliwell, "The Theory
and Practice of Narrative in Plato," in *Narratology and Interpretation: The Content of Narrative Form
in Ancient Literature*, ed. Jonas Grethlein and Antonios Rengakos, Trends in Classics Supplementary
vol. 4 (Berlin: Walter de Gruyter, 2009), 15–41; and Richard P. McKeon, "Literary Criticism and the
Concept of Imitation in Antiquity," in *Critics and Criticism: Ancient and Modern*, ed. Ronald S. Crane
(Chicago: University of Chicago Press, 1952), 147–75.

[47] Aristotle, *Poet.* 1448, 1455, 1460. In this sense Aristotle can be credited with anticipating the
modern narratological distinction between "telling," where the narrator is visible and interprets events
for readers, and "showing," where the story is allowed to tell itself. See Irene J. F. de Jong, "Aristotle
on the Homeric Narrator," *CQ* 55 (2005): 620–21.

[48] For helpful discussions of the role of narrator intrusions in ancient historiography, see Roger
Brock, "Authorial Voice and Narrative Management in Herodotus," in *Herodotus and His World*,
ed. Peter Derow and Robert Parker (Oxford: Oxford University Press, 2003), 3–16; Peter Derow,
"Historical Explanation: Polybius and His Predecessors," in Simon Hornblower, *Greek Historiography*
(Oxford: Clarendon Press, 1996), 73–90; David Gribble, "Narrator Interventions in Thucydides,"
JHS 118 (1998): 41–67; and Thomas P. Hillman, "Authorial Statements, Narrative, and Character in
Plutarch's Agesilaus-Pompeius," *GRBS* 35 (1994): 255–80.

[49] Gerard Genette, *Narrative Discourse: An Essay in Method*, trans. Jane E. Lewin (Ithaca, NY:
Cornell University Press, 1980), 147.

[50] On the role of the narrator in the Lukan prologues, narrative asides, and "we" sections, see

Second, narrators can use summarization as an unfocused narrative bridge between scenes or episodes.[51] Episodes depict specific events, times and places, with characters interacting in them. Summaries, on the other hand, generalize these things through the use of defocalizers, which disperse the particulars of a scene.[52] When the elements of a scene are diffused in this way, the narrator creates more distance between readers and the events of the narrative and allows them to take in the presentation with a sweeping glance. Unfocusing the narrative impacts readers on several levels. First, varying the distance between reader and story through rhythmically changing the degree of focus maintains the interest level of readers. Also, unfocusing provides a momentary respite from immersion in the action of episodes and allows readers to pull up and reflect on what they have been experiencing. Unfocused narration also conveys the impression of omniscience in the narrator. A narrator's comments in a summary often reveal interior knowledge of characters' thoughts and motivations that might not otherwise be known.[53] The most important effect of defocalization, especially when reading biblical narratives with an eye toward application, is that it enables more points of contact between readers and the story. Things may or may not happen in the reader's world exactly the way they did in the particulars of the narrative world of the Bible. Nevertheless, readers are more likely to find analogies to biblical stories in unfocused generalizations that explain concrete events by relating them to common experiences and practices.[54]

Third, summarization accelerates narrative time in relation to discourse time. Discourse time describes the time that passes for readers during the reading process. Narrative time describes the time that passes within the story itself. Narratives unfold before readers as they read them within

---

Vernon K. Robbins, "The Claims of the Prologues and Greco-Roman Rhetoric: The Prefaces to Luke and Acts in Light of Greco-Roman Rhetorical Strategies," in *Jesus and the Heritage of Israel: Luke's Narrative Claim Upon Israel's Legacy*, ed. David P. Moessner (Harrisburg, PA: Trinity Press International, 1999), 63–83; Steven M. Sheeley, "Narrative Asides and Narrative Authority in Luke-Acts," *BTB* 18 (1988): 102–7; and Steven M. Sheeley, "Getting into the Act(s): Narrative Presence in the 'We' Sections," *PRSt* 26 (1999): 203–20.

[51] Narratologists and literary critics often refer to the pattern of focusing and unfocusing a narrative as the alternation between scene and summary. See Mieke Bal, *Narratology: Introduction to the Theory of Narrative* (Toronto: University of Toronto Press, 1997), 104–6; Chatman, *Story and Discourse*, 75–76; Genette, *Narrative Discourse*, 94; and Prince, *Narratology*, 56–58.

[52] Robert W. Funk, *The Poetics of Biblical Narrative* (Sonoma, CA: Polebridge Press, 1988), 116–17.

[53] Michael Kearns, *Rhetorical Narratology* (Lincoln: University of Nebraska Press, 1999), 108–13.

[54] Sternberg, *Poetics of Biblical Narrative*, 120–21; John Goldingay, "How Far Do Readers Make Sense? Interpreting Biblical Narratives," *Them* 18, no. 2 (Jan. 1993): 6–7.

time, and time passes within a narrative itself.[55] The relationship between narrative time and discourse time is called duration.[56] When a narrative enters a scene, narrative time roughly equals discourse time. Readers perceive events transpiring as they read about them and experience time passing only as characters experience it passing in the story. When a narrator summarizes, on the other hand, narrative time accelerates in relation to discourse time. The reader perceives that events abridged in the summary took longer to occur than the time it takes to read about them.[57] The most logical use for accelerating narrative time would be in lengthy histories, when less important material needs to be noted without so much detail.[58] A historian could use summaries to balance his obligation to be informative with his desire to keep his reader's interest. On the other hand, what if a writer wanted to convey the sense that certain activities, which are important to the meaning of his story, were happening continually? We will see shortly that Luke accelerated narrative time in the summary narratives precisely for this purpose.

Fourth, summarization describes ongoing conditions. Summaries move from the particulars of narrated events to general statements about the state of things. For example, in 2 Chr 36:15–16 the narrator reported in a summary that "The LORD God of their ancestors sent word against them by the hand of his messengers, sending them *time and time again*, for He had compassion on His people and on His dwelling place. But they *kept ridiculing* God's messengers, *despising* His words, and *scoffing* at His prophets, until the LORD's wrath was so stirred up against His people that there was no remedy."[59] The summary describes two activities that were happening repeatedly. God continued to show mercy to His recalcitrant people, and His people kept on rejecting His pleas. Rather than say that God sent messengers, and the people rejected them, the statements describe ongoing conditions. They fill up the vision of the reader and create a sense of impending judgment. If one event is reported at face

---

[55] Shimon Bar-Efrat, *Narrative Art in the Bible* (Sheffield: Almond Press, 1989), 141.

[56] Genette, *Narrative Discourse*, 86–112, esp. 95–99. Also see Paul Ricoeur, "The Time of Narrating (Erzählzeit) and Narrated Time (Erzählt)," in Onega and Landa, *Narratology: An Introduction*, 129–42; and Brenda Deen Schildgen, *Crisis and Continuity: Time in the Gospel of Mark, JSNTSup 159* (Sheffield, England: Sheffield Academic Press, 1998), 94–116.

[57] Genette, *Narrative Discourse*, 68–70.

[58] For a comprehensive study of the relationship between narrative time and discourse time in ancient history, biography, epic, fiction, and poetry, see Irene J. F. de Jong and René Nünlist, eds., *Time in Ancient Greek Literature: Studies in Ancient Greek Narrative, Volume 2, Mnemosyne Supplementa: Monographs on Greek and Roman Language and Literature* (Leiden: Brill, 2007).

[59] Italics are mine.

value in an episode, it can be evaluated for its significance. However, if an activity is depicted as ongoing and recurring, the reader is led to ask about the significance of the activities for the overall narrative. If the ongoing action is repeated multiple times through additional summaries, its content is stressed even more.[60] We will see shortly that Luke used all four functions of summarization consistently throughout each summary narrative to create a compelling portrait of a vibrant and dynamic church in Jerusalem.

Summarization functions as a rhetorical strategy. How can narrators influence readers through summaries, especially in an oral culture where the primary mode of reception was hearing Scripture read publicly?[61] The four narratological functions of summarization discussed above provide the writer of narrative discourse with a rhetorical tool that is powerful for its subtlety. By summarizing, a narrator can move quickly through necessary but secondary material. The summary-scene-summary rhythm also preserves readers' (and hearers') interest by varying the tempo and the distance between the implied reader and the mimesis.[62] The absence of elaboration can leave a reader wanting to know more. Also, the choice not to say everything in a summary that could be said in a more detailed scene invites readers (and hearers) to fill in with their imaginations what was left out.[63] Biblical narrative is famous for this aesthetic quality. By using defocalizers to expand the number of characters and their activity, a narrator can fill up the vision of the reader.

Though normally the rhetorical effect of these features of summarization would be to provide a respite between the scenes, it can be much more. If the generalized activity results from the resolution of a conflict, or if it is the effect of an important cause that is emphasized in the previous scene, then the reader is moved to identify with the new narrative situation. Moreover, when narrative time is accelerated in relation to discourse time, this too can impress upon the reader how much activity has been compressed into a brief discourse space, escalating further the impact of the summary and leaving readers wondering why the narrator chose to emphasize the activity.

---

[60] Genette, *Narrative Discourse*, 113–27, esp. 114, 116.

[61] John D. Harvey, "Orality and Its Implications for Biblical Studies: Recapturing an Ancient Paradigm," *JETS* 45 (2002): 101.

[62] D. François Tolmie, *Narratology and Biblical Narratives: A Practical Guide* (Bethesda, MD: International Scholars Publications, 1999), 97.

[63] Theon, *Progymnasmata* 84, encouraged composers of narrative to write concisely by eliminating things that can be supplied by the hearer. See Kathy R. Maxwell, "The Role of the Audience in Ancient Narrative: Acts as a Case Study," *ResQ* 48, no. 3 (2006): 171–80.

The effects of telling, defocalizing, and accelerating narrative time can build upon each other in a summary to emphasize new conditions, especially when the new state has resulted from a cause described in the previous scene. As will be shown in chapter 3, Luke uses this strategy when he places his first summary narrative in Acts 2:42–47 directly on the heels of the coming of the Holy Spirit on Pentecost Day in Acts 2:1–41. On a basic level, summarization is merely a characteristic of realistic narrative where stories resemble life by reporting numerous activities following rapidly one after the other.[64] However, when similar summaries are repeated successively in a narrative, they begin to take on significance for the reader. The exegetical chapters will show how Luke uses this rhetorical strategy to great effect in Acts.

The meaning of the events reported through summaries is not explained directly to readers. Rather, all commentary is implicit and is made through the narrator's emphases so that they remain part of the narrative. The narrator expresses his judgments indirectly.[65] Thus, summaries can guide readers while preserving one of the best aesthetic qualities of mimetic narration. They maintain the representation of the dramatic and do not coerce as one would expect an intrusive and authoritative narrator to do. Instead of expositing the significance of events directly, summaries emphasize things that the author wanted readers to notice and reflect upon within the narrative. Sending rhetorical signals through summaries allows readers to maintain some distance between themselves and the action of the narrative, while reminding readers that the story has a specific meaning toward which the narrator points them. This subtle distinction between explaining directly and emphasizing indirectly is what allows summaries to guide readers implicitly to the author's main points of emphasis.[66] Thus, what might otherwise be a relatively unimportant generalization between episodes can become an important rhetorical indicator of an author's message. Now, we turn to consider how Luke employed summarization as a narrative technique in his rhetorical strategy in Acts in order to emphasize his descriptions of church life in the summary narratives.

---

[64] Charles W. Hedrick, "Realism in Western Narrative and the Gospel of Mark: A Prolegomenon," *JBL* 126 (2007): 348.

[65] Edgar V. McKnight, "Literary Criticism," in *DJG*, 480.

[66] Ryken, *Windows to the World*, 94–98; Robert Alter, *The Art of Biblical Narrative* (New York: Basic Books, 1981), 116–17; Resseguie, *Narrative Criticism*, 130–32.

THE RHETORIC OF SUMMARIZATION IN ACTS

How do the summary narratives function in Luke's rhetorical strategy in Acts? We start with how Luke used summarization in Acts as a narrative technique. Approximately thirty years pass in the narrative of Acts. Yet, the sense of the rapid expansion and advance of the church tends to fill up the vision of the reader. Narrative time moves quickly in relation to discourse time, so that readers are swept into the action of the nascent Christian movement.[67] Summarization is an important part of this sense of rapid expansion of witness to Christ. Numerous summaries move the story along through simple telling. These occur mainly as unfocused abridgements of events following an episode.[68] Sometimes summaries advance the narrative through an unspecified period of time.[69] Many summaries tell as they introduce episodes,[70] intervene midway as pivots within episodes,[71] and conclude episodes.[72] Defocalization is a common feature of summarization in Acts too,[73] as well as iteration.[74] Unfocused summaries that iterate activity over an unspecified period of time contribute to the sense of action and progress in Acts.

The Summary Narratives as a Narrative Technique in Acts

The summary narratives in Acts 2:42–47; 4:32–35; 5:12–16 are the most remarkable use of the summary technique in Acts in that all three paragraphs consistently employ the four features of summarization.

(1) The summary narratives tell about church life as opposed to showing it dramatically. Major episodes precede each summary narrative, where the narrator's voice is largely hidden as Luke shows the actions and dialogue of characters.[75] In the summary narratives, however, the narrator intrudes into the story to speak in his own voice.

(2) The summary narratives are unfocused general statements about church life. Whereas the preceding episodes focus on specific individuals

---

[67] Demosthenes was well known in Luke's day for similar narrative qualities. Cecil W. Wooten, "Dionysius of Halicarnassus and Hermogenes on the Style of Demosthenes," *AJP* 110 (1989): 576–88.

[68] Acts 2:41; 4:31; 5:11,41–42; 8:1–3; 9:31; 11:20–21.

[69] Acts 2:42–47 (esp. 46–47); 4:4,32–35; 5:12–16,42; 6:7; 9:31; 12:24; 15:35; 16:5; 19:20; 28:30–31.

[70] Acts 1:3; 6:1,8; 8:4–5; 10:2; 11:1,19–21; 12:1.

[71] Acts 1:14; 3:11; 4:1–4,13; 5:21,33; 7:54; 8:17; 9:9,19; 10:23; 11:28; 12:5.

[72] Acts 2:40–42; 4:31; 5:11,41; 8:1–4,25,40; 9:31.

[73] Acts 1:3,14; 2:40–47; 4:4,31–35; 5:11–16,42; 6:7–8.

[74] Acts 1:3,14; 2:40,42–47; 4:32–35; 5:12–16,42; 11:19–21,23,28; 12:5,24.

[75] Acts 2:1–40; 3:1–4:31; 4:36–5:11.

and particular circumstances, the summary narratives generalize ongoing activity in the church.

(3) Narrative time accelerates in the summary narratives. In the preceding episodes, readers experience the passage of time at roughly the same rate as the characters do in the story. Narrative time approximates discourse time. However, in the summary narratives, narrative time accelerates greatly in relation to discourse time.[76]

(4) The summary narratives depict an ongoing way of life in the Jerusalem church. The effects of "telling" about the church after "showing" it in the Pentecost episode, of switching from focused to unfocused general statements, and of speeding up narrative time work together to intensify Luke's descriptions of church life.

Luke further emphasized the ongoing state of things in the church by switching from the aorist to the imperfect verb form and remaining in the imperfect throughout each summary narrative.[77] The switch to imperfect affects readers in at least two ways. First, rather than viewing the activities of the Jerusalem church as single events seen in their entirety, the imperfect views them as continuing over an indefinite period of time.[78] This contributes to the sense that the summary narratives describe a way of life. Additional contextual clues discussed in chapters 3–5 will also suggest that the activities depicted in the summary narratives happened regularly in the Jerusalem church.[79] Second, the switch to the imperfect has the effect of highlighting the activities described in the summary narratives and drawing readers' attention to them. In an oral culture, the change in the sound

---

[76] The changing relationship between narrative time (NT) and discourse time (DT) in Acts 2 can be delineated as follows: NT/DT (2:42–47) > NT/DT (2:41) > NT/DT (2:37–40) > NT/DT (2:14–36) < NT/DT (2:1–13).

[77] As noted by C. K. Barrett, *Acts 1–14*, ICC (New York: T&T Clark, 1994), 166–67, 169, 255.

[78] Robert E. Picirilli, "The Meaning of the Tenses in New Testament Greek: Where Are We?" *JETS* 48 (2005): 535–36.

[79] I mention contextual clues in order not to lay too much emphasis on Luke's use of the imperfect tense and become entangled in the debate between traditional grammarians who stress the *aktionsart* of the imperfect (i.e., the iterative imperfect, denoting repeated action) and more recent verbal aspect theorists who see the interpretation of verb forms as more complex and nuanced. Helpful general surveys of the issues can be found in Andrew David Naselli, "A Brief Introduction to Verbal Aspect in New Testament Greek," *Detroit Baptist Theological Seminary Journal* 12 (2007): 17–28; and Picirilli, "Meaning of the Tenses," 533–55. On specific issues surrounding the imperfect verb form, see Constantine R. Campbell, *Basics of Verbal Aspect in Biblical Greek* (Grand Rapids: Zondervan, 2008), 60–82; and Roy R. Millhouse, "The Use of the Imperfect Verb Form in the New Testament: An Investigation into Aspectual and Tense Relationships in Hellenistic Greek" (M.A. thesis, Deerfield, IL: Trinity International University, 1999).

of the inflected verb ending that accompanies a switch from the aorist to the imperfect would not have been missed by the attentive listener.[80]

The concentration of all four features of summarization in the summary narratives makes identifying them as a literary form within Acts, like speeches, prologues, asides, etc., seem plausible. In order for a literary unit to qualify as a form, it must have enough literary and/or thematic features in common with similar texts that readers come to have certain expectations when reading them.[81] The summary narratives certainly have enough in common from a literary and, as we will see, a thematic perspective to be considered a distinct literary form within Acts. To date I have not found any examples of summarization like the summary narratives in ancient history or fiction that would indicate Luke was drawing from a recognizable literary form outside of Acts.[82] They have the appearance of a literary form, but they function like a stylistic device.[83] While not discounting efforts at classification, it makes more sense to view the summary narratives as a creative use of the summary technique by Luke, with a high concentration of distinct discourse markers that set them apart from surrounding material. Several additional features of the summary narratives distinguish them even more clearly from their surroundings.

---

[80] J. W. H. Atkins, *Literary Criticism in Antiquity* (Cambridge: Cambridge University Press, 1934), 119; Witherington, *What's in the Word*, 8; Parsons, "Luke and the Progymnasmata," 60–61; Stanley E. Porter, "Greek Grammar and Syntax," in *The Face of New Testament Studies: A Survey of Recent Research*, ed. Scot McKnight and Grant R. Osborne (Grand Rapids: Baker, 2004), 89–92, 94–96.

[81] Wendell V. Harris, *Interpretive Acts in Search of Meaning* (Oxford: Clarendon Press, 1988), 92. For helpful discussions of the criteria for identifying a literary unit with a particular genre, see James L. Bailey, "Genre Analysis," in Green, *Hearing the New Testament*, 151; Jeannine K. Brown, "Genre Criticism and the Bible," in *Words and the Word: Explorations in Biblical and Literary Theory*, ed. David G. Firth and Jamie A. Grant (Downers Grove, IL: InterVarsity, 2008), 123–25.

[82] My dissertation surveyed a cross section of ancient literature including fiction (*Iliad and Odyssey, Leucippe and Clitophon*, and *Life of Apollonius*), history (Herodotus, Thucydides, and Dionysius of Halicarnassus), OT history (Exodus, Joshua, Judges, Samuel–Kings, Chronicles, and the Apocrypha), the Gospels, and Acts to see how summarization was used (Andy Chambers, "An Evaluation of Characteristic Activity in a Model Church as Set Forth by the Summary Narratives of Acts" (Ph.D. diss., Fort Worth, TX: Southwestern Baptist Theological Seminary, 119–57). I discovered that examples of summarization abound in ancient texts that utilize one or more of the functions enumerated here. See de Jong and Nünlist, *Time in Ancient Greek Literature*; and Scott Richardson, *The Homeric Narrator* (Nashville, TN: Vanderbilt University Press, 1990), 9–35, for additional analyses of the use summarization in ancient narratives.

[83] José Varickasseril, "The Lukan Portrait of the Early Church: A Study of the Major Summaries in the Acts of the Apostles," *Mission Today* 7 (2005): 40.

Additional Features

(5) Acts 2:40–41; 4:31; and 5:11 are brief transitional summaries that allow the summary narratives to stand alone. They resolve the preceding episode and describe its immediate result. They also connect the episode to the summary narratives that follow. However, their transitional nature allows the summary narratives to function independently as generalizations about the community's way of life, even though they remain a part of the ongoing story.

(6) The summary narratives make only general references to time (Acts 2:46,47, *kath' hēmeran*).[84] The surrounding material is more specific with regard to time (2:41, *en tē hēmera ekeinē*; 3:1, *epi tēn hōran...tēn enatēn*). The subtly conveyed timeless quality of the summary narratives contributes to the sense that Luke was describing the way of life of the Jerusalem church, rather than isolated situations.[85]

(7) The summary narratives follow a chiastic A B A' pattern. In Acts 2:42–47, A and A' generalize on aspects of worship and praise in the community of believers (2:43,46–47), while B describes ministry through radical generosity (2:44–45).[86] In Acts 4:32–35, A and A' generalize again on ministry through the giving of possessions to help the needy (4:32,33b–35), while B focuses on the powerful witness of the apostles (4:33a). In Acts 5:12–16, A and A' generalize on signs and wonders through the apostles (5:12,15–16), while B describes the response of the people (5:13–14).[87]

(8) The summary narratives make frequent use of repetition. Numerous themes reoccur from one summary narrative to the next. Repeated themes include numerical growth (Acts 2:47; 5:13), signs and wonders (2:43;

---

[84] See Thucydides, *Hist.* 7.8.1.

[85] H. Alan Brehm, "The Significance of the Summaries for Interpreting Acts," *SwJT* 33, no. 1 (Fall 1990): 33.

[86] I do not include Acts 2:42 in the chiastic pattern of 2:42–47 because its implied subject is αὐτοὺς in 2:40, the immediate respondents to Peter's Pentecost sermon. For this reason, 2:42 could be included with 2:40–41 in the conclusion to Peter's Pentecost, or at least as a transitional summary that looks forward and backward simultaneously. See Mikeal C. Parsons, "Christian Origins and Narrative Openings: The Sense of a Beginning in Acts 1–5," *RevExp* 87 (1990): 410. I include 2:42 in the summary narrative because it begins the pattern of using imperfect tense verb forms. Beginning the imperfect tense here implies the importance of its content for understanding the role of deliberate assimilation of new believers as a part of the ongoing life of the community.

[87] The regnal summaries of King Solomon's reign follow similar chiastic patterns (1 Kgs 4:20–24; 10:23–29; 2 Chr 9:22–28). On the use of chiasm in the summary narratives, see S. Scott Bartchy, "Divine Power, Community Formation, and Leadership in the Acts of the Apostles," in *Community Formation in the Early Church and in the Church Today*, ed. Richard N. Longenecker (Peabody, MA: Hendrickson, 2002), 91; and Josep Rius-Camps, "Las variantes de la Recensión Occidental de los Hechos de los Apóstoles (VI: Hch 2,41–47)," *Filología Neotestamentaria* 8 (1995): 199–208.

5:12,15–16), and generosity (2:44–45; 4:34–35).[88] Nearly all the themes in the summary narratives are repeated later in Acts in the descriptions of church life in the Gentile churches and in the summary statements. Repetition was a popular method in the Old Testament and among ancient writers for calling attention to important themes that tied together various components and established the worldview of a narrative work.[89] Through multiple repetitions of themes within the summary narratives and again throughout Acts, Luke establishes their importance for his portraits of church life.

(9) The summary narratives are relatively culture neutral. This is remarkable considering that the Jerusalem believers were devoted Jews. I do not mean by this that the Jerusalem church's practice was not deeply rooted in first-century Jewish life and culture. As we will see in chapters 3–5, many of the activities of the Jerusalem believers were a continuation of their practice as Jews, only now transformed by faith in Jesus as Messiah. However, Luke does not so much tie his descriptions of church life to Judaism as he ties them to following Jesus. This will be especially important in chapter 6 on exemplary life in the Gentile churches of Acts. We will see that the Gentile believers did not submit to circumcision and become Jews in order to follow Jesus. However, they did adopt the same pattern of church life commended by Luke in the summary narratives.

(10) The summary narratives highlight only positive aspects of life in the Jerusalem congregation.[90] The picture of the church in the early chapters of Acts is that of a Spirit-filled company of committed followers of Christ that is growing rapidly and experiencing the good will of its neighbors.[91] The summary narratives are the focal point of Luke's positive descriptions. Their constant stress on the good things happening in the Jerusalem church is perhaps the summary narratives' most distinctive feature. This characteristic has much in common with the Greek rhetorical device known as the exemplum, and it is the key to Luke's rhetorical strategy.

---

[88] Maria Anicia Co, "The Major Summaries in Acts," *ETL* 68 (1992): 67–68, has demonstrated that nearly every verse of each summary contains a Greek word common to all three summaries.

[89] Alter, *Art of Biblical Narrative*, 95; Resseguie, *Narrative Criticism*, 42–45; Beck, *God as Storyteller*, 82–83; Burke O. Long, "Framing Repetitions in Biblical Historiography," *JBL* 106 (1987): 385–99; Sternberg, *Poetics of Biblical Narrative*, 387–90; David E. Aune, *The Westminster Dictionary of New Testament and Early Christian Literature and Rhetoric* (Louisville, KY: Westminster John Knox, 2003), 399.

[90] Brehm, "Significance of the Summaries," 34.

[91] F. F. Bruce, "The Church of Jerusalem in the Acts of the Apostles," *BJRL* 67 (1985): 643.

THE SUMMARY NARRATIVES IN THE RHETORICAL STRATEGY OF ACTS

The ten characteristics discussed above highlight features of the summary narratives that distinguish them from surrounding material and draw readers into a deeper engagement with their content. The tenth characteristic, their consistent focus on positive aspects of church life in Jerusalem, signals Luke's persuasive agenda for readers. Content selection, what is included and left out, is an important way an author can color his narrative.[92] Why would Luke choose to highlight only exemplary activity in the summary narratives? Surely he does not mean to imply that the church in Jerusalem had no problems. They struggled with duplicity (Acts 5:1–11), discrimination (6:1–7), persecution by Jews (6:8–8:3) and Romans (12:1–24), prejudice (10:2–3), and doctrinal disputes (15:1–6). Luke does not ignore these issues in the surrounding episodes.[93] However, he appears to make a deliberate choice to leave them out of the summary narratives and to focus instead on the good things happening in the Jerusalem church. To comprehend why, we need to understand the role of the rhetorical exemplum in ancient literature.

The Greek word for exemplum, *paradeigma*, can be translated "example" or "precedent."[94] In classical rhetoric, exemplars were used in speechmaking and in literature as examples that helped to prove a point, or as illustrations of behavior to be imitated or rejected.[95] Ancient historians frequently employed them in their writing out of the belief that, in addition to informing, history should promote virtue and moral character through examples that instructed readers.[96] Polybius epitomized this attitude in the preface to his history when he said, "There is no more ready corrective of conduct than knowledge of the past."[97] The rhetorical exemplum provided such knowledge.

---

[92] Beck, *God as Storyteller*, 5.

[93] Witherington, *Acts*, 157.

[94] Aune, *Westminster Dictionary of New Testament*, 173.

[95] On the use of the exemplum in ancient rhetorical theory, see Bennett J. Price, "Paradeigma and Exemplum in Ancient Rhetorical Theory" (Ph.D. diss., Berkeley: University of California, 1975); and Benjamin Fiore, *The Function of Personal Example in the Socratic and Pastoral Epistles* (Rome: Biblical Institute Press, 1986), 26–78. For examples in ancient literature see Abraham J. Malherbe, *Moral Exhortation: A Greco-Roman Sourcebook* (Philadelphia: Westminster Press, 1986), 135–38.

[96] Polybius, 12.25. Also see ibid., 3.31.11–13; Dionysius of Halicarnassus, *Ant. rom.* 1.2.1; 5.56.1; Thucydides, *Hist.* 1.22.4.

[97] Polybius, 1.1. Also see Aristotle, *Rhet.* 1417b; Dion., *Pomp.* 4; Herodotus, *Hist.* 1.1.; Isocrates,

Exemplarity as a rhetorical strategy was not limited to Greek and Roman rhetoricians and historians. Jewish and Christian theologians developed their own traditions that combined Hellenistic rhetorical categories with biblical subjects. In the New Testament, Israel's past history is used positively and negatively as examples for the faith of readers (see Rom 15:4; 1 Cor 10:6; Heb 3:16–19; 11:1–12:2). Luke's noble Bereans are an example of a positive exemplum (Acts 17:10–11). Paul's reference to Cretans as liars, brutes, and gluttons was apparently a well-known negative exemplum in his day (Titus 1:12).[98]

Little direction was given by ancient rhetoricians concerning rules for the literary form of an exemplum or how they should be inserted into a context.[99] Rather, the interest was more in how they functioned. Matthew Roller identifies four key functional elements of exemplary discourse in Roman culture: (1) An action recounted was perceived to be of consequence to the Roman community at large, and it embodied crucial social values. (2) The action should have a primary audience, that is, one for whom the exemplum would have the greatest consequence. (3) The exemplary deed and its consequences must be worthy of commemoration for the primary audience. (4) The primary audience is urged to imitate and even surpass the deeds of the exemplary subject.[100]

Roller's framework for the rhetorical exemplum sheds light on Luke's persuasive agenda in the summary narratives. Luke's positive portraits of church life embody crucial social and spiritual values that would have had positive consequences for the Roman community at large. Readers of Acts familiar with Hellenistic culture likely recognized allusions, especially in the material related to friendship, sharing, and almsgiving (Acts 2:44–45; 4:32,34–35), to the highest ideals of Greek society. Luke shows the church far exceeding these ideals (see Acts 4:34), which were and still today are unattainable in toto, in spite of the sincerest progressive intentions.[101]

Oration 9.77; Quintilian, *Inst.* 10.1.31–34; Lucian, *How to Write History* 9,42; and Thucydides, 1.21.2; 3.82.3–8.

[98] See Annette Yoshiko Reed, "The Construction and Subversion of Patriarchal Perfection: Abraham and Exemplarity in Philo, Josephus, and the *Testament of Abraham*," *JSJ* 40 (2009): 185–212; and Marcel Poorthuis and Joshua Schwartz, eds., *Saints and Role Models in Judaism and Christianity*, Jewish & Christian Perspectives (Leiden: Brill, 2004) for surveys of exemplarity among Jews and Christians during the NT period, in early Christian history, and in Rabbinic Judaism.

[99] Kristoffel Demoen, "A Paradigm for the Analysis of Paradigms: The Rhetorical Exemplum in Ancient and Imperial Greek Theory," *Rhetorica* 15, no. 2 (Spring 1997): 127–29, 138–42.

[100] Matthew B. Roller, "Exemplarity in Roman Culture: The Examples of Horatio Cocles and Cloelia," *CP* 99 (2004): 4–6.

[101] Markus Öhler, "Die Jerusalemer Urgemeinde im Spiegel des antiken Vereinswesens," *NTS* 51

A logical question raised by Roller's framework is, who is Luke's primary audience in the summary narratives? Or to employ the concept of the implied reader, who is the reader called for by the summary narratives? Who would benefit from hearing and embracing Luke's positive descriptions of church life in Jerusalem? Luke's descriptions of the positive social effects of the gospel invited a favorable assessment of the church by Roman society, especially for outsiders to the church who were considering the gospel message. In this sense the summary narratives had an apologetic value for unbelievers. However, another audience is implied in Acts for whom Luke's descriptions of Jerusalem church life were even more important. I speak here of Christian hearers and readers in the Gentile churches described in Acts, and beyond, who would have benefited from Luke's exemplary portraits of church life.

ECHOES OF THE SUMMARY
NARRATIVES LATER IN ACTS

The summary narratives are not the only place in Acts where exemplary church life is described by Luke. Numerous echoes of exemplary life in the summary narratives can be heard repeatedly throughout Acts in Luke's description of life in the Gentiles churches of Acts and in what are commonly referred to as the "summary statements" or "growth notes."

Exemplary Life in the Gentile Churches of Acts

Acts begins with the Jewish church in Jerusalem, but the church quickly spreads and includes churches in numerous Gentile cities. In every city where the gospel is preached and people believe, life in these newly planted churches among the Gentiles echoes aspects of church life

---

(2005): 393–415; David Seccombe, "The New People of God," in *Witness to the Gospel: The Theology of Acts*, ed. I. Howard Marshall and David Peterson (Grand Rapids: Eerdmans, 1998), 355–56. Gregory E. Sterling, "'Athletes of Virtue': An Analysis of the Summaries in Acts (2:41–47; 4:32–35; 5:12–16)," *JBL* 113 (1994): 679–96, argued that summary narratives borrow themes from Hellenistic religious-philosophical groups in order to show the Jerusalem church exemplifying the best of these traditions. Rubén R. Dupertuis, "The Summaries of Acts 2, 4, and 5 and Plato's *Republic*," in *Ancient Fiction: The Matrix of Early Christian and Jewish Narrative*, ed. Jo-Ann Brant, Charles W. Hedrick, and Chris Shea, SBLSymS 32 (Atlanta: Society of Biblical Literature, 2005), 275–95, argues more specifically that Luke's portraits are modeled on Plato's descriptions of the guardians in the *Republic*. Douglas A. Hume, *The Early Christian Community: A Narrative Analysis of Acts 2:41–47 and 4:32–35* (Tübingen, Germany: Mohr Siebeck, 2011), recently argued that Luke depicted the church in Jerusalem as the result of God's community making activity in their midst, as they fulfilled and exceeded the best ideals of the Greek friendship tradition.

in Jerusalem. More will be said on this in chapter 6 on exemplary life in the Gentile churches of Acts, but one example will suffice here. When testimony about the Lord Jesus came to Antioch (cf. Acts 11:19–20 to 4:33a), a great number believed (cf. 11:21,24,26 to 2:47; 5:14; 6:1,7). Note the following parallels between the churches in Jerusalem and Antioch. The church in Antioch was given oversight by apostles (cf. 11:22 to 2:42–43; 4:33a; 5:12). The grace of God rested on both churches (cf. 11:23 to 4:33b). Both churches were committed to being taught (cf. 11:26 to 2:42). Both were generous churches (cf. 11:29–30 to 2:45; 4:34–35). The Holy Spirit was at work in both churches, filling and empowering believers (cf. 11:24,28 to 1:8; 2:1–4,38).

Echoes of exemplary life in Jerusalem occur throughout Acts wherever the gospel is preached and churches are planted.[102] Luke shows the Gentile churches adopting the ideal behavior of the mother church in Jerusalem in the summary narratives. Luke's portraits of church life in the summary narratives serve as the founding case of a general rule that is embodied in subsequent examples that confirm the rule.[103] In this sense the summary narratives function as an exemplum for Gentile readers when they encounter the commonalities between Luke's portraits of the Jerusalem church and the Gentile churches in Acts. The narrative of the spread of the gospel and the planting of churches among the Gentiles keeps guiding readers back to Luke's vision for exemplary life in the summary narratives. Luke's message is implicit, not explicit. The accumulation of echoes of Jerusalem church life in Luke's portraits of Gentile church life points readers back to the summary narratives, rather than direct statements by Luke. Yet, when the summary narratives and the portraits of Gentile church life are considered together, it appears Luke has a high interest in communicating a vision of exemplary church life in his account of the birth of the Christian movement.

Exemplary Life in the Growth Notes

One additional use of the summary technique in Acts further accentuates Luke's descriptions of exemplary church life in the summary narratives, the "summary statements" or "growth notes." These appear at regular intervals throughout Acts. The theme of dramatic growth begins just prior to the

---

[102] In chap. 6 we will consider echoes of exemplary life in Jerusalem in the cities of Samaria, Syrian Antioch, Ephesus, and Troas.

[103] Didier Coste, *Narrative as Communication* (Minneapolis: University of Minnesota, 1989), 303.

first summary narrative in Acts 2:41 when 3,000 believers were baptized and added to the original group of 120 believers (1:15). The summary narratives and several summary statements in the early chapters of Acts emphasize the continual growth of the church in Jerusalem (see 2:47; 4:4; 5:14; 6:1). Afterward, at key intervals, Luke reminds readers of the unstoppable triumph of the gospel through the church with additional growth notes:

Acts 6:7, So the preaching about God flourished, the number of the disciples in Jerusalem multiplied greatly, and a large group of priests became obedient to the faith.

Acts 9:31, So the church throughout all Judea, Galilee, and Samaria had peace, being built up and walking in the fear of the Lord and in the encouragement of the Holy Spirit, and it increased in numbers.

Acts 12:24, Then God's message flourished and multiplied.

Acts 16:5, So the churches were strengthened in the faith and increased in number daily.

Acts 19:20, In this way the Lord's message flourished and prevailed.

Acts 28:30–31, Then he stayed two whole years in his own rented house. And he welcomed all who visited him, proclaiming the kingdom of God and teaching the things concerning the Lord Jesus Christ with full boldness and without hindrance.[104]

---

[104] Additional summary statements in Acts emphasize the growth and spread of the gospel within individual episodes. In Jerusalem, "Many of those who heard the message believed, and the number of the men came to about 5,000" (4:4), and, "In those days, as the number of disciples was multiplying" (6:1). In Samaria, "When they believed Philip, as he proclaimed the good news about the kingdom of God and the name of Jesus Christ, both men and women were baptized" (8:12). In Antioch, "A large number who believed turned to the Lord" (11:21). In Pisidian Antioch, "All who had been appointed to eternal life believed. So the message of the Lord spread through the whole region" (13:48–49). In Iconium, "A great number of both Jews and Greeks believed" (14:1). In Thessalonica, "Some of them were persuaded and joined Paul and Silas, including a great number of God-fearing Greeks, as well as a number of the leading women" (17:4). In Berea, "Consequently, many of them believed, including a number of the prominent Greek women as well as men" (17:12). In Athens, "Some men joined him and believed" (17:34). In Corinth, "Many of the Corinthians, when they heard, believed and were baptized" (18:8). In Rome, "Some were persuaded by what he said" (28:24).

Some interpreters view these growth notes as structural markers that separate the narrative of Acts into major sections or panels.[105] A similar structural scheme has been identified in the summary statements of the Gospel of Mark, which Luke may have used as a model.[106] Such analyses are helpful for readers of Acts as long as we remember that Luke probably was not inviting readers to impose an outline on his narrative using his summary statements.[107] He was more likely utilizing the rhetorical technique of repetition to stress the theme of numerical growth. Repeating the theme of growth in this way made it easier for people in an oral culture listening to a public reading of Acts to follow the theme of growth through the narrative.

The summary statements perform rhetorically in much the same way as the summary narratives, using all four functions of summarization consistently in each one. They *tell* instead of *show* what was happening. They unfocus the episodes that immediately precede them. They speed up narrative time in relation to the discourse time of preceding material. They even consistently utilize the imperfect verb form to signal their connection to the summary narratives. The summary statements, like the summary narratives, describe ongoing conditions in the early Christian movement. These four qualities accent the positive content of the summary statements, and they create a sense of the rapid advance of the gospel and the numerical growth of the church, themes first introduced by Luke in the summary narratives (Acts 2:47; 5:14).[108] The growth notes echo and reinforce Luke's

---

[105] Most recently David Peterson, *The Acts of the Apostles*, PNTC (Grand Rapids: Eerdmans, 2009), vii–xiii; Richard N. Longenecker, *Acts*, EBC vol. 9 (Grand Rapids: Zondervan, 2007), 695–96; and David W. Gooding, *True to the Faith: A Fresh Approach to the Acts of the Apostles* (London: Hodder & Stoughton, 1990). C. H. Turner, "Chronology of the New Testament," in *Dictionary of the Bible*, ed. James Hastings (New York: Charles Scribner's Sons, 1900), 421–23, first articulated the view. See William H. Malas, "The Literary Structure of Acts: A Narratological Investigation into Its Arrangement, Plot, and Primary Themes" (Ph.D. diss., Richmond, VA: Union Theological Seminary and Presbyterian School of Christian Education, 2001); Floyd V. Filson, *Three Crucial Decades* (Richmond, VA: John Knox, 1963), 11–13; J. de Zwaan, "Was the Book of Acts a Posthumous Edition?" *HTR* 17 (1924): 101; Michael Green, *Evangelism in the Early Church* (Grand Rapids: Eerdmans, 1970), 110; Paul Hertig and Robert L. Gallagher, "Introduction: Background to Acts," in *Mission in Acts: Ancient Narratives in Contemporary Context*, ed. Robert L. Gallagher and Paul Hertig (Maryknoll, NY: Orbis Books, 2004), 8–12; and A. Q. Morton and G. H. C. MacGregor, *The Structure of Luke and Acts* (New York: Harper and Row, 1964), 40–41, for surveys and proposals for seeing the summary statements as structural markers in Acts.

[106] F. G. Lang, "Kompositionalyse des Markusevangeliums," *ZTK* 74 (1977): 1–24; Wilhelm Egger, *Frohbotschaft und Lehre: Die Sammelberichte des Werkens Jesu im Markusevangelium* (Frankfurt: Joseph Knecht, 1976), 1–26; and James A. Brooks, *Mark*, NAC (Nashville: Broadman, 1991), 31–32.

[107] Henry J. Cadbury, *The Making of Luke-Acts* (New York: Macmillan, 1927), 324–25.

[108] Thematic parallels to ancient historians have been cited, like Dionysius of Halicarnassus who

descriptions of exemplary life in the summary narratives much like his portraits of exemplary life in the Gentile churches.[109]

WHO IS THE IMPLIED READER OF THE SUMMARY NARRATIVES?

Inquiring after the implied reader of Acts is to ask about the reader called for by Luke's discourse. What clues do the summary narratives provide concerning what Luke thinks is important for readers to understand and embrace? When combined with Luke's portraits of exemplary life in the Gentile churches, and exemplary life in the summary statements, a cumulative picture emerges. Together they engage readers with a portrait of exemplary life in the community of believers in Jesus and its missional results. It is hard to think it coincidental that these three sets of texts in Acts share so much in common on the subject of church life. More likely, Luke desires to impress upon his readers and hearers a vision of what happens in an exemplary church. He casts his vision initially in the summary narratives, and he reinforces it in the echoes of church life in his descriptions of Gentile churches and in the summary statements. I will say more about echoes of the summary narratives in chapter 6.

It remains to ask, why? Here we come up against a limitation of narrative and rhetorical criticism. These approaches can tell us much about what Luke says, how he says it, and the impact he seeks to have on readers. However, they cannot tell us specifically why Luke crafts the summary

---

emphasized the growth of the Roman Empire at several points in his history (*Ant. rom.* 1.76–84; 2.73.4). See David L. Balch, "The Genre of Luke-Acts: Individual Biography, Adventure Novel, or Political History," *SwJT* 33, no. 1 (1990): 18–19. However, Dionysius's history is much too long and the occurrence of growth notes too rare to justify seeing a Lukan allusion here. Rather, it appears Luke is alluding to the theme of divine causation of growth which runs throughout the Bible. God revealed Himself to the patriarchs as a God of numerical increase (cf. Gen 1:28; 15:5; 17:2; 26:4,24; 28:14, to Acts 7:17). Individual growth in stature is also stressed in the OT in persons like Samson (Judg 13:24), Samuel (1 Sam 2:21,26; 3:19), David (1 Sam 18:14; 2 Sam 3:1), and Jehoshaphat (2 Chr 17:12), as well as in the NT in John the Baptist (Luke 1:80), Jesus (Luke 2:42,52), and Paul's writings (1 Cor 3:6; Eph 4:16; Col 1:6). See Jerome Kodell, "The Word of God Grew: The Ecclesial Tendency of ΛΟΓΟΣ in Acts 1,7 [*sic* read 6,7]; 12,24; 19,20," *Bib* 55 (1974): 505–19, for the view that the growth of the λόγος motif in the summary statements is rooted in the parable of the sower in Luke 8:4–15, where the seed that grows is the word of God (Luke 8:11).

[109] For more on the summary statements, see Brehm, "Significance of the Summaries," 38–39; Brian S. Rosner, "The Progress of the Word," in Marshall and Peterson, *Witness to the Gospel*, 215–33; José Varickasseril, "Short Summaries in the Acts of the Apostles: Lukan Presentation of Features that Are the Hallmark of the Early Church," *Mission Today* 6 (2004): 377–95; and Jens-W. Taeger, *Der Mensch und sein Heil: Studien zum Bild des Menschen und zur Sicht der Bekehrung bei Lukas* (Gütersloh: Gütersloher Verlagshaus Gerd Mohn, 1982), 163–83.

narratives the way he does for the response they seem designed to provoke, because Luke does not tell us why. However, the emphases he makes by their use do lend themselves to reasonable, though tentative, speculation. Certainly they possess a historical value for providing readers with an account of the earliest stages of the church's history. They possess an apologetic value that may have been helpful in Paul's defense or in explaining "the Way" to an uninformed Roman audience, especially the comments that share affinities with aspects of Greek utopian ideals and the friendship tradition. They also possess evangelistic value for people who needed to hear the gospel and see the way Jesus changed the lives of those who followed Him.

These possibilities have much to commend them. However, if that is all Luke wants to do with his emphasis on church life in the summary narratives, he goes to exorbitant lengths to make his point. It makes more sense to think about how Luke's portraits of church life might be instructive for believers in Jesus reading Acts. Theophilus was likely a believer, for whom Luke provides an account of Jesus' ministry in his Gospel and an account of what Jesus continued to do through His followers and the churches they planted in Acts (Acts 1:1). Readers are told nothing about when Theophilus, or Luke for that matter, came to Christ. In Acts, the mission catches up to Luke in the "we" passages, which occur deep into the Gentile mission. Luke was a coworker with Paul in the work of proclaiming the gospel and gathering converts into newly planted churches among the Gentiles. When he sat down to record the beginnings of this movement, his descriptions of life in the Gentile churches keep echoing his portraits of the mother church in Jerusalem.

Believers in Jesus, like Theophilus, can read Luke and Acts and learn much about Jesus and the early years of the Christian movement. They will also hear what exemplary church life looks like from Luke's perspective. I believe this is Luke's primary purpose for the summary narratives. Much of what Luke says about church life does appear in seams that serve the literary purpose of dividing and connecting episodes. Form and redaction critics like Dibelius, Cadbury, Conzelmann, and Haenchen get that much right. Nevertheless, we must refuse to follow them in separating the summary narratives from the rest of Acts and ask instead what the summary narratives contribute to the overall message of Acts. When we do this, an emphasis on the theology of church life emerges that runs throughout Acts as one of its major themes. Readers of Acts have in Luke's narrative a treasure chest of theological resources, which they can access for the faithful formation of their own churches. When it comes to discerning Luke's convictions about what an exemplary church should look like, the summary narratives should be the first place that readers turn.

SUMMARY

Chapter 1 argued that the summary narratives were overshadowed in twentieth-century scholarship by the historical-critical method. Consequently their theology of church life has been underemphasized in efforts to articulate the major themes and theological emphases of Acts. Chapter 2 sought to overcome this weakness by considering how summarization functions as a narrative technique in a writer's rhetorical strategy. These insights were applied to Luke's narrative style in order to understand how he seeks to impact readers through the summary narratives. What emerged was the sense that Luke uses the technique of summarization, modified to suit his own rhetorical purposes in the summary narratives, to present his portraits of the church in Jerusalem in an exemplary fashion. His vision for life together in the church provides believers in Jesus with a rich theological resource for the faithful formation of churches in any generation and cultural context. The next three chapters will provide a close reading of the summary narratives as a foundation for articulating Luke's theology of church life.

CHAPTER THREE

EXEMPLARY LIFE PORTRAIT 1:
ACTS 2:42-47

T he summary narratives form three portraits of life together in
Christ that can ignite the imagination of believers who seek God's
direction for their own churches. Chapters 3 through 5 will pursue
a close reading of Acts 2:42–47; 4:32–35; and 5:12–16. The insights gained
will form the foundation for a theology of church life in Acts. Before the
first portrait of church life can be considered in chapter 3, however, the
creation of the church at Pentecost must be considered.

THE BIRTH OF THE CHURCH

Luke's account of Pentecost immediately precedes the first summary
narrative in Acts 2. The Pentecost narrative emphasizes the coming of the
Holy Spirit (2:1–13), the preaching of the gospel (2:14–36), and the call to
a response as central features in Luke's theology of church life (2:37–41).

The Holy Spirit and the Birth of the Church

The role and the effects of the reception of the Holy Spirit in Luke–Acts have received much attention in modern scholarship. Was the Holy Spirit given primarily to empower the witness and mission of the apostles and the early church? Was the Spirit given to enable believers to perform signs and wonders or to speak in tongues? Was the Spirit given to empower personal spiritual growth? What is the Spirit's role in the ethical formation of the community of believers?[1] These questions stir lively debate in both the academy and the church. In 1926 Heinrich von Baer's pioneering study set the direction for twentieth-century scholarship by arguing that although one can speak of many functions of the Holy Spirit in Luke–Acts, His main role is to empower believers for proclaiming the gospel.[2] He also noted the Spirit's role in the formation of the church but did little to develop this theme.[3] However, no attentive reading of Acts can miss the position of the first summary narrative immediately following the coming of the Holy Spirit on Pentecost Day in Acts 2.[4] Though the Pentecost episode may climax in Acts 2:41 with the response of the 3,000, the narrative does not end until Acts 2:47, after the new believers are fully assimilated into the ongoing life of the church. The arrival of the Holy Spirit on Pentecost in Acts 2:1–4 then is vitally related to the first portrait of church life in Acts 2:42–47.[5]

Luke's placement of the first summary narrative on the heels of the outpouring of the Holy Spirit on Pentecost reveals his belief that the

---

[1] George Kwame Agyei Bonnah, *The Holy Spirit: A Narrative Factor in the Acts of the Apostles* (Stuttgart: Katholisches Bibelwerk, 2007), 12. Bonnah's survey of research into Luke's pneumatology is the most thorough and up to date available currently (11–61).

[2] Heinrich von Baer, *Der Heilige Geist in den Lukasschriften* (Stuttgart: W. Kohlhammer, 1926). Also, Robert P. Menzies, *Empowered for Witness: The Spirit in Luke–Acts* (Sheffield, England: Sheffield Academic Press, 1994).

[3] von Baer, *Der Heilige Geist*, 186, 188, 190–91, 204.

[4] Matthias Wenk, *Community-Forming Power: The Socio-Ethical Role of the Spirit in Luke–Acts* (Sheffield, England: Sheffield Academic Press, 2000), 21–31, 40–46, helpfully surveys contemporary scholarly interest in the connection between the outpouring of the Spirit and the birth of the church in Acts 2. See also, James D. G. Dunn, *Baptism in the Holy Spirit* (Philadelphia: Westminster Press, 1970), 49–51; D. Hamm, "The Mission Has a Church: Spirit, World, and Church in Luke–Acts," in *The Spirit in the Church and the World*, ed. Bradford E. Hinze (New York: Orbis, 2004), 68–80, esp. 75–78; Peter T. O'Brien, "Mission, Witness, and the Coming of the Spirit," *BBR* 9 (1999): 210; and Max Turner, "The Work of the Holy Spirit in Luke–Acts," *WW* 23, no. 2 (2003): 152.

[5] Morris Inch, "Manifestation of the Spirit," in *The Living and Active Word of God: Studies in Honor of Samuel J. Schultz*, ed. Morris Inch and Ronald Youngblood (Winona Lake, IN: Eisenbrauns, 1983), 151, went so far as to call the appearance of Christian community in Acts 2:41–47 "the critical indicator of the Spirit at work."

Holy Spirit gives birth to the church. The Spirit of God takes the initiative and drives events throughout Luke and Acts. In the Gospel the Holy Spirit filled those who heralded the Messiah's coming (Luke 1:15,41,67; 2:25–27). The Spirit enabled Mary to conceive Jesus (Luke 1:35), and He empowered Jesus for ministry (Luke 3:22; 4:1,18; Acts 1:2; 10:38). Jesus' disciples were to minister in the power of the Holy Spirit (Luke 12:12), and before Jesus left He told His disciples to wait in Jerusalem until they were clothed with power from on high (Luke 24:49; Acts 1:4–5). Jesus also promised His disciples that when the Holy Spirit arrived they would receive power and be His witnesses to the ends of the earth (Acts 1:8). When the Spirit arrived on Pentecost, He filled the believers and enabled them to declare the mighty acts of God in the languages of Jews present in Jerusalem from all over the Empire (Acts 2:1–11). The role of the Spirit in Acts does not end at Pentecost. He appears frequently in Acts empowering witness to Christ and the planting of churches to the ends of the earth.[6] However, the Holy Spirit does not operate in Acts in the creation of churches apart from proclaiming the gospel and calling for a response.

Proclaiming the Gospel and Calling for a Response

The Holy Spirit brought the church into existence through the Spirit-filled preaching of the good news about Jesus Christ.[7] Peter was filled with the Holy Spirit on Pentecost Day (Acts 1:8; 2:4) as he told the crowd that God was pouring out His Spirit on His people (Acts 2:16–18,33; cf. Joel 2:28–29). Peter's sermon was an exposition of several Old Testament texts from Joel and the Psalms, which he applied to the risen Jesus.[8] In his sermon Peter confronted the complicity of his hearers in the death of Jesus (Acts 2:22–23,35). His message culminated in a call for an obedient response. He commanded his hearers to repent and be baptized in the name of Jesus Christ for the forgiveness of sins, and they would receive the gift of the Holy Spirit (Acts 2:37–38).[9] The call to repentance is a call

---

[6] See Acts 4:8,31; 6:10; 7:55; 8:15–17,29,39; 9:31; 10:19,44; 11:28; 13:3–4,9; 16:7; 19:6; 20:23, 28. Also Malcolm B. Yarnell III, "The Person and Work of the Holy Spirit," in *A Theology for the Church*, ed. Daniel L. Akin (Nashville: B&H Academic, 2007), 617.

[7] Leo O'Reilly, *Word and Sign in the Acts of the Apostles: A Study in Lukan Theology* (Rome: Editrice Pontificia Universita Gregoriana, 1987), 76–87; Jerome Kodell, "The Word of God Grew: The Ecclesial Tendency of ΛΟΓΟΣ in Acts 1,7 [*sic* read 6,7]; 12,24; 19,20," *Bib* 55 (1974): 505–19.

[8] In Acts, the Holy Spirit is even acknowledged as the One speaking the Scriptures of the OT through their respective writers (1:16; 4:25; 28:25).

[9] Not only did Peter preach from the prophets, his call to repentance reflected the posture of the prophets, whose essential pattern was to point out Israel's unfaithfulness and God's patience,

to a decisive turning away from sin that leads to forgiveness through faith in Jesus.[10] The baptism preached by Peter was the same as that of John the Baptist, who proclaimed a baptism of repentance for the forgiveness of sins (Luke 3:3). All three Synoptic Gospels reference John's call to a baptism of repentance, but Luke describes in greater detail what repentance looks like for various people such as the crowd, tax collectors, and soldiers (Luke 3:3–18; cf. Mark 1:4–5; Matt 3:7–12). Baptism expresses true repentance that leads to a changed life (see esp. Luke 3:7–14). Repentance and baptism are tied together so closely in Luke–Acts, that it would be fair to say Luke could not have imagined someone repenting and professing faith in Christ without a willingness to be baptized.[11] As a result of Peter's preaching 3,000 believed in Jesus Christ and were baptized (Acts 2:41a).

Not only did the new believers identify with Jesus in baptism, they also identified with the other believers in the new church. Acts 2:41 tells us they were "added to them." Repentance and baptism separated them from a "corrupt generation" (2:40) and brought them into the new people of God. Together they became the church described in the first summary narrative.[12] The Holy Spirit formed them into a community, not merely an aggregation of autonomous individuals.[13] This fits with Luke's consistent use of plural verb forms in the summary narratives, as opposed to singular verbs that are common elsewhere in Acts. As with baptism above, it would be fair to say that Luke could not have imagined someone following Jesus apart from a commitment to do so with other believers in the church.[14] He

---

culminating in a call to repentance. See Hans F. Bayer, "The Preaching of Peter in Acts," in *Witness to the Gospel: The Theology of Acts*, ed. I. Howard Marshall and David Peterson (Grand Rapids: Eerdmans, 1998), 262–67. This pattern accords with Jesus' teaching that the Holy Spirit would convict people of sin, righteousness, and judgment (John 16:8–11).

[10] Though the call to faith is not included in the call to repent here, repentance and faith are linked elsewhere in the NT (see Acts 20:21; Mark 1:15) such that they can be called two sides of the same coin (I. Howard Marshall, *The Acts of the Apostles*, New Testament Guides [Sheffield, UK: Sheffield Academic Press, 2001], 81). On the relationship between repentance, faith, baptism, and forgiveness in Acts, see Robert H. Stein, "Baptism in Luke-Acts," in *Believer's Baptism: Sign of the New Covenant in Christ*, ed. Thomas R. Schreiner and Shawn D. Wright (Nashville: B&H Academic, 2006), 47–52; Luther B. McIntyre, "Baptism and Forgiveness in Acts 2:38," *BSac* 153 (1996): 53–62. For a general survey of baptism in Acts see the classic statement in George R. Beasley-Murray, *Baptism in the New Testament* (Grand Rapids: Eerdmans, 1962), 93–125.

[11] F. F. Bruce, *The Book of the Acts*, NICNT, rev. ed. (Grand Rapids: Eerdmans, 1988), 70.

[12] Robert L. Brawley, "Social Identity and the Aim of Accomplished Life in Acts 2," in *Acts and Ethics*, ed. Thomas E. Phillips, New Testament Monographs (Sheffield, England: Sheffield Academic Press, 2005), 32–33.

[13] Beverly Roberts Gaventa, *The Acts of the Apostles*, ANTC (Nashville: Abingdon, 2003), 81.

[14] Arthur G. Patzia, *The Emergence of the Church: Context, Growth, Leadership, and Worship* (Downers Grove, IL: IVP Academic, 2001), 241–42; Beverly R. Gaventa, "'You Will Be My

would scarcely recognize the individualism that characterizes so much of American church life today.[15] Together, repentance, faith, baptism, and being added to the church indicate Luke's strong conviction that the early church was composed of persons who were thoroughly converted to Christ and committed to one another in the church.

LIFE TOGETHER IN THE FELLOWSHIP OF BELIEVERS (ACTS 2:42–47)

Immediately following the response of the 3,000, Luke launched into his first description of church life, beginning with four commitments made by the new believers in Acts 2:42.

Four Commitments New Believers Make

No definite subject is mentioned in Acts 2:42, which means Luke intends for readers to identify the new believers of 2:41 as the proper subject of the verb in 2:42.[16] Beginning in 2:42, Luke begins to employ all the rhetorical features of summarization discussed in chapter 2 above to create the sense that his portrait describes an ongoing way of life among the believers, beginning with the four commitments made by the new believers. He characterizes their commitment with the Greek verb *proskartereō*, which means to be engaged in or to persevere in something.[17] The verb stresses an intentional and serious commitment. The new believers went

---

Witnesses': Aspects of Mission in the Acts of the Apostles," *Missiology: An International Review* 10 (1982): 421. Jesus taught His disciples the importance of community from the very beginning of their journey with Him. In Luke's Gospel Jesus chose twelve from a larger group of disciples to be apostles (Luke 6:13–16). Though Luke did not call them a church, the twelve apostles composed the first community of Christ followers in the NT, with Jesus among them as their leader. They traveled with Jesus and were sent by Him to proclaim the kingdom of heaven (9:1–2). He taught them to serve together as those who would one day lead the church. Jesus exposed their rivalry and pride, and He called them to love those whom they perceived as enemies (9:46–56). He also welcomed women as fellow travelers and students (8:1–3; 10:38–42), and He had a larger group of seventy disciples whom He trained and sent out to minister (10:1–23).

[15] Bruce J. Malina and Jerome H. Neyrey, "First-Century Personality: Dyadic, Not Individual," in *The Social World of Luke-Acts*, ed. Jerome H. Neyrey (Peabody, MA: Hendrickson, 1991), 72–74, 80–83.

[16] Maria Anicia Co, "The Major Summaries in Acts," *ETL* 68 (1992): 59.

[17] BAGD, 715. In the phrase ἦσαν δὲ προσκαρτεροῦντες, Luke used προσκαρτερέω periphrastically as a participle following the imperfect plural form of εἰμί, which implies an ongoing state rather than a one-time decision. These believers committed themselves to these practices as a way of life. See Acts 1:14; 2:46; 6:5; Rom 12:12; 13:6; Col 4:2; Josephus, *J.W.* 6.27; idem. *Ant.* 5.130 for additional examples of the verb's use.

after following Jesus with passion and determination. Some have suggested that the four commitments form for Luke the basic liturgical elements of the early church's worship service, in which teaching and fellowship were followed by the Lord's Supper and corporate prayer.[18] While such activities would likely be a part of corporate worship rooted in synagogue services, the immediate context does not demand it here. Others have inferred that Luke is describing the duties of new believers in the Jerusalem church, or perhaps even Luke's own ecclesial context.[19] Luke does not tell us this explicitly. However, it makes sense to see Acts 2:42 describing what Luke believes should characterize newly baptized converts, considering its location following the conversion of the great majority of them in Acts 2:41.

In the list of characteristics of exemplary life that follows, the church will be referred to primarily as "the believers," which is Luke's preferred designation for the community in the summary narratives (Acts 2:44; 4:32; 5:14).[20]

The believers committed themselves to the apostles' teaching (Acts 2:42). Teaching and being taught are major themes in Luke and Acts.[21] With the phrase "the apostles' teaching" Luke stresses both the authority of the apostles and the authoritative content of their teaching. The events

---

[18] James D. G. Dunn, *The Acts of the Apostles* (Valley Forge, PA: Trinity Press International, 1996), 35; Joachim Jeremias, *The Eucharistic Words of Jesus*, trans. Norman Perrin (New York: Charles Scribner's Sons, 1966), 118–21; I. Howard Marshall, *Luke: Historian and Theologian* (Grand Rapids: Zondervan, 1989), 204–6; H. Alan Brehm, "The Significance of the Summaries for Interpreting Acts," *SwJT* 33, no. 1 (Fall 1990): 34–35; Jean-Marc Prieur, "Actes 2, 42 et le Culte Réformé," *Foi et Vie* 94, no. 2 (1995): 61–72.

[19] Gerhard Schneider, *Die Apostelgeschichte*, vol. 1 of *Herders theologischer Kommentar zum Neuen Testament* (Freiburg: Herder, 1980), 286; Rudolf Pesch, *Die Apostelgeschichte, Apg. 1–12* (Köln: Benzinger, 1986), 130.

[20] On Luke's use of the term "believers" (*pisteuontes*) to refer to the church, see Paul Trebilco, *Self-designations and Group Identity in the New Testament* (Cambridge, UK: Cambridge University Press, 2012), 103–11. The word appears in the present tense here and in 5:14, consistent with Luke's emphasis on continuing action through his preference for imperfect tense verb forms throughout the summary narratives. The early church was made up of those who believed in Jesus for salvation and who *continued* to trust in Jesus for faith and life. They were thoroughly converted to Jesus Christ. The use of an aorist tense participle for "those who believed" in 4:32, *pisteusantōn*, is an exception to the pattern, but its emphasis on the ongoing state of the believers' faith is not. See C. K. Barrett, *Acts 1–14*, ICC (New York: T&T Clark, 1994), 167; Bruce M. Metzger, *A Textual Commentary on the Greek New Testament* (Stuttgart: United Bible Societies, 1971), 302–3.

[21] Jesus was called Teacher thirteen times in Luke's Gospel by both friends and enemies (Luke 7:40; 8:49; 9:38; 10:25; 11:45; 12:13; 18:18; 19:39; 20:21,38,39; 21:27; 22:11). His ministry of teaching was referenced thirteen times (7:40; 8:49; 9:38; 10:25; 11:45; 12:13; 18:18; 19:39; 20:21,38,39; 21:27; 22:11). Jesus' goal in teaching was that His students would be like Him (6:40). Teaching by the apostles is referenced 17 times in Acts, making the apostles' teaching an important theme in Luke's second volume too (Acts 2:42; 4:2,18; 5:21,25,28,34,42; 11:26 (in Antioch); 13:12; 15:35; 17:19; 18:11; 20:20 (in Ephesus); 21:21,28; 28:31).

of Pentecost firmly established the authority of the apostles as leaders in the Jerusalem church as Jesus intended (Luke 22:24–30).[22] At this early date, a formal ecclesiastical structure did not exist. However, the apostles were already recognized as leaders through their prior association with Jesus and their commission by Him as apostles (Luke 6:12–16), as well as by the signs and wonders that accompanied their ministry (Acts 2:43; 5:12).[23] The new believers were eager to be taught and were willing to submit to the apostles' teaching as Christ's authoritative spokesmen.[24] From the earliest days of the church, the believers prioritized gathering together to sit under the teaching of the apostles (Acts 2:46; 5:12,42).[25] Even years later in Gentile churches that did not have the benefit of an apostle among them, believers gathered together to hear letters from the apostle Paul read (Col 4:16).

Luke also stresses the doctrinal content of the apostles' teaching. Their message would have included an exposition of the Old Testament from the perspective of their fulfillment in Christ. No doubt much time was also spent repeating, explaining, and applying the teachings of Jesus, as well as recounting His life and ministry.[26] Decades later at least two of the original twelve apostles, Matthew and John, would commit the words and deeds of Jesus to writing in their own Gospel accounts. Luke's placement of submission to the apostles' teaching as the first of four commitments should not be overlooked at the start of the first summary narrative.[27] The apostles' teachings, and later their writings (2 Pet 3:15–16), were the doctrinal foundation for church life that would undergird every other belief and practice. Any attempt to articulate a theology of church life in Acts must reckon with Luke's concern to establish the apostles' teaching as fully authoritative in the church.

The believers committed themselves to the fellowship (Acts 2:42). The term for "fellowship" (*koinōnia*) comes from the word for "common"

---

[22] Robert L. Brawley, *Centering on God: Method and Message in Luke-Acts* (Louisville, KY: Westminster/John Knox, 1990), 92–93; J. Bradley Chance, *Jerusalem, the Temple, and the New Age in Luke-Acts* (Macon, GA: Mercer University Press, 1988), 66–73, 81.

[23] David S. Dockery, "The Theology of Acts," *CTR* 5, no. 1 (1990): 54; Joseph B. Tyson, "Authority in Acts," *TBT* 30, no. 5, *CTR* 5 (1992): 279–83.

[24] Luke 24:48; Acts 1:3,8; 11:26; 20:7–9; 28:30–31.

[25] Andrew C. Clark, "The Role of the Apostles," in *Witness to the Gospel: The Theology of Acts*, ed. I. Howard Marshall and David Peterson (Grand Rapids: Eerdmans, 1998), 179.

[26] James D. G. Dunn, *Beginning from Jerusalem*, vol. 2 of *Christianity in the Making* (Grand Rapids: Eerdmans, 2009), 189–96.

[27] Steven J. Lawson, "The Priority of Biblical Preaching: An Expository Study of Acts 2:42–47," *BSac* 158 (2001): 200–201.

(*koinē*) and can be translated "association" or "society."[28] The word could be used in a secular sense to refer to a social club or to the mutual obligations of a partnership between persons, or between a person and a group.[29] Although *koinōnia* is translated "fellowship" in Acts 2:42, the word is barely adequate for all it implies.[30] The believers in Jerusalem shared many things, including their possessions (2:44–45), but the meaning is much broader. The word in its context encompasses the totality of relationships in the community of believers, including fellowship between members, between individual believers and God, and even fellowship between the believing community and God.[31] What this fellowship should look like is fleshed out for readers in the summary narratives, but Luke wants to make one thing clear at the beginning of his three portraits of church life. A commitment to follow Jesus includes a commitment to His people.

The believers committed to breaking bread together (Acts 2:42). The most basic meaning of the phrase "the breaking of bread" is to share a meal. Luke may be using it to refer to eating meals together as a normative church practice (see Acts 2:46; 20:11).[32] This practice originated in Judaism, where the head of a household would begin a meal by breaking bread and passing it around to his guests.[33] The phrase has also been interpreted as a shorthand way by which Luke, or perhaps the early church, referred to the Lord's Supper (see Luke 22:19; Acts 20:7).[34] The

---

[28] κοινωνία occurs only here in Acts. For other uses see 1 Cor 1:9; 2 Cor 8:14; Phil 2:1; 3:10; Col 1:24; 1 John 1:3; 1:9; 2:9; Rev 1:9.

[29] Bruce J. Malina and John J. Pilch, *Social-Science Commentary on the Book of Acts* (Minneapolis, MN: Fortress, 2008), 36. The concept was similar to the ancient Israelite's perception of his relationship to the community of Israel as his extended family. See Paul M. Joyce, "The Individual and the Community," in *Beginning Old Testament Study*, ed. John Rogerson, John Barton, David J. A. Clines, and Paul M. Joyce, 2nd ed. (Danvers, MA: Chalice Press, 1982), 77–78.

[30] Arthur Carr, "The Fellowship (Κοινωνία) of Acts II.42 and Cognate Words," *The Expositor* 29, no. 8 (1913): 461.

[31] Robrecht Michiels, "The Model of Church in the First Christian Community of Jerusalem: Ideal and Reality," *Louvain Studies* 10 (1985): 309; George Panikulam, *Koinōnia in the New Testament: A Dynamic Expression of the Christian Life* (Rome: Biblical Institute Press, 1979), 123–24.

[32] Dunn, *Beginning from Jerusalem*, 198–200; Johannes Munck, *The Acts of the Apostles*, AB (Garden City, NY: Doubleday, 1967), 22, 283–84; David Peterson, *The Acts of the Apostles*, PNTC (Grand Rapids: Eerdmans, 2009), 161.

[33] John Lightfoot, *A Commentary on the New Testament from the Talmud and Hebraica*, vol. 4, *Acts–1 Corinthians* (Peabody, MA: Hendrickson, 1979, orig. 1859), 35–36.

[34] The view of F. F. Bruce, *The Acts of the Apostles: The Greek Text with Introduction and Commentary* (Grand Rapids: Eerdmans, 1990), 132; Joseph A. Fitzmyer, *The Acts of the Apostles*, AB (New York: Doubleday, 1998), 271; John Paul Heil, *The Meal Scenes in Luke-Acts: An Audience-Oriented Approach* (Atlanta: Society of Biblical Literature, 1999), 237–38; Mikael C. Parsons, *Acts*, Paideia: Commentaries on the New Testament (Grand Rapids: Baker, 2008), 49.

second-century church understood it this way.[35] The problem is that Luke does not clarify what he means. He may assume that his readers understand, or perhaps Luke deliberately leaves its meaning ambiguous so that both sharing meals and remembering the death of Christ are implied.[36] It is unnecessary to choose one over the other, because the early church often took the Lord's Supper in the context of a shared meal (1 Cor 11:20–34). Sharing meals and sharing the Lord's Supper were both extensions of table fellowship with Jesus among His disciples.[37]

Separating the possible meanings too sharply also overlooks how meals possessed both social and spiritual significance in ancient Jewish culture.[38] To show hospitality by welcoming others into one's home to share a meal was to accept them as friends. For believers in Jesus, eating together declared that no matter what social group a person belonged to outside of the church, everyone was part of the family in the church. On a spiritual level, to take the Lord's Supper together is to share in God's hospitality and welcome. He is the God that the elders of Israel saw, and before whom they ate and were accepted (Exod 24:9–11). Jesus looked forward to eating the Passover meal with His disciples before He suffered (Luke 22:15). Even after His resurrection, in an astonishing act of humility before His ascension, Jesus prepared breakfast for His disciples on the shore of the Sea of Galilee (John 21:9–13). For believers to eat together as the church is an act of worship in the presence of the Lord. To take the Lord's Supper together, in remembrance of the death of Christ, is to experience God's hospitality and to show each other hospitality in the church.[39] More will be said later on the spiritual and social significance of meals when Acts 2:46 is discussed.

---

[35] See *Did.* 9–10; 14.1; Ignat. *Smyrn.* 7.1; 8.1–2 *Eph.* 20.2; *Phld.* 4.1; Justin *1 Apol.* 65–66. See Geoffrey Wainwright, "Lord's Supper, Love Feast," in *DLNT*, 690–92.

[36] See Barrett, *Acts 1–14*, 164–65; Darrell L. Bock, *Acts*, BECNT (Grand Rapids: Baker Academic, 2007), 150–51; Brehm, "Significance of the Summaries," 35; J. Bradley Chance, *Acts*, SHBC (Macon, GA: Smyth & Helwys, 2007), 59; Ernst Haenchen, *The Acts of the Apostles*, trans. R. McL. Wilson (Philadelphia: Westminster Press, 1971), 191; William J. Larkin, *Acts*, CBC (Carol Stream, IL: Tyndale House, 2006), 392–93; John Polhill, *Acts*, NAC (Nashville: Broadman, 1992), 119; Ben Witherington III, *The Acts of the Apostles: A Socio-Rhetorical Commentary* (Grand Rapids: Eerdmans, 1998), 161; Pesch, *Die Apostelgeschichte*, 165.

[37] Charles H. Talbert, "The Place of the Resurrection in the Theology of Luke," *Int* 46 (1992): 26–28.

[38] Reta Halteman Finger, *Of Widows and Meals: Communal Meals in the Acts of the Apostles* (Grand Rapids: Eerdmans, 2007), 230, 169–82.

[39] Justo L. González, *Acts: The Gospel of the Spirit* (Maryknoll, NY: Orbis Books, 2001), 53–54; Michiels, "The Model of Church," 310.

The believers committed themselves to prayer (Acts 2:42). The phrase *tais proseuchais* is translated variously: "to prayers" (HCSB), "to . . . the prayers" (ESV, NRSV), "prayed together" (CEV, NCV).[40] Establishing a private prayer life surely was implied, following Jesus' example (Luke 5:16; 6:12; 9:28–29), as well as spontaneous praying whenever the need arose (Acts 4:23–30; 12:5). However, the emphasis of the plural form for prayer here is on the practice of meeting together at set times for corporate prayer and worship.[41] In this the Jerusalem church simply followed their practice as Jews (Acts 3:1; 10:2–3,30), only now they prayed with fellow believers in Christ.

Prayer is a major theme in Luke–Acts.[42] Luke portrays Jesus as a person in constant communion with His heavenly Father through prayer.[43] Jesus taught His disciples to pray too (Luke 11:1–13; 18:1–8), although they struggled at times to remain focused in prayer (Luke 22:40,46). After the resurrection of Jesus and the coming of the Holy Spirit, however, the believers are devoted to prayer, both individual and corporate, as a major theme that runs throughout Acts.[44] Though praying together is not elevated above devotion to the apostles' teaching, the fellowship, and the breaking of bread, it is accorded the same level of importance as the other three foundational commitments new believers make.

---

[40] The NASB and NLT render *tais proseuchais* "to prayer." While adequate, this translation sacrifices the nuanced emphasis of the plural form on gathering together for worship and prayer, which the context implies.

[41] Timothy C. G. Thornton, "Continuing Steadfast in Prayer," *ExpTim* 83, no. 1 (1971): 23–24.

[42] Of the thirty-six NT uses of the noun for prayer (*proseuchais*), twelve are in Luke–Acts, nine of which are in Acts. Of the eighty-five occurrences of the verb for pray (*proseuchomai*), thirty-four are in Luke–Acts, sixteen of which are in Acts, making prayer an important theme in Luke's writings (Bock, *Acts*, 151).

[43] Luke 3:21; 5:16; 9:18,28–29; 11:1,5–8; 18:1–8; 22:31–32,40; 23:34,46.

[44] Acts 1:14; 4:23–30; 6:4,6; 8:15,22–24; 9:11,40; 10:2,5,9; 12:5,12; 13:3; 14:23; 16:13,16,25; 20:36; 21:5; 22:17; 27:29; 28:8. The *Didache* (c. AD 90) challenged Christians to pray three times per day (8.2–3). See also Dan 6:10. On the theme of prayer in Luke–Acts, see Craig G. Bartholomew and Robby Holt, "Prayer in/and the Drama of Redemption in Luke," in *Reading Luke: Interpretation, Reflection, and Formation*, ed. Craig G. Bartholomew, Joel B. Green, and Anthony C. Thiselton (Grand Rapids: Zondervan, 2006), 350–75; Joel B. Green, "Persevering Together in Prayer: The Significance of Prayer in the Acts of the Apostles," in *Into God's Presence: Prayer in the New Testament*, ed. Richard N. Longenecker (Grand Rapids: Eerdmans, 2001), 183–202; Steven F. Plymale, "Luke's Theology of Prayer," in SBLSP (1990): 529–51; and Peter T. O'Brien, "Prayer in Luke-Acts," *TynBul* 24 (1973): 111–27. On the first-century Jewish practice of corporate prayer, see Asher Finkel, "Prayer in Jewish Life of the First Century as Background to Early Christianity," in *Into God's Presence*, ed. Longenecker, 43–65.

Signs and Wonders and the Fear of the Lord

The subject of the verb in Acts 2:42 refers specifically to the new believers in Acts 2:41. However, in 2:43 the subject is broadened to include "everyone," or literally "every soul" (*pasē psuchē*). Acts 2:43–47 expands on the commitments of the new believers described in Acts 2:42. Luke continues to exploit the narrative technique of summarization in these verses to create the sense of a way of life among the believers.

The believers experienced the fear of the Lord (Acts 2:43). The word for fear (*phobos*) signifies amazement, awe, and reverence, especially when it is used to speak of the fear of the Lord (Acts 9:31).[45] The term can also refer to fright or terror, like Zechariah's reaction to the angel Gabriel (Luke 1:12), the Gerasenes' reaction to Jesus (Luke 8:37), or the church's reaction to the death of Ananias and Sapphira (Acts 5:5,11).[46] The latter use is more common in Luke's writings, but in Acts 2:43 there is room for both meanings. Rendering *phobos* as "awe" is appropriate (ESV, NASB, NIV), but the word "fear" (HCSB, NKJV, RSV) better captures the grip that God's presence and power had on His people.[47] God was doing something clearly beyond anyone's power to predict or control. The fellowship of believers was overwhelmed by the realization that God was on the move in Jerusalem and ruling over the affairs of His people.

The fear of which Luke speaks was not the kind that made believers run from God either. Instead, they stood in stunned amazement at what God was doing among them. By using the imperfect tense Luke conveys that the fear people felt was not merely a momentary panic. It was an ongoing reverence for God. Fear did not suddenly wash over the believers and move on as quickly as it came. It lay upon them as a continuous condition.[48] Some interpreters have understood "everyone" in Acts 2:43 to refer to the people of Jerusalem outside the church. They see Luke saying that fear came over the city.[49] Others see Luke referring to the church only.[50]

---

[45] See Acts 5:11; 2 Cor 5:11; Eph 5:21; 1 Clement 3:4; 21:6. Compare to *T. Levi.* 13:7; 1QH 4.26 on the topic of fear in the holy congregation.

[46] Also see Acts 19:17. Aristotle spoke of fear as an emotion caused when we face whatever has the power to destroy us or cause us great pain (*Rhet.* 1382a 28–29).

[47] The NCV renders the phrase, "Everyone felt great respect for God," which, while acceptable, hardly does justice to what the statement implies.

[48] Curtis Vaughan, *Acts* (Grand Rapids: Zondervan, 1974), 30; Barrett, *Acts 1–14*, 166.

[49] Bock, *Acts*, 151; Larkin, *Acts*, 398; Richard N. Longenecker, *Acts*, EBC vol. 9 (Grand Rapids: Zondervan, 2007), 757; Marshall, *Acts*, 84.

[50] Fitzmyer, *Acts*, 271; Peterson, *Acts*, 162; Robert W. Wall, "The Acts of the Apostles," in *NIB*, 71.

Both may be in view, but in light of the rhetorical context of emphasizing exemplary behavior in the church, the emphasis is more on the church's disposition. Times of testing, the worries, riches, and even pleasures of life (Luke 8:13–14) can dull the spiritual senses to the things of God. An entire church can become lukewarm (Rev 3:16). But an exemplary church maintains reverence and the fear of the Lord.

God performed many wonders and signs through the apostles (Acts 2:43).[51] The apostles are not spoken of as causing wonders and signs. God performed them "through the apostles" (*dia tōn apostolōn*).[52] The term for wonders (*terata*) can also be translated "miracles" and describes an occurrence so out of the ordinary that it causes people to take note. Wonders can be positive occurrences, or they can denote events that frighten because they so contradict the ordered unity of nature.[53] The term for signs (*sēmeia*) describes a miracle by which God validates His message and the person who brings it.[54] Signs in Acts also point to the reality of God's saving power in His church. Both senses are implied in Luke's use of the word here. The immediate precursor to wonders and signs in Acts is Peter's declaration of their meaning in his Pentecost sermon. He said that the miracles witnessed on Pentecost Day fulfilled Joel's prophecy of what would accompany the outpouring of the Holy Spirit in the last days (Acts 2:19; Joel 2:28–32). Peter also said that Jesus' ministry was attested by "miracles, wonders, and signs" (Acts 2:22).[55] The statement about wonders and signs through the apostles in Acts 2:43 seems strategically placed by Luke right after Peter's sermon to indicate that what Joel prophesied and what Jesus began to do, He continued to do through His apostles (1:1; 2:43; 5:12). The apostles are mentioned five times in the summary narra-

---

[51] Some uncertainty exists over the wording of Acts 2:43. The NA27 (followed by most English translations) follows B, cop^sa, it^d, syr^h. However, some early manuscripts (p^74, ℵ, vg, geo) add ἐν Ἰερουσαλὴμ φόβος τε ἦν μέγας ἐπὶ πάντας καί. A, C, and 2127 read ἐγένετο διὰ τῶν ἀποστόλων ἐν. See Barrett, *Acts 1–14*, 167; and Richard I. Pervo, *Acts*, Hermeneia (Minneapolis: Fortress, 2009), 93, for discussion.

[52] Andreas Lindemann, "The Beginnings of Christian Common Life in Jerusalem according to the Summaries in the Acts of the Apostles (Acts 2:42–47; 4:32–37; 5:12–16)," in *Common Life in the Early Church: Essays Honoring Graydon F. Snyder*, ed. Julian Hills (Harrisburg, PA: Trinity Press International, 1998), 206.

[53] Wilhelm Mundle, Otfried Hofius, and Colin Brown, "Miracle, Wonder, Sign," in *NIDNTT*, 2:633.

[54] Robert L. Hamblin, "Miracles in the Book of Acts," *SwJT* 17, no. 1 (Fall 1974): 20–21; Peterson, *Acts*, 162; Witherington, *Acts*, 161.

[55] Luke anticipated this theme in his Gospel when he stressed Christ's power to heal and drive out demons both in his summaries of Jesus' ministry and in individual episodes. See Luke 4:33–39,40–41; 5:12–15,17–26; 6:17–19; 7:1–16; 8:2,22–56; 9:10–17,37–43; 13:10–17; 17:11–19; 18:35–42; 22:51.

tives (2:42,43; 4:33,35; 5:12), six when the reference to Peter's shadow is included (5:15). The link between signs and wonders through the apostles and Jesus combined with their predominance in the summary narratives indicates Luke's concern that readers recognize the unique position of the apostles as Jesus' designated representatives in the early church.

One additional detail connects Christ's ongoing ministry to the apostles. The order of most occurrences of the phrase in Scripture is "signs and wonders."[56] However, in Peter's reference to Joel and to the ministry of Christ (Acts 2:19,22) and here in his reference to the apostles' ministry (2:43), the word "wonders" appears first, followed by "signs" (2:18–19,22; 2:43), which suggests a natural correspondence between them.[57] This connection would not have been missed by attentive readers/hearers of Acts. More will be said on the issues raised by Luke's emphasis on signs and wonders when Acts 5:12,15–16 are discussed in chapter 5.

Sharing Lives and Possessions

The believers shared in each other's lives (Acts 2:44). Luke describes the way the believers shared in each other's lives with two phrases. First, they were "together" (*epi to auto*), which is a prepositional phrase meaning "in the same location." Luke may be referring to their meetings in Solomon's Colonnade at the temple (5:12). The believers often met together in a large group at the temple complex for worship, instruction, and fellowship (2:46; 5:12).[58] A figurative sense also seems to be implied concerning the believers' identity as a people who belonged to God and to each other. They saw themselves as the society of those who believed in Jesus.[59] Faith in Christ and sharing in each other's lives are inseparable in Luke's theology of church life. The *Didache* expressed a similar conviction, "If we share in the immortal things, should we not share in those that are mortal?"[60]

---

[56] For examples see Deut 6:22; 7:19; Neh 9:10; Ps 135:9; Isa 8:18; Jer 32:21; Matt 24:24; John 4:48; Rom 15:19; 2 Cor 12:12; Heb 2:4. In Acts see 4:30; 5:12; 14:3; 15:12.

[57] Robert B. Sloan, "'Signs and Wonders': A Rhetorical Clue to the Pentecost Discourse," in *With Steadfast Purpose: Essays on Acts in Honor of Henry Jackson Flanders*, ed. Naymond H. Keathley (Waco, TX: Baylor University Press, 1990), 156.

[58] Everett F. Harrison, *Acts: The Expanding Church* (Chicago: Moody, 1975), 66.

[59] Barrett, *Acts 1–14*, 167; Jacques Dupont, "Community of Goods in the Early Church," in *The Salvation of the Gentiles: Essays on the Acts of the Apostles*, trans. John R. Keating (New York: Paulist Press, 1979), 102.

[60] *Did.* 4.8.

Luke's second phrase describing the believers' sharing is that they had "everything in common" (*eichon hapanta koina*). A popular Greek proverb said something similar, "Friends have all things in common."[61] However, friendship alone did not produce such openness and unselfishness toward each other. Rather, it was the presence and power of the Holy Spirit and the impact of a new standing with Christ, whose death many of these converts recently cheered (Acts 2:36; Luke 23:21,23,35).

Believers in Jesus gather together for the purpose of sharing in each other's lives. The physical location is not as important as practice of meeting often. Meeting together enables believers to share life's joys and burdens with each other (Gal 6:2; 1 Cor 12:26), and it helps us know how we can encourage one another toward love and good deeds (Heb 10:24–25).

The believers practiced radical generosity in giving to meet needs (Acts 2:45). The believers' commitment to the fellowship and to sharing in each other's lives (Acts 2:42,44) is fleshed out here in their sacrificial giving. They regularly sold their possessions and goods and gave to anyone among the believers who had a need. The word for possessions (*ktēma*) can also be translated "property" and is often used to refer to a field or tract of land.[62] A person who owned land would be perceived as having great wealth. The word for goods (*huparxeis*) refers to the belongings of any person no matter how many or few.[63] The collective sense of the "possessions and property" is that everyone in the church, whether rich or poor, gave generously to meet each other's needs.

Some have suggested that Luke refers to a sense of collective ownership. The believers gave up the idea of private property and pooled their possessions formally, so that the church functioned, at least temporarily in Jerusalem, as a sort of alternative family structure.[64] There was precedent

---

[61] Compare εἶχον ἅπαντα κοινά in Acts 2:44 to κοινὰ τὰ φιλῶν and in Plato, *Resp.* 4.424a; 5.449c. Also see Aristotle *Eth. nic.* 8.9; 1159b.31; Philo, *Abr.* 235; Ps. Clem., *Recog.* 10.5; Ael. Arist., 27.24. κοινά can refer adjectivally to objects that were considered common, or it can be used to designate a common fund. See LSJ, 968; and Pieter W. van der Horst, "Hellenistic Parallels to the Acts of the Apostles (2.1–47)," *JSNT* 24 (1985): 59.

[62] See Josephus, *Jewish War* 4.574; Prov 23:10; 31:16; Acts 5:1. κτῆμα is interchangeable with χωρίον, which is found in Acts 5:3,8 (Haenchen, *Acts*, 192 n. 5).

[63] See 2 Chr 35:7; Ps 77:48; Prov 18:11; 19:14; Jer 9:9; Hos 1:5; *T. Levi* 17:9; Heb 10:34. Also, note similar attitudes toward property and helping people in need in 1 John 3:17–18 and Jas 2:1–6,14–17. Both John and James were leaders in the Jerusalem church.

[64] N. T. Wright, *The New Testament and the People of God* (Minneapolis: Fortress Press, 1992), 448–49; and Bruce, *Book of the Acts*, NICNT, 74. D. K. Bornhäußer, *Studien zur Apostelgeschichte* (Gütersloh: Bertelsmann, 1934), 55, argued that Luke was merely reporting the Jerusalem situation, rather than advocating a specific approach to property among believers. Joachim Jeremias, *Jerusalem*

for this among the original twelve disciples, who traveled extensively with Jesus and lived from the same money bag (John 12:6; 13:29). However, it is unlikely that all the believers liquidated their assets and practiced a form of primitive communism. That church members were able to sell possessions continually and give as needs arose implies that private property was not immediately renounced when the church was born. However, Luke makes it clear that the experience of forgiveness of sins and the gift of the Holy Spirit led the believers to embrace a radical generosity that put the needs of others before their own (1 Cor 10:24,33; 13:5; Phil 2:4). Because of Christ, people suddenly became far more important than earthly treasures (Luke 19:8). More will be said on the generosity of the believers in chapter 4 when Acts 4:34–35 is discussed.

Meeting Together and Sharing Meals

The believers devoted themselves to gathering daily in the temple complex (Acts 2:46). The lengthy sentence in Acts 2:46 locates the two main gathering places of the early church in the temple complex and in their homes. Luke places the phrase "every day" (*kath' hēmeran*) in an emphatic position at the start of the sentence to stress that in the earliest days the church met daily.[65] Their gatherings were not haphazard either. They "devoted themselves [to meeting] together" (*proskarterountes homothumadon*). The word for devoted here is the same verb that appears in v. 42. The church made an intentional commitment to gathering together in a large public setting. The entire fellowship, as many as 5,000 or more (4:4; 6:1,7), could meet together "in the temple complex" (*en tō hierō*) to hear the apostles teach and to share the experience of being a part of a movement.

Attendance at the temple indicates that they did not abandon their claim to the temple or see themselves as forsaking their heritage as Jews in order to follow Jesus.[66] Worshippers could watch the priests as they went about their duties and hear the apostles explain how what they saw had

---

in the Time of Jesus, trans. F. H. and C. H. Cave (Philadelphia: Fortress, 1967), 130, thought Luke was actually advocating a form of Christian communism.

[65] καθ᾿ ἡμέραν is an idiomatic expression that means "daily." Eleven of its seventeen NT occurrences appear in Luke–Acts (Peterson, *Acts*, 163).

[66] J. Julius Scott Jr., "The Church's Progress to the Council of Jerusalem according to the Book of Acts," *BBR* 7 (1997): 208–9; Haenchen, *Acts*, 154; Hans Conzelmann, *Acts of the Apostles*, trans. James Limburg, A. Thomas Kraabel, and Donald H. Juel, Hermeneia (Philadelphia: Fortress, 1987), 31–32.

its fulfillment in the death of Jesus.[67] Luke's comment on meetings at the temple complex allowed him to make clear that the first church believed itself to be rooted in Judaism, especially the theology of temple sacrifices.

The practice of meeting daily at the temple may well have abated after a period of time, as believers returned to their homes and jobs, many of them in Galilee and the surrounding towns of Judea. However, it is remarkable how the believers were conscious of both their commitment to worshipping together and of their continual connection to each other. The temple eventually became an unsafe place for believers to meet as Jewish opposition to the new movement grew (Acts 4:1–21; 5:17–42; 6:9–8:3).

The believers devoted themselves to the practice of hospitality in their homes (Acts 2:46). Not only did the Jerusalem church meet as one body in the temple complex, it also gathered in smaller bodies in believers' homes (Acts 2:46; 5:42).[68] Luke's mention of home meetings indicates that a transition away from the temple toward meeting in homes was underway from the first days of the church's existence.[69] Though the believers were indebted to the temple, the practice of hospitality in homes enabled them to develop a distinctively Christian worship and fellowship.[70] The transition away from the temple would later accelerate as the believers were scattered away from Jerusalem, and the Christian movement moved outside of Judea (8:1–5,40). Homes would eventually become the focal point of church life in Acts (16:40; 17:7; 18:26; 20:8,20).[71] Gathering in private homes would continue to be the norm for church meetings for the next

---

[67] Marshall, *Acts,* 85.

[68] Roger W. Gehring, *House Church and Mission: The Importance of Household Structures in Early Christianity* (Peabody, MA: Hendrickson, 2004), 83.

[69] S. K. Kisirinya, "Re-Interpreting the Major Summaries (Acts 2:42–46; 4:43–35; 5:12–16)," *African Christian Studies* 18, no. 1 (2002): 67–74, argues that a major role of the summary narratives is to show a gradual detachment of believers from the temple in favor of the community meal as the gathering place for the church as the new people of God. See also Dunn, *Acts,* 36; Luke Timothy Johnson, *The Acts of the Apostles,* SP (Collegeville, MN: Michael Glazier, 1992), 59; Finger, *Of Widows and Meals,* 238; and John H. Elliott, "Temple Versus Household in Luke-Acts: A Contrast in Social Institutions," in *The Social World of Luke-Acts,* ed. Jerome H. Neyrey (Peabody, MA: Hendrickson, 1991), 216.

[70] Abraham Malherbe, *Social Aspects of Early Christianity* (Baton Rouge, LA: LSU Press, 1977), 61, 67.

[71] Also see Rom 16:5; 1 Cor 16:19; Col 4:15; Phlm 2; John Reumann, "One Lord, One Faith, One God, but Many House Churches," in Hills, *Common Life in the Early Church,* 106–17; John Koenig, *New Testament Hospitality: Partnership with Strangers as Promise and Mission* (Philadelphia: Fortress, 1985), 106; and John E. Stambaugh and David L. Balch, *The New Testament in Its Social Environment* (Philadelphia: Westminster Press, 1986), 138–40.

three centuries until Constantine began constructing the first Christian basilicas.[72]

Because the phrase "broke bread" (klōntes . . . arton) in Acts 2:46 is actually a participle that modifies the main clause verb, "They ate their food," it likely refers to sharing meals rather than to the Lord's Supper.[73] The phrase "from house to house" (kat' oikon) implies that these smaller gatherings were spreading across Jerusalem through believers' homes. Their meals were accompanied by the dispositions of "gladness" and "simplicity of heart." The term gladness (agalliasei) expresses an intense form of joy that can be rendered "great joy" or "transcendent gladness." The word for simplicity of heart (aphelotēti) conveys the related ideas of "humility" and "sincerity." They did not eat together merely to satisfy their need for nourishment. They genuinely enjoyed one another's company and chose to gather in each other's homes often. The practice of hospitality enabled both host and guests to participate in a practice taught by Jesus as a crucial means of spreading the message about the kingdom of heaven (Luke 10:1–9) and of welcoming the stranger (Luke 24:13–32).

Breaking bread together also implied an openness and acceptance of each other. Table sharing was a universal symbol of friendship, for one might eat with a stranger but never with an enemy.[74] As the Jewish church moved outside of Judea later in Acts, a major barrier to reaching out through hospitality would be that Jews would not eat with Gentiles, because they and their food were considered unclean. However, God would soon instruct Peter no longer to consider the Gentiles' food unclean (Acts 10:15) and then send him to the home of a Gentile centurion named Cornelius. There Peter would witness many Gentiles receiving the gift of

---

[72] Bradley B. Blue, "Architecture, Early Church," in *DLNT*, 91. The evolution of the physical architecture of pre-Constantinian churches is usually divided into three phases: private homes, homes remodeled for use as churches, and larger meeting halls, which were predecessors to the churches constructed by Constantine (Daryl D. Schmidt, "The Jesus Tradition in the Common Life of Early Christian Communities," in Hills, *Common Life in the Early Church*, 138). A fascinating survey of the famed Dura-Europa house church, a large third-century home in Syria that was converted into a church complete with meeting hall and baptistry, can be found in Ramsay MacMullen, *The Second Church: Popular Christianity A.D. 200–400*, Writings from the Greco-Roman World Supplement Series 1 (Atlanta: Society of Biblical Literature, 2009), 1–10. Excellent surveys of research into archeological and literary evidence for early house churches can be found in Bradley B. Blue, "Acts and the House Church," in *The Book of Acts in Its Graeco-Roman Setting*, ed. David W. J. Gill and Conrad Gempf (Grand Rapids: Eerdmans, 1994), 119–222; and Gehring, *House Church and Mission*, 1–27.

[73] William A. Dowd, "Breaking Bread: Acts 2:46," *CBQ* 1 (1939): 358–62.

[74] Santos Yao, "Dismantling Social Barriers through Table Fellowship," in *Mission in Acts: Ancient Narratives in Contemporary Context*, ed. Robert L. Gallagher and Paul Hertig (Maryknoll, NY: Orbis, 2004), 32; William L. Blevins, "The Early Church: Acts 1–5," *RevExp* 71 (1974): 473–74.

the Holy Spirit. Peter would stay for several days, enjoying their hospitality and no doubt sharing meals together (Acts 10:24–48). For Peter, a Palestinian Jewish Christian, and Cornelius, a Gentile Roman centurion, hospitality would provide the means by which these two strangers could overcome their differences in Christ.[75] The Jerusalem church's devotion to hospitality set an example for readers of Acts that the divisions that occur between people in a fallen world now have been overcome in Christ (Gal 3:28; Eph 2:14; Col 3:11). Luke places the practice of hospitality and the shared meal at the relational center of exemplary church life.[76]

Worship, Neighbor Love, and Growth

The believers were continually praising God (Acts 2:47). The Greek term for praising (*ainountes*) means "to speak in praise of" or "to recommend." Their praise involved talking about the great things God had done, like Anna who saw Jesus at the temple and began to praise God and talk about Jesus to others (Luke 2:38). Six of the eight New Testament occurrences of this way of praising God appear in Luke–Acts.[77] While the term could refer to formal gatherings for worship and praise, the context suggests that Luke is describing a general characteristic of the believers.[78] Their home meetings, indeed their very lives, were characterized by gratitude and praise. The church attributed everything it had and was to God, which is the only appropriate response to grace.[79]

Luke's emphasis on praise shines additional light on the believers' generosity. Humanitarian interest, though laudable in any age, was not primarily what drove these believers to sacrifice their possessions the way they did. Their giving was in direct response to God, who had done so much for them.[80] They recognized that they were living in a time when God's eschatological promises to Israel were being fulfilled (Acts 2:16,25,34). Of course, it must be acknowledged that not all of God's promises to Israel were fulfilled (1:7), and there was much left to be accomplished (1:8).

---

[75] Andrew Arterbury, "The Ancient Custom of Hospitality, The Greek Novels and Acts 10:1–11:18," *PRSt* 29 (2002): 65–66; Halvor Moxnes, "The Social Context of Luke's Community," *Int* 48 (1994): 379–89.

[76] Also see Rom 12:13; Heb 13:2; 1 Pet 4:9.

[77] Luke 2:13,20; 19:37; Acts 2:47; 3:8–9 (twice); Rom 15:11; Rev 19:5. Bock, *Acts*, 154.

[78] Graham H. Twelftree, *People of the Spirit: Exploring Luke's View of the Church* (Grand Rapids: Baker, 2009), 132.

[79] González, *Acts*, 54.

[80] Richard P. Thompson, *Keeping the Church in Its Place: The Church as Narrative Character in Acts* (New York: T&T Clark, 2006), 57.

Doug Hume has noted that there is a tension in the believer's prayer life between a yearning for fulfillment and the "essentially unknowable quality of the future."[81] The early church's desire was that God's kingdom would be established on earth, and their daily sharing of bread in meals together (Acts 2:42,46) expressed the life of God's kingdom reign as Jesus taught His disciples to pray (Luke 11:2–3). And yet so many of the particulars of this kingdom, especially as they relate to the concrete realities of everyday life, must be revealed in their proper time. A posture of praise and devotion to Christ remains open to what God might do in the particulars of life, but it does not have to have this tension resolved.[82] The exemplary church does not depend on circumstances in order to maintain a posture of praise. Rather, it praises God for what He has already done for us in Christ, what He is doing in and through us today, and what He will do when all things reach their consummation in the reign of Christ. All of this is now and will be to the praise of His glorious grace (Eph 1:6).

The believers cared for the people of Jerusalem (Acts 2:47). We see in Acts 2:47 both the vertical and horizontal dimensions of following Jesus.[83] The believers praised God, and they had good will toward the people. The Greek word for "favor" (*charin*) can be translated "grace," "kindness," or "good will." Translating the phrase "having favor with all the people" (*echontes charin pros holon ton laon*) raises the following question: Who was showing favor to whom—the church to the city of Jerusalem or the city to the church? Most English translations and commentators see the church experiencing the good will of the city of Jerusalem,[84] although a few recognize both possibilities.[85] The preposition "with" (*pros*) can also be translated "toward," making it difficult to state with certainty what Luke means beyond what the context suggests.

Two clues in the context can be put forward as evidence for seeing the church as the recipient of Jerusalem's good will. First, several statements in surrounding narratives indicate the positive disposition of the people of Jerusalem toward the church (Acts 4:21; 5:13–16,26). Second, Luke's next

---

[81] Douglas A. Hume, *The Early Christian Community: A Narrative Analysis of Acts 2:41–47 and 4:32–35* (Tübingen, Germany: Mohr Siebeck, 2011), 104.

[82] Ibid.

[83] Parsons, *Acts*, 49.

[84] For example, "having favor with all the people" (NASB, HCSB, NKJV, ESV) and, "enjoying the favor of all the people" (NIV). Also, see the RSV, NJB, NRSV, NLT, NCV, NAB, and CEV translations of Acts 2:47. For commentaries that hold this view, see Fitzmyer, *Acts*, 273; Haenchen, *Acts*, 193; Johnson, *Acts*, 59; Pervo, *Acts*, 94; Polhill, *Acts*, 122; Witherington, *Acts*, 163.

[85] Bock, *Acts*, 154; Bruce, *Acts of the Apostles: The Greek Text*, 133; Peterson, *Acts*, 164.

statement that people were being saved daily fits with the positive attitude of the people toward the church. However, neither of these clues requires that *pros* be translated "with." One could just as easily argue that the surrounding notes about Jerusalem's good will call for seeing Acts 2:47 as an affirmation by Luke that the reverse was true too. Favor flowed from the church toward Jerusalem, and the church's concern for others was used by God to bring salvation to the people of Jerusalem.

Rhetorical and linguistic reasons suggest that the phrase should be understood as the church having good will toward the city of Jerusalem. All of the preceding statements are a part of Luke's strategy of using the rhetorical exemplum in his portrait of the Jerusalem church, which focuses on the exemplary behavior of believers. They gave generously. They met daily. They ate together with glad and sincere hearts. They praised God. And they had good will toward all the people. It makes sense to see Luke's emphasis on the positive behavior of the church continuing, rather than shift toward the attitude in Jerusalem, which he waits until Acts 5:13–16 to describe.

Additionally, there are strong linguistic grounds for translating *pros* as "toward" rather than "with." The word *charis* appears with the preposition *pros* only here in the New Testament, but the pair occurs six times in Josephus and three times in Philo.[86] In each occurrence the object of the preposition *pros* is in the accusative case and is always the person(s) toward whom the good will (*charis*) is directed. In Acts 2:47 the object of *pros* in the accusative case is "all the people" (*holon ton laon*). Thus, the people of Jerusalem are the ones toward whom the good will of the church is directed.[87]

Luke's exemplary portrait makes clear that not only did the believers love one another, they also loved their neighbors (Lev 19:18; Luke 10:27), the people of Jerusalem. God's grace changed their lives, and it caused them to love the city where they lived and to practice hospitality toward her people.

---

[86] In Josephus: *Life* 252,339; *Ant.* 6.86; 12.124; 14.146,148. In Philo: *Confusion* 116; *Abraham* 118; *Gaius* 296.

[87] T. David Andersen, "The Meaning of ΕΧΟΝΤΕΣ ΧΑΡΙΝ ΠΡΟΣ in Acts 2:47," *NTS* 34 (1988): 607. Also see F. P. Cheetham, "Acts ii.47: ἐχοντες χαρίν πρὸς ὅλον τὸν λαόν," *ExpTim* 74, no. 7 (1963): 214–15; Thompson, *Keeping the Church in Its Place*, 57–59; Peterson, *Acts*, 164; Pervo, *Acts*, 94–95; and Bradley B. Blue, "The Influence of Jewish Worship on Luke's Presentation of the Early Church," in Marshall and Peterson, *Witness to the Gospel*, 486 n. 43.

People were saved and added to the fellowship daily (Acts 2:47). The first summary narrative closes with a statement about God's activity in daily saving and adding new believers to the church in Jerusalem. A major theme in Acts is expressed by this statement, which is that the continued growth of the church is the result of divine action.[88] By placing a note about growth at the end of his exemplary portrait Luke reminds readers that what was happening in the church was the direct result of the Lord's sovereign initiative and plan.[89] Luke stresses this with both the subject and the object of the verb "added." The subject is "the Lord" (*ho kurios*). Israel's covenant-making God was performing the action of adding to His people. The object of the verb is the participle "those who were being saved" (*sōzomenous*), which is in the passive voice.[90] The people of Jerusalem were being acted upon by God as the object of His gracious action through the apostles' preaching.

Luke begins a theme here at the end of the first summary narrative that runs throughout Acts, which is that God is taking His salvation to the ends of the earth through the witness of His people (Acts 1:8; 13:47; Isa 49:6).[91] To be sure, witness to Christ in Acts is always accompanied by the expectation of obedient response and participation in God's mission. The call to obedience is not ignored or minimized in the least in Acts. Peter urged his listeners to repent, to be baptized and save themselves (2:38,40; also 3:19). Only those who believed and were willing to be baptized (2:41) became the church at the beginning of the summary narrative that Luke credited God with creating at the end of his portrait (2:47). Nevertheless, the more encompassing focus in Acts is on God's mission to save.[92]

Luke does not explain the mystery or resolve any tension that may arise from his affirmations of God's sovereignty and human duty in salvation and mission. Both are affirmed without qualification throughout Acts. Paul affirmed human duty when he declared in Athens that "God now commands all people everywhere to repent" (Acts 17:30) and when

---

[88] John T. Squires, "The Plan of God," in Marshall and Peterson, *Witness to the Gospel*, 28, calls this statement the "interpretive key" for every subsequent statement about growth in Acts.

[89] Thompson, *Keeping the Church in Its Place*, 59–60.

[90] The use of the Greek participle σωζομένους for "those who were being saved" appears three times in the NT as a designation for Christians (see Luke 13:23; 1 Cor 1:18). See Fitzmyer, *Acts*, 273.

[91] Joel B. Green, "God as Saviour in the Acts of the Apostles," in Marshall and Peterson, *Witness to the Gospel*, 84–85.

[92] Beverly R. Gaventa, "Initiatives Divine and Human in the Lukan Story World," in *The Holy Spirit and Christian Origins: Essays in Honor of James D. G. Dunn*, ed. Graham N. Stanton, Bruce W. Longenecker, and Stephen C. Barton (Grand Rapids: Eerdmans, 2004), 81.

he called the Philippian jailor to believe in the Lord Jesus, if he desired to be saved (16:30–31). The responsibility for responding to the gospel is placed squarely on the shoulders of those being confronted with the apostles' testimony to Christ. On the other hand, equal stress is laid in Acts on God's sovereignty in salvation. In Antioch of Pisidia, Luke reported that "all who had been appointed to eternal life believed" (13:48). When Paul spoke to Lydia in Philippi, the Lord "opened her heart" to respond to his message (16:14). And in Corinth Jesus spoke to Paul in a vision and told him to keep on speaking because "I have many people in this city" (Acts 18:9–10). In Acts, those who are saved were appointed to eternal life, even before the apostles preached to them or knew who they were. They were simply called to testify to Christ. The story line of Acts traces the deliberate witness of the apostles and those who believed their message. Yet, the power that opened hearts to respond to their witness was God's.[93]

Another theme expressed by Luke in his note about growth is that people were coming to Christ regularly. Believers were not added on Pentecost only to congeal into a fellowship with a fixed number of participants. People were saved "every day" (*kath hēmeran*), which indicates that the believers were witnessing to Christ daily and people were responding daily. The verb for "added" (*prosetithei*) appears in the imperfect tense too, which stresses God's ongoing activity in bringing people to salvation. The church quickly grew to 5,000 men (Acts 4:4), not counting women and children, which would be no small number in a city whose population was around 120,000 in the middle of the first century AD.[94] These many features taken together cause Luke's description to take on the character of a movement as much as it is a description of a local church.

The final theme expressed by Luke in Acts 2:47 is that the people being saved by the Lord were also added to the church. The prepositional phrase *epi to auto* functions adverbially to modify "added" and is translated "to them" (HCSB) or "to their number" (NIV, ESV, NRSV, NASB, NAB)

---

[93] On the twin themes of divine sovereignty and human responsibility in Acts see Robert Banks, "The Role of Charismatic and Noncharismatic Factors in Determining Paul's Movements in Acts," in Stanton, Barton, and Longenecker, *The Holy Spirit and Christian Origins*, 117–30; Gaventa, "Initiatives Divine and Human"; Robert L. Mowery, "Direct Statements Concerning God's Activity in Acts," in SBLSP (1990), 196–211; and Jens-W. Taeger, *Der Mensch und sein Heil: Studien zum Bild des Menschen und zur Sicht der Bekehrung bei Lukas* (Gütersloh: Gütersloher Verlagshaus Gerd Mohn, 1982), 155–56.

[94] Wolfgang Reinhardt, "The Population Size of Jerusalem and the Numerical Growth of the Jerusalem Church," in *The Book of Acts in Its Palestinian Setting*, ed. Richard Bauckham (Grand Rapids: Eerdmans, 1995), 263–65.

and expresses an important nuance.[95] In the Septuagint, *epi to auto* often translates the Hebrew *yahad* (LXX Pss 2:2; 4:9; 33:4; 36:38), which was a quasitechnical term for the gathered community (*1QS* 1:1,12; 8:2; 9:2).[96] If this sense was commonly understood in Luke's day, the phrase could be a reference to the gathered church. It would not be a stretch then to render it "to the church."[97] The point Luke makes is that when God saves people, He adds them to His people in the church.

SUMMARY

To speak of exemplary church life in Acts is to consider first God's purpose in sending the Holy Spirit to empower witness to Christ and give birth to the church. The Spirit came on Pentecost Day and filled the 120 believers with power for witness (Acts 1:8; 2:1–4). Peter's sermon promised forgiveness of sins and the gift of the Holy Spirit to everyone who would repent of sin, show their repentance through baptism, and believe in Jesus Christ. The 3,000 who believed were baptized and added to their number, and for a time they became the first and only church anywhere in the history of the world.

The first summary narrative in Acts 2:42–47, coming on the heels of the Pentecost narrative, describes Luke's vision for exemplary life in the local church. New believers make four deliberate and serious commitments as they begin to follow Jesus as His disciples (Acts 2:42). First, believers commit to the apostle's teaching by recognizing their authority as Jesus' designated spokespersons for His life and ministry. Second, believers commit to the fellowship of other believers. Just as repentance is not considered in Acts apart from a willingness to be baptized, so Acts does not countenance faith in Jesus without a commitment to be a part of God's people in the local church. Third, believers commit to gathering

---

[95] Luke may have also included it for reasons of rhythm, because it is not demanded by the context (Haenchen, *Acts*, 193 n. 4).

[96] Johnson, *Acts*, 60. Many copyists apparently thought readers needed help seeing this nuance, so they added the equivalent phrase "to the church" to the sentence for clarification [τῇ ἐκκλησίᾳ (E, P, Ψ, *Byz.*), ἐν τῇ ἐκκλησίᾳ (D, it^d)]. The KJV and NKJV follow this tradition. Most major witnesses, however, have only ἐπὶ τὸ αὐτό (p^74, ℵ, A, B, C, vg, cop^sa,bo).The abbreviation 1QS refers to the Qumran Scroll *Serek Hayaḥad* or *Rule of the Community*.

[97] Similarly "to their group" (NLT), or "to their community" (NJB). See the helpful discussions in Everett Ferguson, "'When You Come Together': *Epi To Auto* in Early Christian Literature," *ResQ* 16 (1973): 202–8; Metzger, *Textual Commentary*, 304–5; Polhill, *Acts*, 122 n. 155; Peterson, *Acts*, 164 n. 120.

together often to share meals and to remember the death of Christ in the Lord's Supper. Fourth, believers commit to meeting regularly to pray.

According to Luke, life together in the exemplary church will be marked by the following qualities described in Acts 2:43–47. The fear of the Lord will pervade the fellowship as believers recognize God's presence and power among them ruling over His church. The message and ministry of Christ's apostles will be authenticated by God before His people, through signs and wonders if He is pleased to perform them. Believers in Jesus meet together often so that they can share in each other's lives. They hold their possessions loosely and are possessed with a radical generosity that seeks to meet the needs of fellow believers. They meet together regularly in a large group setting for worship and hearing the teaching of the apostles, and they share meals together in smaller groups in each other's homes. The practice of hospitality and the shared meal is at the relational center of exemplary church life. Such gatherings in homes are characterized by an attitude of praise, gladness, and sincerity as believers experience one another's hospitality and the welcome of God. Believers enjoy each other's company and accept each other as friends. The practice of hospitality also sets an example and a context in which to learn that the divisions that occur between people in a fallen world have been overcome in Christ. The exemplary church loves the city where it lives, and it regularly sees people saved.

CHAPTER FOUR

EXEMPLARY LIFE PORTRAIT 2:
ACTS 4:32-35

A t the end of Acts 2:42–47 Luke plunges readers into a dramatic episode that emphasizes the witness and authority of Peter and the realization that following Jesus will arouse hostility (3:1–4:31). The attack on Peter and John by the Jewish leaders threw the young church upon God's faithfulness (4:25–26). They cried out to God for boldness and that He would perform signs and wonders through the name of Jesus. God answered them by shaking the place where they met and by filling them with the Holy Spirit. The believers all began to speak God's word boldly (4:31).

Luke's characteristic switch to the imperfect tense occurs in Acts 4:31 with "began to speak" (*elaloun*). The exemplary character of the believers' witness plus the tense of the verb could justify including 4:31b in the second summary narrative.[1] Bold proclamation in the face of opposition is

---

[1] The preference of Ernst Haenchen, *The Acts of the Apostles*, trans. R. McL. Wilson (Philadelphia: Westminster Press, 1971), 232.

affirmed as exemplary behavior elsewhere in Acts like it is here (5:42; 8:4; 11:19–20). The statement unfocuses the preceding episode by dispersing its characters. Also, narrative time speeds up considerably compared to previous verses. However, the primary purpose of 4:31b is to bring closure to the extended episode that began in 3:1. Also, 4:32 begins with the particle *de*, which is Luke's usual way of transitioning to a new section.[2] Rather than include it in the second summary narrative, 4:31b should be considered a transitional summary statement that both closes the previous episode and looks ahead to Luke's second portrait of church life in 4:32–35.

LIFE TOGETHER IN THE FELLOWSHIP OF BELIEVERS (ACTS 4:32–35)

Acts 4:32–35 repeats several emphases from 2:42–47, especially the unity of the believers in 4:32 (cf. 2:42b,44) and sharing possessions in 4:32b,34–35 (cf. 2:44–45). The use of repetition in the summary narratives enabled Luke to contribute to the persuasive effect of his portraits of exemplary church life.[3]

Living as One and Sharing Possessions

The community of believers was knit together in unity (Acts 4:32). The Greek word for multitude (*plēthous*) can refer to a large number of objects (John 21:6; Heb 11:12; Jas 5:20) or people (Luke 23:27; Acts 2:6). The term can also possess a more definitive sense of an assembly (Luke 1:10; 19:37; Acts 6:2; 15:12), which is the case in Acts 4:32.[4] For this reason, it might best be translated "the whole congregation" (MSG) or simply "the congregation" (NASB).[5] This was not an indiscriminate crowd. It

---

[2] Douglas A. Hume, *The Early Christian Community: A Narrative Analysis of Acts 2:41–47 and 4:32–35* (Tübingen, Germany: Mohr Siebeck, 2011), 120–21; Maria Anicia Co, "The Major Summaries in Acts," *ETL* 68 (1992): 61–62.

[3] Robert C. Tannehill, *The Narrative Unity of Luke-Acts: A Literary Interpretation, Volume 1: The Gospel According to Luke* (Minneapolis: Fortress, 1986), 75.

[4] Joseph A. Fitzmyer, *The Acts of the Apostles: A New Translation with Introduction and Commentary*, AB (New York: Doubleday, 1998), 313, suggested that *plēthous* may be a reflection of various Hebrew terms that denote the gathered assembly of an Essene community (1QS 5:2,9,22; 6:1,7–9,11–19,21,25). For additional information on the use of *plēthous* to refer to the community of disciples, see Justin Taylor, "The Community of Jesus' Disciples," in PIBA 21 (1998): 25–32.

[5] F. F. Bruce, *The Acts of the Apostles: The Greek Text with Introduction and Commentary* (Grand Rapids: Eerdmans, 1990), 159.

was specifically the company of those who believed in Jesus that was knit together in unity.[6]

Luke emphasized their unity by saying that the believers were "of one heart and soul" (*kardia kai psuchē mia*). Combining the words "heart" and "soul" into a doublet allowed Luke to stress the depth of the church's unity.[7] Luke's Hellenistic readers would have immediately recognized in these words an allusion to their own friendship tradition.[8] Aristotle said that a friend is "one soul dwelling in two bodies" (*Diog. Laert.* 5.20). Cicero said that at the heart of friendship was the formation of "one soul" out of several (*Amic.* 25.92). Plutarch spoke of friends who "unite and fuse their souls together" (*Amat.* 21:9).[9] Plato wrote in the *Republic* of an ideal city led by guardians whose goal was to achieve a state of unity where the members were all of "one mind" (*Resp.* 4.431e).[10]

Of course, an allusion to a well-known secular tradition does not imply equivalence for Luke, whose description goes beyond the Greek friendship tradition in several important ways. First, Luke portrays the unity of the church as the result of submission to the lordship of Jesus. The greatness of a king in Greco-Roman culture was tied to his ability to unite all of his subjects as one community. Such unity did exist occasionally, but it was usually enforced by the sword. Luke critiques the Roman understanding by showing how the Holy Spirit brings unity to the church under the reign of King Jesus.[11] Second, Luke shows believers united across social and

---

[6] Justin Taylor, "The Community of Goods among the First Christians and among the Essenes," in *Historical Perspectives: From the Hasmoneans to Bar Kokhba in Light of the Dead Sea Scrolls*, Proceedings of the Fourth International Symposium of the Orion Center, 27–31 January 1999, ed. David Goodblatt, Avital Pinnick, and Daniel R. Schwartz, STDJ 37 (Leiden: Brill, 2001), 151.

[7] Martin M. Culy and Mikeal C. Parsons, *Acts: A Handbook on the Greek Text* (Waco, TX: Baylor University Press, 2003), 81. Bruce M. Metzger, *A Textual Commentary on the Greek New Testament* (Stuttgart: United Bible Societies, 1971), 325, notes that there was such a concern to stress the unity of the early church among copyists in the Western tradition that several witnesses (D, E, Cyprian, Ambrose) added, "and there was no quarrel among them at all" to Acts 4:32. Would that this could be said of all our churches!

[8] See Hume, *Early Christian Community*, 48–77. For an extensive treatment of friendship language in Hellenistic literature, see especially Aristotle's *Nicomachean Ethics*; Plutarch's *Advice to Brides and Grooms*; Diogenes Laertius's three biographies *Life of Bion, Life of Pythagoras,* and *Life of Epicurus*; and Iamblicus's *On the Pythagorean Way of Life*.

[9] These quotes are taken from Charles H. Talbert, *Reading Acts: A Literary and Theological Commentary on the Acts of the Apostles* (New York: Crossroads, 1997), 63.

[10] On Lukan allusions to the guardian tradition in Plato, see Rubén R. Dupertuis, "The Summaries of Acts 2, 4, and 5 and Plato's *Republic*," in *Ancient Fiction: The Matrix of Early Christian and Jewish Narrative*, ed. Jo-Ann Brant, Charles W. Hedrick, and Chris Shea, SBLSymS 32 (Atlanta: Society of Biblical Literature, 2005), 288–89.

[11] Alan J. Thompson, *One Lord, One People: The Unity of the Church in Acts in Its Literary Setting*, Library of New Testament Studies (New York: T&T Clark, 2008), 19–30, 63–74, esp. 70–74.

economic lines. Those with means willingly helped those in need, regardless of social status.[12] Third, though the allusions to the aspirations of the
Greek friendship tradition are obvious, the friendship of the believers was
not rooted in Greek philosophy. Rather, Luke's ethic is rooted in God's
covenant with Israel as found in her Scriptures and in the teachings of
Jesus. Jesus called His followers to go beyond reciprocal relationships by
learning to love and do good to enemies (Luke 6:27–36), to forgive others
(6:37), and to show mercy to the neighbor who is different (10:25–37). The
believers' unity hearkens back to the great commandment in the *Shema* to
love God with all of one's heart and soul (Deut 6:5), which Jesus said is
like the command to neighbor love (Matt 22:34–40).[13] The fourth major
difference is that unity in the church was not created by the resolve and
good will of the believers. Their unity was the result of God's grace and
the filling with the Holy Spirit (Acts 4:31,33). Certainly Acts shows the
church actively pursuing unity too. When disputes over the needs of widows or the reception of Gentiles arose, the church took action to identify
and solve the problems that threatened their unity (Acts 6:2–4; 15:2–6).
Paul challenged churches to make the pursuit of unity a priority (1 Cor
1:10; Eph 4:3; Phil 2:2). Nevertheless, ultimately unity comes from God
(Rom 15:5; cf. 2 Chr 30:12; Jer 32:39) in answer to the prayer of Jesus
(John 17:21–23). Because of remaining sin, no church has ever modeled
unity perfectly. However, God's people should rejoice and confess that
true faith in Christ creates unity between believers that is the gift of God.

*The believers made their belongings available to other believers in
need (Acts 4:32).* The deep unity of the believers led them to consider
their possessions as belonging to each other. The theme of generosity from
the first summary narrative (Acts 2:44) is repeated here with the wording
slightly modified. In this verse Luke states that "no one said that any of
his possessions was his own." Instead, they "held everything in common."
The word for common (*koina*) conveys the idea of active participation with
others in sharing, rather than the passive idea of delivering one's possessions into a communal storehouse.[14] The believers' practice flowed from a

---

For examples of the connection in Greco-Roman political thought between state unity and having a
successful king, see Herodotus, *Hist.* 5.3, 3.82; Dionysius of Halicarnassus, *Ant. rom.* 2.2.2; Plutarch,
Alex. fort. 329; Diodorus, *Hist.* 18.4.4; 1 Maccabees 8:16.

[12] Alan C. Mitchell, "The Social Function of Friendship in Acts 2:44–47 and 4:32–37," *JBL* 111
(1992): 266–67.

[13] Birger Gerhardsson, "Einige Bemerkungen zu Apg 4,32," *ST* 24 (1970): 145.

[14] Ben Witherington III, *The Acts of the Apostles: A Socio-Rhetorical Commentary* (Grand Rapids:
Eerdmans, 1998), 206 n. 33.

disposition that said in effect, "What's mine is yours." The second-century
Gospel of Barnabas probably referred to Acts 4:32 when it said, "You
shall share everything with your neighbor and not claim that anything is
your own" (*Barn.* 19.8).[15]

That no one spoke of their possessions as their own indicates that a
profound reorientation had occurred among believers toward this world's
goods. The filling of the Holy Spirit spilled over into every area of life,
including their attitude toward possessions. The Greek friendship tradition
aspired to such a level of unselfishness. Euripedes said, "True friends cling
not to private property; their wealth is shared in close community" (*Andr.*
376–377).[16] However, in Christ this noble aspiration became a dynamic
reality. The question of whether believers in the early church liquidated
all of their private property and lived communally will be addressed when
Acts 4:34–35 is discussed below.

Great Power and Great Grace

*The apostles bore powerful witness to the resurrection of the Lord
Jesus (Acts 4:33).* Jesus told His disciples to wait in Jerusalem until they
were clothed with power from on high (Luke 24:49). He promised that
when they received power, they would be His witnesses (Acts 1:8). When
Pentecost came, the apostles began to witness to the resurrection of Jesus
with great power (Acts 2:6–11). Luke places their witness at the center of
his second summary narrative, which makes proclaiming the resurrection
of Jesus a major emphasis of his portrait of church life.[17] The context of
the verb "giving" (*apedidoun*) conveys the sense that the apostles were
regularly witnessing to the resurrection of Jesus in public, in homes, and
anywhere God opened the door (Acts 5:42). The word for "witness" (*marturion*) denotes "that which serves as testimony or proof."[18] The apostles
were eyewitnesses of Jesus' ministry, especially after His resurrection
(Acts 1:21–22), and they offered their unified testimony as proof that Jesus
had risen from the dead.[19]

---

[15] Also see Lucian, *Peregr.* 13.

[16] Talbert, *Reading Acts*, 64.

[17] S. Scott Bartchy, "Divine Power, Community Formation, and Leadership in the Acts of the
Apostles," in *Community Formation in the Early Church and in the Church Today*, ed. Richard N.
Longenecker (Peabody, MA: Hendrickson, 2002), 91.

[18] BAGD, 493–94. The word for witness eventually took on the meaning of martyr in the early
church. For discussion, see Hermann Strathman, "μάρτυς, μαρυρέω, μαρτυρία," in *TDNT*, 4:504–8.

[19] See Acts 2:32; John 21:24; 1 Cor 15:5; 2 Pet 1:16–18; 1 John 1:1–3.

The word for power (*dunamei*) can be rendered "might" or "strength." It is often associated in the New Testament with the power of God (Rom 1:16; 1 Cor 1:18,24) and with the Holy Spirit (Acts 1:8; Eph 3:16).[20] In this context the word refers to the effect of the apostles' preaching.[21] In Acts 2 Peter spoke boldly about the resurrection of Jesus, and 3,000 responded (Acts 2:1–4,24–32,41).[22] The very existence of the church at the conclusion of Peter's sermon was a display of the power of God. In Acts 3 Peter healed a man who was crippled from birth in the name of the risen Jesus (3:1–10,15–16; 4:10). This was one of many signs and wonders that occurred through the apostles (2:43; 5:12,15–16,26). The courage of the apostles and all the believers in their witness to Christ was an example of God's power (4:31b). They kept boldly proclaiming Jesus until the Jewish authorities were provoked and arrested the apostles. Nevertheless, people kept responding and the apostles refused to stop witnessing (4:1–4,19–20; 5:29). The authorities finally admitted that these courageous but unschooled and ordinary men had been with Jesus (4:13).[23] Believers in Jesus in an exemplary church believe and know that the gospel is the power of God for salvation (Rom 1:16). God's power accompanies the proclamations of the death and resurrection of Jesus.

The power of God also went beyond the apostles' testimony into the power of new life in Christ. The Holy Spirit's power transformed the believers and possessed them with a radical love and generosity toward each other (Acts 4:32b,34–35), the kind Jesus said would convince the world that they were His disciples (John 13:34–35).[24] It is no surprise then that Luke goes on to say in Acts 4:33 that great grace was upon them all.

Great grace rested on all the believers (Acts 4:33). Luke places the powerful witness of the apostles and great grace on the church in the middle of Acts 4:32–35, making both central to his second portrait of church life. The term for grace (*charis*) can be rendered "kindness," "favor," and

---

[20] BAGD, 207.

[21] I. Howard Marshall, *The Acts of the Apostles*, New Testament Guides (Sheffield, UK: Sheffield Academic Press, 2001), 108; John Polhill, *Acts*, NAC (Nashville: Broadman, 1992), 152; C. K. Barrett, *Acts 1–14*, ICC (New York: T&T Clark, 1994), 254.

[22] Peter's preaching had the same effect as Jesus who amazed the crowds with His teaching (Luke 4:32). Like Peter, Jesus was anointed with the Holy Spirit and with power for His public ministry of proclamation (Luke 4:18; Acts 10:38).

[23] Compare the boldness and authority of the apostles' witness in Acts to their behavior before Jesus' resurrection when they fled after He was arrested (Mark 14:50) and Peter denied knowing the Lord three times (Luke 22:54–62).

[24] Richard N. Longenecker, *Acts*, EBC vol. 9 (Grand Rapids: Zondervan, 2007), 311.

even "thanks."[25] Grace is normally associated with Paul and his letters. Luke uses the word to speak of the essence of the gospel message (Acts 14:3). He may have learned the term from Paul's teaching, since they often traveled together (20:24,32).[26] Like Paul, Luke speaks of grace as the means by which God saves and by which sinners are able to believe in Jesus (15:11; 18:27).[27]

The grace Luke speaks of in Acts 4:33 could refer to the good will of Jerusalem toward the church, "much favor was accorded them all."[28] This view is plausible, especially if 2:47 is understood to be saying that the church had favor with all the people (a view I have rejected above). Or, it could refer to the favor of God resting on the fellowship.[29] The latter view is more likely what Luke means. In this sense the experience of the church echoes a summary of Jesus' childhood years during which He "grew up and became strong . . . and God's grace was on Him" (Luke 2:40; also John 1:14). The inclusion of the adjective "great" (*megalē*) along with grace intensifies the statement. Luke wants to convey that the fellowship of believers was flooded with the kindness of God. Great grace from God overflowing in believers' lives enables them to become ministers of grace to one another and gracious givers (cf. 2 Cor 8:1–7; 9:1; 1 Pet 4:10).

Giving Motivated by Grace

The believers gave generously to help fellow believers in need (Acts 4:34–35). The grace that rested on the believers led to an astonishing development. There was not a needy person among them.[30] All those who owned lands or houses were selling them and bringing the proceeds to the apostles for distribution among the needy in the church. Luke could

---

[25] BAGD, 877–78.

[26] Justo L. González, *Faith and Wealth: A History of Early Christian Ideas on the Origin, Significance, and Use of Money* (San Francisco: Harper and Row, 1990), 86; Walther Zimmerli and Hans Conzelmann, "χάρις, χαρίζομαι, χαριτόω, ἀχάριστος," in *TDNT*, 9:391.

[27] Cf. Rom 3:24; 4:16; Gal 1:6; 2:21; Eph 2:8.

[28] Fitzmyer, *Acts*, 313–14.

[29] Barrett, *Acts 1–14*, 254; Luke Timothy Johnson, *The Acts of the Apostles*, SP (Collegeville, MN: Michael Glazier, 1992), 86; Culy and Parsons, *Acts*, 81–82.

[30] Paul makes a similar argument about the effect of grace on the Macedonian churches in 2 Corinthians 8–9. God gave grace to the churches, and out of severe trial their joy and poverty welled up in rich generosity (8:1) and grace toward others (8:6). The grace of the Lord Jesus toward His church is that though He was rich, He became poor so that through His poverty His people might become rich in His grace (8:9). God makes His grace abound to believers so that they always have enough to abound in every good deed (9:8). God's grace causes our hearts to go out to those in need (9:14).

have used the more common Greek term *ptōchoi* to refer to needy persons (see Luke 6:20; Jas 2:2). Instead, he chooses to use *endeēs*. Both words describe persons who were impoverished or lacking. However, *endeēs* is used in the LXX translation of Deut 15:4, "There will be no poor among you." By doing this, Luke skillfully weaved an Old Testament mandate concerning the Sabbath year with an allusion to the highest ideals of Greek Utopianism.[31] The Sabbath year commands were designed to provide food for Israelites who fell on hard times and could not take care of themselves. Every seven years the land was to lie fallow so that the poor could eat (Exod 23:10–11). Harvests were not to be reaped to the edge of fields, so that the poor might find food (Lev 19:9–10; 23:22). When a brother became poor, God wanted His people to strengthen him (Lev 25:35–38).[32] There is little evidence in the Old Testament that these laws were consistently implemented. Yet, when the Holy Spirit arrived and the church was born, the believers began to do spontaneously for the poor what the Sabbath laws required and what Greek idealists aspired to but could never achieve.

Luke especially emphasizes here the generosity of the more well-to-do members of the church, those who owned "lands or houses."[33] The plural form for lands (*chōriōn*) can refer to small parcels of property or fields, or it can refer to an entire estate. The word for houses (*oikiōn*) can refer to a person's home(s) or, more generally, to their wealth and goods. These possessions would hold great value for their owner under most circumstances, but no longer in the face of such a great salvation (Heb 2:3). God's grace stirred the believers to give extravagantly to help others in need. Later in Acts, Paul reminded the Ephesian elders of Jesus' words, "It is more blessed to give than to receive" (Acts 20:35). Here were members

---

[31] See Lev 25:1–43; Deut 15:1–11. Luke's skill at simultaneously orienting readers to a Jewish context in the Septuagint and to a Greco-Roman context is designated "double signification" by Daniel Marguerat, "Luc-Actes entre Jérusalem et Rome: Un Procédé Lucanien de Double Signification," *NTS* 45 (1999): 70–87, see esp. 78–79. Also see David L. Mealand, "Community of Goods and Utopian Allusions in Acts II–IV," *JTS* 28 (1977): 96–99; Mitchell, "Social Function of Friendship in Acts 2:44–47 and 4:32–37," 272; David Peter Seccombe, *Possessions and the Poor in Luke-Acts*, SNTSU B/6 (Linz: Fuchs, 1982); Markus Öhler, "Die Jerusalemer Urgemeinde im Spiegel des antiken Vereinswesens," *NTS* 51 (2005): 393–415; Talbert, *Reading Acts*, 63–64; Jacques Dupont, "Community of Goods in the Early Church," in *The Salvation of the Gentiles: Essays on the Acts of the Apostles*, trans. John R. Keating (New York: Paulist Press, 1979), 88–91.

[32] David L. Baker, *Tight Fists or Open Hands? Wealth and Poverty in Old Testament Law* (Grand Rapids: Eerdmans, 2009), 223–51. On the appropriation of the principles of the Jubilee year in the Qumran community and in Acts 2:44–45; 4:32–37, see James Parker, *The Concept of Apokatastasis in Acts: A Study in Primitive Christian Theology* (Austin, TX: Scholars Press, 1978), 104–13.

[33] Witherington, *Acts*, 207.

of a close-knit Jewish community enjoying a level of mutual concern that effectively eliminated poverty among them. The Jerusalem church experienced the blessing Jesus taught about as a way of life. Their loose grip on land is especially remarkable considering these were Jews for whom land was a part of the inheritance God gave them (Gen 12:7; Josh 14:1–5). For a Jew to lose possession of his land due to financial hardship was a tragedy (Lev 25:25–27), but here are Jewish believers in Jesus selling land for the sake of the poor! Jerusalem is, in the words of William D. Davies, "honorably demoted."[34]

Once property was sold, the believers would lay the proceeds "at the apostles' feet" (Acts 4:35). This action symbolized submission to their leadership (4:37; 5:2,10; 10:25).[35] The apostles administered the growing fund as needs arose. In 2:45 the believers gave directly to each other. However, by 4:35 it appears the apostles served as a kind of clearinghouse that connected resources to needs in the fellowship. Soon the church would be so large that the apostles would have to delegate this noble work to others, so they could remain focused on the ministry of the word and prayer (6:1–7). The summary narratives focus more on the activity of the church than its organizational structure. However, we do see in the changes in 2:45; 4:35; and 6:1–7 an incipient form of organization as a pragmatic response to the growing size of the ministry.

Luke follows his second summary narrative (Acts 4:32–35) with a positive and a negative example in 4:36–5:11 that illustrate his comments on the generosity of the Jerusalem church. Barnabas serves as a positive example of generosity (4:36–37). He sold one of his fields and laid the money at the apostles' feet, demonstrating how Jesus Christ had changed

---

[34] William D. Davies, *The People and the Land* (Berkeley, CA: University of California Press, 1974), 252. For more on the role of possessions in Luke–Acts, see Luke Timothy Johnson, *The Literary Function of Possessions in Luke-Acts* (Atlanta: Scholars Press, 1977). Johnson sees possessions functioning as a symbol, along with other elements, of the spiritual unity of the believers (187). Also see Thomas E. Phillips, "Reading Recent Readings of Issues of Wealth and Poverty in Luke and Acts," in *Acts within Diverse Frames of Reference* (Macon, GA: Mercer University Press, 2009), 78–117, a slightly revised version of his earlier article with the same title in *Currents in Biblical Research* 1, no. 2 (2003): 231–69; Stephen C. Barton, "The Communal Dimension of Earliest Christianity: A Critical Survey of the Field," *JTS* 43 (1992): 410–14; Gene A. Getz, *A Biblical Theology of Possessions* (Chicago: Moody, 1990), 43–49; Edgar Haulotte, "La vie en communion, phase ultime de la Pentecôte, Acts 2,42–47," *Foi et Vie* 80, no. 1 (1981): 69–75; Peter Liu, "Did the Lucan Jesus Desire Voluntary Poverty of His Followers?" *EvQ* 64 (1992): 291–317.

[35] Johnson, *Literary Function of Possessions in Luke-Acts*, 201–2; J. Bradley Chance, *Jerusalem, the Temple, and the New Age in Luke-Acts* (Macon, GA: Mercer University Press, 1988), 72. For examples of similar actions, see Deut 33:3; Ruth 3:4; 1 Sam 25:24; 1 Kgs 5:3; Pss 8:6; 45:5; 47:3; Isa 60:14; Luke 7:38–46; 8:35,41; 10:39; Acts 10:25; 22:3.

him. His action also showed that he recognized the unique leadership role of the apostles in the early church. Ananias and his wife Sapphira are a negative example whose behavior is the opposite of what Luke commends in his exemplary portraits (5:1–11). Like Barnabas, they too sold a piece of property and brought some of the proceeds to the apostles. However, they lied about the price they obtained and tried to make others think that they had brought all the money they earned from the sale. Their behavior is not unlike Simon the sorcerer who spoke of helping others, but what he wanted was to purchase the gift of God with money (8:18–23); or Cain who brought "some" of the fruits of the soil to the Lord, but not in faith (Gen 4:3; Heb 11:4). God's response through Peter was swift and dramatic, but not unheard of in the early church (1 Cor 11:30–31). The deaths of Ananias and Sapphira sent great fear throughout the church (Acts 5:11). Luke wants to make clear that gifts given duplicitously displeased God, and He was willing to protect His name and the church He created. God worked through His apostles, but the events of this episode reveal that ultimately He was the One directing the affairs of His people.

Excursus: Property Sharing in the Jerusalem Church

Acts 4:34–35, along with 2:44–45 and 4:32b, raises important questions about the relationship of owning property to the church's ministry to the poor. These questions have been wrestled with throughout the history of interpretation of the summary narratives, with little consensus emerging.[36] Is Luke (1) describing, a formal sharing of posses-

---

[36] For a general survey of the issues, see Daniel B. McGee, "Sharing Possessions: A Study in Biblical Ethics," in *With Steadfast Purpose: Essays on Acts in Honor of Henry Jackson Flanders*, ed. Naymond H. Keathley (Waco, TX: Baylor University Press, 1990), 163–78. For their use in the patristics, with a special emphasis on poverty and the community of goods, see Pier Cesare Bori, *Chiesa Primitiva: L'immagine della comunità delle origini—Atti 2,42–47; 4,32–37—nella storia della chiesa antica*, Dipartimento di scienze religiose (Brescia, Italy: Paideia Editrice, 1974), 213–87; and Francis Martin, "Monastic Community and the Summary Statements in Acts," in *Contemplative Studies: An Interdisciplinary Symposium*, ed. M. Basil Pennington (Washington, DC: Consortium Press, 1972), 26–38. Also see Gildas H. Hamel, *Poverty and Charity in Roman Palestine, First Three Centuries C. E.*, University of California Publications, Near Eastern Studies 23 (Berkeley: University of California Press, 1990), 224–38. On their interpretation in the Middle Ages, see Glenn W. Olsen, "The Image of the First Community of Christians at Jerusalem in the Time of Lanfranc and Anselm," in *Les Mutations Socio-Culturelles Au Tourant Des XI-XII Siècles*, ed. Raymonde Foreville (Paris: Éditions du Centre National de la Recherche Scientifique, 1984), 341–53. From the Reformation to modern times, with an emphasis on Anabaptists and the radical reformers, see Reta Halteman Finger, "Cultural Attitudes in Western Christianity toward the Community of Goods in Acts 2 and 4," *Mennonite Quarterly Review* 78 (2004): 235–70, esp. 242–45; and Reta Halteman Finger, *Of Widows and Meals: Communal Meals in the Acts of the Apostles* (Grand Rapids: Eerdmans, 2007), 12–47.

sions, where believers actually liquidated their assets and lived from a common fund?[37] (2) Is he suggesting that a temporary community of possessions actually existed due to the unique circumstances of the earliest believers in Jerusalem? (3) Or is Luke idealizing through hyperbole in a nonhistorical way, knowing that there was a clear difference between his portraits and the actual practice of the Jerusalem church?

Under the historical-critical paradigm, interpreters have generally dismissed the historicity of the summary narratives with little qualification (see chapter 1). This view argues that Luke never intended to say that a true community of goods actually occurred.[38] Richard I. Pervo's successor to Hans Conzelmann's commentary on Acts in the Hermeneia series follows Conzelmann on this point. Like Conzelmann, Pervo simply declares Luke's descriptions to be fiction and dismisses those like Brian Capper who disagree by declaring that the issue is not whether the account describes what actually happened, because this cannot be determined from Acts.[39] I recognize that no interpreter can go back in time behind the text of Acts to the actual situation of the Jerusalem church to verify that what Luke says happened. Most of Luke's first readers were probably not there either. However, neither can Pervo determine from the text of Acts that Luke's record is untrue. We must both acknowledge that worldviews are at work below the surface of our reading that impact our instincts when it comes to questions of historicity.

Narrative critics and several recent commentators have suggested that Luke's descriptions are somewhat idealized, at least in a literary sense. In their view the historicity of the community of possessions does not matter for Luke's point about radical generosity to be valid.[40] This view is unsatisfying for two reasons. First, accounts of communal living and actual property sharing can be found in first-century Judaism, making Luke's descriptions plausible within their historical context. The Essenes were well known for their intentional approach

---

[37] This is the view of Barrett, *Acts 1–14*, 168–69, 253; Bruce, *Acts*, NICNT, 74, 108–9; and Parsons, *Acts*, 48. Longenecker suggests that the believers did live communally, reflecting a practice common to various sects in the first century but not necessarily formal property sharing (*Acts*, 758).

[38] Hans Conzelmann, *Acts of the Apostles*, trans. James Limburg, A. Thomas Kraabel, and Donald H. Juel, Hermeneia (Philadelphia: Fortress, 1987), 24; Haenchen, *Acts*, 110, 234–35, 246; Gerhard A. Krodel, *Acts*, Proclamation Commentaries (Philadelphia: Fortress Press, 1981), 25–26; Gerd Lüdemann, *The Acts of the Apostles: What Really Happened in the Earliest Days of the Church?* (Amherst, NY: Prometheus, 2005), 58–59, 77.

[39] Richard I. Pervo, *Acts*, Hermeneia (Minneapolis: Fortress, 2009), 89 n. 8. See Brian J. Capper, "The Palestinian Cultural Context of Earliest Christian Community of Goods," in *The Book of Acts in Its Palestinian Setting*, ed. Richard Bauckham (Grand Rapids: Eerdmans, 1995), 323–56.

[40] Johnson, *Acts*, 15, 61–62; Tannehill, *Narrative Unity of Luke-Acts: Acts*, 46; also see James D. G. Dunn, *The Acts of the Apostles* (Valley Forge, PA: Trinity Press International, 1996), 34–36, 58.

to possessions and the life of faith.[41] The community in Qumran was likely an Essene group, albeit a more radical and isolated sect, that had many similarities to the church in Jerusalem.[42] The Dead Sea Scrolls that come from this community reveal a society that formally renounced all claims to property and lived communally.[43] Experiments in communal living were doubtless attempted for spiritual reasons. However, the economic uncertainty faced by many Jews in first-century Judea may have influenced some toward a pooling of resources in the interest of survival.[44]

The earliest believers in Jerusalem faced their own unique circumstances that may have prompted them to pool resources temporarily. Many Diaspora Jews came to Jerusalem on a pilgrimage for the Passover-Pentecost season and remained for some time after they became Christians (Acts 2:9–11). Additionally, the disciples of Jesus came originally from Galilee, but they and perhaps many of their family members were lodging in Jerusalem in the days before and after Pentecost (Luke 24:52–53; Acts 1:13). These people were likely unprepared for an extended stay. That some level of sharing of possessions actually occurred among these early believers is certainly plausible.

Second, it is hard to see how Luke could be teaching that the gospel transforms lives if he does not also mean to say that those whose lives he draws from in his exemplary portraits were not actually changed in their attitude toward possessions. Where is the power of the gospel Luke writes about if the narrative of the founding church is grounded not in history but on hyperbole or wishful utopian thinking?

I believe Luke's descriptions of the church are historically reliable. I do not, however, think Luke is saying that the Jerusalem believers actually liquidated all of their assets and lived communally.[45] Nor do

---

[41] For example, Josephus admired the Essenes for their practice of community of goods, whereby new members surrendered their property to the order, with the result that among them one would not find abject poverty or inordinate wealth (*J.W.* 2.122). He also wrote that the Essenes, "hold their possessions in common, and the wealthy man receives no more enjoyment from his property than the man who possesses nothing" (*Ant.* 18.20).

[42] Richard Bauckham, "The Early Jerusalem Church, Qumran, and the Essenes," in *The Dead Sea Scrolls as Background to Postbiblical Judaism and Early Christianity*, ed. James R. Davila (Leiden: Brill, 2003), 63–89; Taylor, "Community of Goods," 155–56.

[43] For discussions of similarities between the Qumran community and the church in Jerusalem, see the chapter "The Dead Sea Scrolls and Early Christianity," in F. F. Bruce, *A Mind for What Matters: Collected Essays of F. F. Bruce* (Grand Rapids: Eerdmans, 1990), 49–64, esp. 52, 59; and Joseph A. Fitzmyer, "Jewish Christianity in Light of the Qumran Scrolls," in *Studies in Luke-Acts*, ed. Leander E. Keck and J. Louis Martyn (Philadelphia: Fortress, 1966), 241–44.

[44] Brian J. Capper, "Holy Community of Life and Property amongst the Poor: A Response to Steve Walton," *EvQ* 80, no. 2 (2008): 114–15.

[45] See Bock, *Acts*, 153; Chance, *Acts*, 59; Marshall, *Acts*, 84–85; Peterson, *Acts*, 163; Polhill, *Acts*, 121; Witherington, *Acts*, 162.

I think he is trying to convince readers to forsake all private property and live in the manner of the Essenes.[46] Instead, the context suggests that the believers were selling property "from time to time" (NIV, NCV), especially Barnabas's one-time sale of a field (Acts 4:36–37), and the fact that Ananias and Sapphira's proceeds from their sale of land was considered theirs to keep (5:4). Communally held property would undermine the very principle of giving, which requires that what is given really be the possession of the one giving it.[47] Moreover, if all members of the community of believers disposed of their possessions, they too would join the ranks of the poor. If a man sold his home, his family would be homeless. If a farmer sold off all his fields, he would lose the ability to generate income that could be used to help others. Property and assets can serve as a means of building wealth, so the poor can be helped. Rather than see Luke saying that the believers gave up their belongings, it makes more sense to say that they gave up their claim on them and placed them at the disposal of all.[48] Luke's portrait both acknowledges property (understood as stewardship) and demands generosity.

The late-second-century church father Clement of Alexandria addressed the challenges created for Christians by possessions in his homily "Who Is the Rich Man That Shall Be Saved?" He took his title directly from a question asked by Jesus' disciples, "Who then can be saved?" The disciples had just witnessed a rich young ruler turn away from Jesus because he clung to his wealth and heard Jesus say that it is easier for a camel to pass through the eye of a needle than for a rich man to enter the kingdom of heaven (see Matt 19:16–30, esp. 24–25). Clement's answer to the question came from the parable of the Good Samaritan and how the innkeeper used his inn to serve others (Luke 10:35). Of the innkeeper Clement wrote, "If no one had anything, what room would be left among men for giving?"[49] Equally important to

---

[46] José Miranda vastly overstated Luke's intentions when he said, "No one has come up with a better definition of communism than Luke in Acts 2:44–45 and 4:32–35." José Porfirio Miranda, *Communism in the Bible*, trans. Robert R. Barr (Maryknoll, NY: Orbis, 1982), 1–2.

[47] González, *Faith and Wealth*, 8.

[48] Andreas Lindemann, "The Beginnings of Christian Life in Jerusalem according to the Summaries in the Acts of the Apostles (Acts 2:42–47; 4:32–37; 5:12–16)," in *Common Life in the Early Church: Essays Honoring Graydon F. Snyder*, ed. Julian Hills (Harrisburg, PA: Trinity Press International, 1998), 210–11, 216 (esp. 211 n. 46).

[49] Clement of Alexandria, "Who Is the Rich Man That Shall Be Saved?" in *ANF* 2:591–604, esp. 2:594. See Jaroslav Pelikan, *Acts*, BTCB (Grand Rapids: Brazos, 2005), 81; and Annewies van den Hoek, "Widening the Eye of the Needle: Wealth and Poverty in the Works of Clement of Alexandria," in *Wealth and Poverty in Early Church and Society*, ed. Susan R. Holman, Holy Cross Studies in Patristic Theology and History (Grand Rapids: Baker Academic, 2008), 67–75.

Clement's interpretation of this passage is that the rich man who is saved will show it by his concern for the hurting (Jas 1:27).

The Law of Moses affirmed the right to own property although God made it clear that the land of Canaan belonged to Him. Owners of property were to see themselves in reality as God's tenants and the stewards of His possessions (Lev 25:23; Ps 24:1; also Matt 25:14–20).[50] The New Covenant did not undo property rights, but it did radically transform them. Luke does not teach a formal group ownership of property, but the force of his statements should not be softened either.[51] Luke shows a people whose grip on possessions was dramatically transformed by Jesus Christ. These grateful believers followed the example of a risen Savior who taught them how to care for each other, especially the poor.[52] They freely gave themselves to God and what they owned for each other so that the needs of the poor could be met.[53] The social and economic impact of the Jerusalem church on the families that joined with them became a powerful witness to people around them that Jesus changes lives.

Summary

Luke's second portrait of exemplary church life (Acts 4:32–35) repeats some material from his first portrait (2:42–47), especially the comments about generosity.[54] Luke introduces new material too, beginning with unity. An exemplary church is characterized by a deep unity among its members. This unity rings with the best aspirations of human society, especially the Greek friendship tradition, which strives in relationships for oneness in

---

[50] Baker, *Tight Fists or Open Hands*, 15–36, 310–11.

[51] Lindemann, "Beginnings of the Christian Common Life," 218.

[52] Robert C. Tannehill, "Do the Ethics of Acts Include the Ethical Teaching in Luke?" in *Acts and Ethics*, ed. Thomas E. Phillips, New Testament Monographs (Sheffield, England: Sheffield Academic Press, 2005), 116–21. The poor were important in Luke's theology. Mary's song spoke of the hungry being filled (Luke 1:52–53). Jesus was born into humble circumstances (2:7), and His parents could only afford the offering for Jesus that poor parents would make (2:24). The poor were a focal point of the Lukan beatitudes (6:20–21). That the good news was preached to the poor was a sign that the "Expected one" had come (4:18; 7:22). The poor were invited to the banquet Jesus spoke of (14:21). The parable of the rich man and Lazarus showed Christ's concern for the poor (16:20), and Zacchaeus's repentance involved giving to the poor (19:8).

[53] For arguments for and against the idea that Luke taught a formal community of possessions, see the excellent exchange between Steve Walton, "Primitive Communism in Acts? Does Acts Present the Community of Goods (Acts 2:44–45; 4:32–35) as Mistaken?" *EvQ* 80, no. 2 (2008): 99–111; and Capper, "Holy Community," 113–27. Walton argues that Luke taught that a radical generosity existed in the Jerusalem church but not communal living. Capper argues that the Jerusalem church practiced a formal community of goods, much like the well-known Essenes of Judea in the first century.

[54] Compare Acts 4:33b to 2:44 and Acts 4:34–35 to 2:45.

soul and mind. Unfortunately, unity cannot finally be attained in a fallen world through philosophy, a strong king, or good intentions. The unity believers have is a gift from God by the Holy Spirit that comes to those who submit to the Lordship of Christ. It unites people across social and economic lines and is rooted in the Old Testament and the teachings of Jesus. The unity of believers in the church leads to a profound reorientation toward worldly possessions. No longer do people think of their possessions as their own. Instead, they think of what they own as belonging to anyone in need.

In an exemplary church the apostles' testimony about the resurrection of the Lord Jesus goes forth with power. Great grace from God rests upon the church and floods His people with an awareness of His exceeding goodness to them in Christ. This grace has the power to transform people into gracious givers and ministers of grace to others. The impact of such a spirit of generosity in an exemplary church is that the poor are effectively helped. People who are blessed with possessions continually sell them and bring the proceeds to church leaders with no strings attached, for the benefit of anyone in need. Church leadership then distributes help to people who need it. The result is that there are no impoverished persons within the fellowship of believers. Every local church has resources in the gospel of Jesus Christ and the transformed lives of His people to make a truly significant impact on the problem of poverty in its community.

CHAPTER FIVE

EXEMPLARY LIFE PORTRAIT 3:
ACTS 5:12–16

L uke's third and final portrait of church life in Acts 5:12–16 is connected to its surrounding context in several ways. It has been identified as the conclusion of a larger unit (4:32–5:16) that repeats and expands on the material on church life in the first summary narrative (esp. 2:43–47).[1] Acts 5:12–16 has also been compared to a "hinge" that recalls and then closes an even larger section of Acts (3:1–4:31) and prepares readers for what follows in 5:17–42.[2] Acts 5:12–16 recalls and closes 3:1–4:21 by referring to the church's regular meetings in Solomon's Colonnade (5:12; cf. 3:11), to signs and wonders prayed for by the church and God's response (5:12; cf. 4:30), to the rapid growth of the church

---

[1] Sijbolt J. Noorda, "Scene and Summary: A Proposal for Reading Acts 4,32–5,16," in *Les Actes des Apôtres: traditions, redaction et théologie*, ed. Jacob Kremer (Louvain, Belgium: University Press, 1979), 481–83; David Peterson, *The Acts of the Apostles*, PNTC (Grand Rapids: Eerdmans, 2009), 207.
[2] Richard I. Pervo, *Acts*, Hermeneia (Minneapolis: Fortress, 2009), 135.

(5:14; cf. 4:4), and to healings (5:15–16; cf. 3:1–10).[3] Acts 5:12–16 prepares readers for what follows in 5:17–42 by alluding to the theme of persecution. Peter and John were already arrested and warned to stop speaking in the name of Jesus (4:3,17–21), which caused many to avoid identifying with the church (5:13). In the next episode all the apostles were thrown in jail by the high priest and the Sadducees (5:17–18). The temple leadership was furious and wanted to kill them (5:33). Instead, they had them flogged and let go (5:40). By alluding to the fear of joining the church in Acts 5:13, Luke anticipates a theme that builds in subsequent chapters: that as the church grew, persecution grew too. Opposition came first from the Jews (6:9–14; 7:54–8:3) and then from the Romans (12:1–5).[4]

LIFE TOGETHER IN THE FELLOWSHIP OF BELIEVERS (ACTS 5:12–16)

Acts 5:12–16 depicts the miraculous power of God through the apostles and describes the impact of the church on the city of Jerusalem.[5] Purged of the hypocrisy exposed in Acts 5:1–11, the church was living in the fear of the Lord (5:11) and experienced a resurgence of spiritual power.[6] The fear that came upon the church and all who heard about the deaths of Ananias and Sapphira doubtless led to a greater respect for the apostles' authority. Luke's third portrait further affirms the divine authentication of their leadership role by emphasizing the signs and wonders done through them.

Signs and Wonders through the Apostles

God performed many signs and wonders through the apostles among the people (Acts 5:12a). Luke's statement repeats nearly verbatim what he said in 2:43, with minor modifications. Acts 2:43 and 5:12 both indicate that signs and wonders occurred regularly in the Jerusalem church and that God was the One performing them. Luke makes this clear in 5:12 with the passive voice of the verb "were being done" (*egineto*) and with the preposition "through" (*dia*), which shows that the apostles were God's instruments for performing miracles and not the cause (see 19:11). Both

---

[3] Mikael C. Parsons, *Acts*, Paideia: Commentaries on the New Testament (Grand Rapids: Baker, 2008), 76.

[4] French L. Arrington, *The Acts of the Apostles* (Peabody, MA: Hendrickson, 1988), 60.

[5] J. Bradley Chance, *Acts*, SHBC (Macon, GA: Smyth & Helwys, 2007), 90; H. Alan Brehm, "The Significance of the Summaries for Interpreting Acts," *SwJT* 33, no. 1 (Fall 1990): 37.

[6] Curtis Vaughan, *Acts* (Grand Rapids: Zondervan, 1974), 38.

statements also emphasize the apostles as the focal point of God's miracle working power in the Jerusalem church. Acts 5:12 intensifies the emphasis in 2:43 by adding that the miracles were done through "the hands of the apostles" (*tōn cheirōn tōn apostolōn*). That the miracles happened through the hands of the apostles is as important in the summary narratives as the fact that they happened at all. Luke's reference to the apostles' hands could refer to the action of laying hands on the sick the way Jesus did when He healed people (Luke 4:40; 13:13; also Paul in Acts 28:17).[7] It could also be an allusion to the believers' prayer in Acts 4:30 that God would stretch out His "hand for healing, signs, and wonders." The language of 5:16 supports this connection by stressing healings through the apostle Peter in addition to the signs and wonders noted in 5:12. Both ideas might have been intended by Luke. More will be said on signs and wonders through the apostles in Acts when 5:15–16 is discussed below.

Meeting Together

The believers committed to meeting together regularly (Acts 5:12b). The subject of Acts 5:12b, "they," is not identified explicitly. It could be the apostles, but it more likely refers to the entire community of believers (so NIV, CEV, KJV).[8] They met together by common consent in the temple complex. The Greek word for "common consent" (*homothumadon*) appears in the New Testament almost exclusively in Acts.[9] The term can denote being present "in the same place" (2:46), or it can refer to a group action that proceeds from the united effort of the group's members (8:6; 12:20; 18:20). Both senses seem to be implied in 5:12. However, the immediate context suggests the stronger connotation of a united action that stems from a common mind and heart (also 1:14; 15:25; Rom 15:6).[10]

---

[7] The laying on of hands in Acts also accompanied the impartation of the Holy Spirit (8:17; 19:6) and consecration to service (6:6; 13:3). See also 1 Tim 4:14; 2 Tim 1:6.

[8] Joseph A. Fitzmyer, *The Acts of the Apostles: A New Translation with Introduction and Commentary*, AB (New York: Doubleday, 1998), 328, and Luke Timothy Johnson, *The Acts of the Apostles*, SP (Collegeville, MN: Michael Glazier, 1992), 95, see the subject of Acts 5:12b as the apostles only. John Polhill, *Acts*, NAC (Nashville: Broadman, 1992), 163, and William J. Larkin, *Acts*, CBC (Carol Stream, IL: Tyndale House, 2006), 418, see the believers as the implied subject.

[9] Acts 1:14; 2:46; 4:24; 5:12; 7:57; 8:6; 12:20; 15:25; 18:12; 19:29. See also Rom 15:6.

[10] See the discussion in Steve Walton, "*Homothumadon* in Acts: Co-location, Common Action, or 'Of One Heart and Mind'?" in *The New Testament in Its First Century Setting: Essays in Context and Background in Honor of B. W. Winter on His 65th Birthday*, ed. P. J. Williams, Andrew D. Clarke, Peter M. Head, and David Instone-Brewer (Grand Rapids: Eerdmans, 2004), 90, 99–105; and BAGD, 566. Culy and Parsons see *homothumadon* as an adverb that merely expresses the sense of location in Acts 5:12 and 1:14 (Martin M. Culy and Mikeal C. Parsons, *Acts: A Handbook on the Greek Text* (Waco,

Solomon's Colonnade became an increasingly hostile place, but the believers decided that they would continue to meet there regardless of the threat. The Colonnade was a large covered porch that ran along the eastern portion of the temple precinct.[11] Jesus spent time there (John 10:23), and Peter preached his second sermon there too (Acts 3:11). In the first summary narrative the believers met in the temple complex and moved about freely (Acts 2:46). As opposition developed in the episodes surrounding the summary narratives, it became more risky to meet together publicly. However, they made a united commitment that they would keep gathering as a church (Heb 10:25). Meeting together was a high priority for the Jerusalem church, no matter how difficult or dangerous it was to do.

In the twenty-first century, technology and ease of transportation make getting together easier, but people feel more hurried and disconnected than ever. The exemplary church, however, recognizes the downside of some aspects of modern society and resists the loss of community and fragmentation of relationships. To be the church described in the summary narratives, believers in Jesus must commit to meeting together regularly.

The believers in Jerusalem likely lost access to the temple complex as a meeting place after persecution broke out against the church in Jerusalem (Acts 8:1). However, by noting that the church first met at the temple, Luke reminds Gentile readers that their gospel was rooted in the faith of Israel even as their practice of meeting in homes (16:40; 17:7; 18:7–8; 20:20) transcended temple attendance and observances.[12]

Costly Membership

The potential cost of joining the church caused many to stay away (Acts 5:13a). Luke's statement in Acts 5:12 about the commitment of the believers to meet together stands in contrast to the fear that kept others from joining. His mention of "the rest" (*tōn loipōn*) refers to Jews in Jerusalem who would not profess Christ publicly and identify with His followers. Jews who visited the temple could observe the believers and

---

TX: Baylor University Press, 2003), 90), but the statement in its context seems more forceful than merely an indicator of location.

[11] Richard N. Longenecker, *Acts*, EBC vol. 9 (Grand Rapids: Zondervan, 2007), 758.

[12] S. K. Kisirinya, "Re-Interpreting the Major Summaries (Acts 2:42–46; 4:43–35; 5:12–16)," *African Christian Studies* 18, no. 1 (2002): 68–72. Also, see Bruce W. Longenecker, "Rome's Victory and God's Honour: The Jerusalem Temple and the Spirit of God in Lukan Theodicy," in *The Holy Spirit and Christian Origins: Essays in Honor of James D. G. Dunn*, ed. Graham N. Stanton, Stephen C. Barton, and Bruce W. Longenecker (Grand Rapids: Eerdmans, 2004), 99–102.

hear the apostles' preaching, but they feared the temple leadership. Add to that the fear caused by the deaths of Ananias and Sapphira (5:11), and many Jews did not dare join the believers.[13] The Greek term for dared (*etolma*) can be translated "had the courage." It is associated with a willingness to do something that could lead to severe repercussions.[14]

A fully developed sense of formal church membership probably did not exist at this early stage.[15] However, the growing risk associated with identifying with the believers does suggest the emergence of a line that separated the church from the rest of the Jerusalem. On one side of the line was safety and anonymity. On the other was visibility and association with the apostles whose boldness had put them in the crosshairs of the Sanhedrin. The declaration of the apostles that Jesus was the fulfillment of Jewish hope and that the church was the true heir of God's promises to Israel cut to the heart of Jewish faith.[16] Luke wanted readers to understand that joining the church can be costly. Association with the church in Jerusalem was dangerous enough to keep some people away.

Too often the cost of discipleship is underemphasized in an effort to make Christianity as appealing as possible. Yet, Jesus challenged would-be followers to count the cost before becoming His disciples (Luke 14:25–35). He warned that true disciples must deny themselves and take up their cross in order to follow Him (9:23; 14:27). Following Jesus may lead to rejection (6:22), persecution (11:53; 12:11), division within families (12:49–53), even death (21:12–16). It seems strange in a positive portrait of church life that Luke would also note that the cost was too high for some. In reply it should be asked whether a church is really following Jesus if the opposition Jesus promised is never stirred. Persecution should not be considered an abnormality for the believer (2 Tim 3:12; Acts 14:22). If a church is experiencing exemplary life, some will not have the courage to join.

Respect and Growth

The people of Jerusalem spoke well of the church in their city (Acts 5:13b). Even though many were afraid to join with them, the people

---

[13] Daniel R. Schwartz, "Non-Joining Sympathizers (Acts 5.13–15)," *Bib* 64 (1983): 550–55.

[14] Mark 14:53; Rom 5:7; Phil 1:14; Jude 9. See BAGD, 821–22; LSJ, 1803.

[15] Johnson, *Acts*, 95.

[16] N. T. Wright, *The New Testament and the People of God* (Minneapolis: Fortress Press, 1992), 449–51. On the development of the theme of persecution in Acts, see Brian Rapske, "Opposition to the Plan of God and Persecution," in *Witness to the Gospel: The Theology of Acts*, ed. I. Howard Marshall and David Peterson (Grand Rapids: Eerdmans, 1998), 235–56.

esteemed the church highly. The Greek word for "people" (*laos*) refers
to the general populace of Jerusalem. Their attitude stands in stark contrast to that of the Jewish leaders.[17] The people of Jerusalem observed the
boldness of the believers and the way they treated each other and praised
them highly. The Greek verb for "praised highly" (*emegalunen*) means to
"extol" or "make great by word."[18] Genesis 12:2 (LXX) uses the verb in a
similar way when God declared to Abram, "I will make your name great."
Four of the eight New Testament occurrences of the verb speak of esteem-
ing God and making His name great (Luke 1:46; Acts 10:46; 19:17; Phil
1:20).[19] In Acts 5:13 the people of Jerusalem spoke highly of the church.
Luke wanted his readers to know that even though the Jewish leadership opposed the apostles (Acts 4:1–22; 5:17–42; 6:8–8:4), the people of
Jerusalem respected their way of life as seen in the rapid growth of the
church in 5:14.[20]

More and more believers were being added to the Lord (Acts 5:14).
The response of new believers was overwhelming in spite of the risks
involved in joining the church. The statement in Acts 5:14a is difficult
to translate precisely. The prepositional phrase *tō kuriō* can be translated
"to the Lord" or "in the Lord," depending on whether it functions as an
adverbial or adjectival phrase. If it functions adverbially, it modifies the
verb "added" (*prosetithento*) and means believers were added "to the Lord"
(NKJV, ESV, HCSB, RSV).[21] If it functions adjectivally, then it modifies
the participle "believers" (*pisteuontes*) and means believers "in the Lord"
were added to their number (NASB, NIV).[22] Though I prefer the former
translation, it is probably best not to draw a hard and fast line between the
options. Perhaps Luke meant to convey both ideas to readers. Certainly for
him, believing in the Lord and being added to His church went together
(Acts 2:41).

In Acts 2:47 Luke notes that people were being saved and daily
"added" to the church; in 5:14 he intensifies his emphasis on growth in

---

[17] Justo L. González, *Acts: The Gospel of the Spirit* (Maryknoll, NY: Orbis Books, 2001), 81.

[18] In Acts 5:13 the term includes attitudes like "respect" (NCV) and "high esteem" for the believers (NASB, ESV), but it goes beyond them to include speaking highly of them (GNT) (LSJ, 1088).

[19] See Matt 23:5; Luke 1:58; 2 Cor 10:15 for the three other occurrences of μεγαλύνω. See the
discussion in Walter Grundmann, "μέγας, μεγαλεῖον, μεγαλειότης, et al.," in *TDNT*, 4:543.

[20] See also Acts 4:4; 6:1,7; 9:31; 12:24; 16:5; 19:20.

[21] C. K. Barrett, *Acts 1–14*, ICC (New York: T&T Clark, 1994), 275; Darrell L. Bock, *Acts*,
BECNT (Grand Rapids: Baker Academic, 2007), 231; Ben Witherington III, *The Acts of the Apostles:
A Socio-Rhetorical Commentary* (Grand Rapids: Eerdmans, 1998), 226.

[22] F. F. Bruce, *The Acts of the Apostles: The Greek Text with Introduction and Commentary* (Grand
Rapids: Eerdmans, 1990), 168; Fitzmyer, *Acts*, 328; Parsons, *Acts*, 76.

two additional ways. First, Luke does not begin his sentence in Greek with the subject "believers." Instead, he leads with *mallon*, an adverb that intensifies the action of "added." Placing *mallon* at the beginning of the sentence positions it in strong contrast to the preceding statement in 5:13 and means "now more than ever."[23] In spite of the many who stayed away, believers were "all the more" (NASB) or "more than ever" (ESV) being added to their number. Second, rather than speak of individuals, Luke refers to "crowds" (*plēthē*) of men and women believing. The steady stream of new believers coming into the church had now taken on the feel of a great movement in Jerusalem.

Acts 5:14 also mentions women along with men as a vital part of the growth of the church.[24] Luke has been criticized by some as insensitive to women, either unwittingly because he was a product of a highly patriarchal society, or deliberately out of concern not to offend Roman readers he wanted to reach with the gospel.[25] Luke does not ignore the social or political implications of his message. Instead, he focuses on how the gospel, as it moved through the Mediterranean world, brought women from all levels of Roman society into the churches as partners with men in service to Christ. Prominent women are noted among the believers (Acts 13:50; 17:4,12), as well as a servant girl named Rhoda (12:13). Lydia was a businesswoman who hosted the church in Philippi in her home (16:14,40). Priscilla worked with her husband Aquila to explain the way of God to Apollos more adequately (18:24–26; see also Rom 16:3–4; 1 Cor 16:19). Philip's daughters prophesied (Acts 21:8–9). Though it is not a major theme of Acts, the progress of women in Roman society is one of the effects of the gospel, in which both women and men are divine image bearers and are of equal worth in Christ (Gen 1:27; Gal 3:28).[26]

Healings through Peter and the Apostles

The believers brought multitudes who were sick and tormented by unclean spirits to Peter and the apostles, and they were healed (Acts 5:15–16). The final two verses of the third summary narrative expand on Luke's

---

[23] BAGD, 489. According to LSJ, 1076, this adverb strengthens the word with which it stands and thus the assertion the verb makes.

[24] Also see Luke 8:1–3; 24:10,22,24; Acts 1:14; 8:12; 9:2 for this emphasis in Luke–Acts.

[25] See Jane Schaberg, "Luke," in *The Women's Bible Commentary*, ed. Carol A. Newsom and Sharon H. Ringe (Louisville, KY: Westminster/John Knox, 1992), 275–92, esp. 291; and Gail R. O'Day, "Acts," in ibid., 305–12, esp. 311–12.

[26] Witherington, *Acts*, 338–39.

comments on signs and wonders through the apostles in Acts 5:12 and 2:43. A crescendo is reached here as people (5:15) and soon a multitude (5:16) from the towns surrounding Jerusalem brought people to Peter for healing.

If we read Acts 5:15 as modifying the verb "added" in v. 14, then we see that Luke records one of the results of the great numbers of people added to the church. The crowd at Solomon's Colonnade grew so large that many of the sick had to be brought out into the streets on beds and pallets in anticipation of Peter passing by so that his shadow might at least fall on them. Quite a scene must have ensued as believers in Jerusalem learned of Peter's travel routes and rushed to place their loved ones in the path of his shadow.[27] The shadow in ancient popular belief was thought to be an extension of the soul or essence of a person. Many believed that to come into contact with a person's shadow, especially the shadow of a man of God like Peter, put one in contact with the healing power operating through him.[28]

The text does not clarify whether Luke believes Peter's shadow actually had a healing effect, or if he is simply reporting the behavior and belief of the people.[29] C. K. Barrett suggests that these people may not have even been Christians, in which case Luke would be referring to those in Acts 5:13 who chose not to join the church.[30] Acts 5:14 then would stand on its own as a parenthesis, which is a statement that has no syntactical connection to its immediate context, and the people were likely not healed by this practice.[31] If this is the case, then 5:15 cannot function adverbially to modify "added" in 5:14. Either option is acceptable on grammatical grounds. Positively this view avoids the awkwardness of portraying believers follow-

---

[27] The believers' determination is similar to that of the friends of the paralytic in Mark 2:1–12. They could not get their friend to Jesus because of the crowd, so they dug a hole in the roof above Jesus and lowered the mat he was laying on into the room with him on it. Jesus forgave his sins and healed him.

[28] See the chapter "The Shadow in Hellenistic Popular Belief" in Pieter W. van der Horst, *Jews and Christians in Their Graeco-Roman Context: Selected Essays on Early Judaism, Samaritanism, Hellenism, and Christianity* (Tübingen: Mohr Siebeck, 2006), 234–41. Also, see W. Bieder, "Der Petruschatten, Apg. 5:15," *TZ* 16 (1960): 407–9; Johnson, *Acts*, 96; Charles H. Talbert, *Reading Acts: A Literary and Theological Commentary on the Acts of the Apostles* (New York: Crossroads, 1997), 67; and Bruce J. Malina and John J. Pilch, *Social-Science Commentary on the Book of Acts* (Minneapolis, MN: Fortress, 2008), 50.

[29] Polhill, *Acts*, 164; Witherington, *Acts*, 227.

[30] Barrett, *Acts 1–14*, 276. Also C. S. C. Williams, *A Commentary on the Acts of the Apostles*, HNTC (New York: Harper & Brothers, 1957), 103.

[31] On Acts 5:14 as a possible parenthesis, see A. T. Robertson, *A Grammar of the Greek New Testament in the Light of Historical Research* (Nashville: Broadman, 1934), 433–35, esp. 435; BDF, 243.

ing a practice that had parallels in ancient popular belief. However, if they were not believers, it would interrupt Luke's consistent focus on the behavior of believers in the summary narratives. It therefore makes more sense to view them as believers.[32] That certain superstitions were associated with a person's shadow in the ancient world does not require us to conclude that the believers in Jerusalem held to these views, or that Luke affirms them. These were extraordinary times due to the resurrection of Jesus and the sending of the Holy Spirit. Things were happening that were utterly unique. Jesus earlier indicated that power for healing had gone out from Him after a woman merely touched His garment (Luke 8:43–48). Later in Acts handkerchiefs and aprons that Paul had touched were carried to the sick, and they were healed or delivered from demons (Acts 19:11–12). Amazing miracles were occurring that simply had no precedent in Jewish faith and practice.[33] John Chrysostom suggested that healing through Peter's shadow was an example of the apostles doing even greater works than Jesus, as He promised (John 14:12).[34] Perhaps Luke simply wants to show that God responded to the faith of His people, expressed in this unique manner, and graciously worked through Peter's shadow to heal.[35]

In Acts 5:16 we see the first hint that the geographic program outlined by Jesus in Acts 1:8 is beginning to be fulfilled as news of the apostles' ministry spread beyond Jerusalem.[36] The word went out, and a multitude of people came from the towns of Judea surrounding the city. Luke's reference to the growing crowd, though part of his historical description, is also a narrative technique that contributes to the crescendo of momentum in his narrative. The people were not passive observers. In increasing numbers they actively sought out the apostles and engaged their ministry.[37]

---

[32] One might respond by pointing to the unbelievers in Acts 5:13 as an exception to Luke's focus on believers in the summary narratives. However, I have already demonstrated above that Luke's mention of those who dared not join not only highlights the potential cost to believers of joining the church, it indirectly commends the exemplary behavior of those who did join, because of the opposition already endured by the apostles and the more intense persecution yet to come.

[33] Although no OT precedent exists, Luke may have alluded to the statement of the angel Gabriel to Mary, "The Holy Spirit will come upon you, and the power of the Most High will *overshadow* you" (Luke 1:35; italics are mine). Also see Luke 9:34. Cf. Pieter W. van der Horst, "Shadow," in *ABD*, 5:1149. On the Jewish and Hellenistic background of belief in the efficacy of the shadow for healing, see Pieter W. van der Horst, "Peter's Shadow: The Religio-Historical Background of Acts 5:15," *NTS* 23 (1977): 204–12.

[34] John Chrysostom, *Hom. Act.* 12.

[35] Bock, *Acts*, 232.

[36] See Acts 9:31. Cf. Dunn, *Acts*, 66.

[37] Richard S. Ascough, "Narrative Technique and Generic Designation: Crowd Scenes in Luke-Acts," *CBQ* 58 (1996): 76.

The verb "came together" (*sunērcheto*) means "to assemble" and can refer to any gathering together of people for a specific purpose (John 18:20; Acts 10:24).[38] Interestingly, it often refers to the coming together of the church (1 Cor 11:17; 14:23,26). Though the boundary line between those who joined the church and those who were afraid to join was clear (Acts 5:13), the ministry of the church clearly had broken out into the city and was carried on quite literally in the streets of Jerusalem.

People brought the sick (*astheneis*) and those who were tormented by unclean spirits. Tormenting spirits are normally described by Luke as evil spirits (Luke 7:21; 8:2; Acts 19:12–16). Here he calls them "unclean" (*akathartōn*), a word which means defiled or impure. An impure life was thought by many to be what opened the door to being tormented by this kind of spirit.[39] The word for "tormented" (*ochloumenous*) implies that the attacks of these unclean spirits were personal. Satan's desire to devour is not an impersonal force (1 Pet 5:8). It is a malevolence that flows from his hatred of persons created in God's image whom he wants to destroy (John 10:10). However, Jesus came to conquer him. Numerous episodes in Luke's Gospel demonstrate Jesus' authority over Satan and the demonic realm (Luke 4:1–13; 8:26–39; 9:37–43; 10:17–19; 11:24–26). Acts echoes this theme by showing the apostles exercising the same authority through the name of Jesus (Acts 8:9–25; 13:4–12; 19:11–20). Several summary statements in Acts on the exorcism of unclean spirits also echo summary statements in Luke's Gospel about Jesus' authority over Satan (Luke 4:41; 6:18; 8:2; 9:1; cf. Acts 5:16; 19:11–12).[40] Acts 5:16 brings the final summary narrative to a close by declaring that every sick and demon harassed person who came to Peter for help was healed.

Luke stresses two things in his final statements about the apostle Peter's ministry of healing in Jerusalem. First, God was displaying tremendous miracle-working power in the church. The power of God was demonstrated in His total victory over every disease and unclean spirit. No one who came to be helped went away disappointed. Second, this power was focused on and through the ministry of the apostle Peter.

---

[38] BAGD, 788.

[39] The use of unclean to describe the tormenting spirits could also denote the view that these spirits led people into an unclean life, or that a person's wandering in a state of demonic possession led them into places where ceremonial defilement could occur (Mark 5:2–5). See Williams, *Acts*, 104; Bock, *Acts*, 232–33.

[40] Numerous summary statements in Luke's Gospel also declare Jesus' absolute power to heal (Luke 4:40; 5:15; 6:17–19), which are echoed in Acts in the ministry of the apostles (Acts 5:16; 8:7; 28:9).

Excursus: Signs and Wonders in the Summary Narratives

The ministry of the apostles is mentioned frequently in the summary narratives, both with and without accompanying signs and wonders (Acts 2:42–43; 4:33,35; 5:12,15–16). However, signs and wonders are not mentioned in the summary narratives apart from the apostles' ministry (Acts 2:43; 5:12). This raises the question of where the emphasis on signs and wonders lies in the summary narratives. Do they stand on their own as aspects of exemplary church life that Luke wants all churches to expect to see? Or do they authenticate the leadership and doctrine of the apostles for the faith and life of the church? A few comments about the role of miracles in Acts generally must be made before this question can be answered.

Acts does not distinguish sharply between natural and supernatural occurrences the way modern people do, because the entire book is suffused with God's sovereign and purposeful intervention in the world. These interventions range from ordinary providences that are the outworking of His will in history, to exceptional events or miracles that are visible evidence of His power and purpose.[41] Miracles are not a greater manifestation of God's power than providence is, but they are a different manifestation.[42]

The regular occurrence of miracles is a dominant feature of the book of Acts. The phrase "signs and wonders" occurs nine times in Acts, more often than any other Bible book.[43] Four of the nine reports of signs and wonders occur in summaries that create the sense that miracles occurred regularly in the early years of the Christian movement (Acts 2:43; 5:12; 6:8; 14:3).

Peter Davids organizes the miracle accounts in Acts into four basic categories. First, Acts contains many miracles of *inspiration*. Examples include the miracle of speaking in tongues on Pentecost (Acts 2:1–13), divine guidance through prophecies (11:28; 21:10–11), through direct speech by the Holy Spirit (13:2–3), and through visions (16:9; 18:9–10). Second, there are miracles of *physical restoration* including the healing of sick persons (3:1–10; 14:8–10), raising the dead (9:37–41; 20:7–12), and the expulsion of an unclean spirit from a slave girl (16:16–8). Third, we see miracles of *protection and deliverance* like the release of the

---

[41] See Witherington, *Acts*, 221; and G. W. H. Lampe, "Miracles in the Acts of the Apostles," in *Miracles: Cambridge Studies in Their Philosophy and History*, ed. C. F. D. Moule (London: A. R. Mowbrays, 1965), 171.

[42] Robert L. Hamblin, "Miracles in the Book of Acts," *SwJT* 17, no. 1 (Fall 1974): 20.

[43] See Acts 2:19,22,43; 4:30; 5:12; 6:8; 7:36; 14:3; 15:12. The word *sign* does appear in Luke's Gospel (Luke 2:12,34; 11:16,29–30; 21:7,11,25).

apostles from jail (5:17–20; 16:25–26), deliverance from shipwreck (27:13–44), and protection from a snakebite (28:3–6). Fourth, miracles of *judgment* also appear, like the deaths of Ananias and Sapphira (5:1–11) and King Herod (12:20–23), and temporary blindness inflicted on Saul (9:1–9) and Bar-Jesus (13:6–12).[44] All of these accounts have in common an association with one of God's messengers and the word that went forth from them.

The expression "signs and wonders" is Luke's favorite way of referring to the numerous reports of miracles in Acts. In Hellenistic literature the phrase generally refers to ancient superstitions and beliefs about the abilities and exploits of various gods.[45] In Acts, however, signs and wonders are rooted in the Old Testament, especially the miracles Yahweh performed through Moses. God sent Moses to Israel and to Pharaoh with signs and wonders that served several purposes. First, God sent signs and wonders as judgments against Egypt (Exod 7:3–4; Deut 6:22; 29:3; 34:11; Neh 9:10; Pss 105:27; 135:9). Second, God rescued His people by means of signs and wonders (Deut 4:34; 26:8; Jer 32:21; Dan 6:27). Third, God provided signs and wonders to stimulate the faith of Israel (Exod 10:1–2; Deut 7:19; Ps 78:43; Isa 8:18).[46] Fourth, through these signs and wonders God certified Moses to Israel as His spokesperson and chosen leader (Exod 4:1–8,30).[47]

Each of the miracles in Acts could be related to one or more of these four purposes. However, the fourth purpose fits more of them than any purpose, because they tend to certify the apostles the way signs and wonders certified the leadership of Moses. The miracles in

---

[44] Peter H. Davids, "Miracles in Acts," in *DLNT*, 746–47. More precise groupings of the miracles in Acts can be found in Colin J. Hemer, *The Book of Acts in the Setting of Hellenistic History* (Tübingen: J. C. B. Mohr, 1989), 434–37; Matti Myllykoski, "Being There: The Function of the Supernatural in Acts 1–12," in *Wonders Never Cease: The Purpose of Narrating Miracle Stories in the New Testament and Its Religious Environment*, ed. Michael Labahn and Bert Jan Lietaert Peerbolte (New York: T&T Clark, 2006), 154–59; and Witherington, *Acts*, 220.

[45] Polybius, *Hist.* 3.112.18; Plutarch, *Alex.* 75.1. See Graham H. Twelftree, "Signs, Wonders, Miracles," in *DPL*, 875; Molly Whittaker, "Signs and Wonders: The Pagan Background," *SE* 5 (1968): 155–58; and A. H. McDonald, "Herodotus on the Miraculous," in Moule, *Miracles*, 83–91. Miracles are pictured in ancient mythology as "divine instruments to exact worship, obedience, and submission" (Henk J. Versnel, "Miracles," in *OCD*, 989).

[46] The word *wonders* appears without *signs* in the OT primarily to refer to miracles that revealed God's judgment against Pharaoh (Exod 4:21; 11:9,10; 15:11; 18:11) and as a means of stimulating the faith of his people (Exod 15:11; 34:10). On *wonders* see also Josh 3:5; Judg 6:13; 1 Chr 16:12; Neh 9:17.

[47] Philo spoke twice in his writings of "signs and wonders" as validation of the divine origin of an accompanying statement or revelation through his servant (Philo, *Moses* 1.95; *Spec. Laws* 2.218). See Graham H. Twelftree's *People of the Spirit: Exploring Luke's View of the Church* (Grand Rapids: Baker, 2009), 201. Paul also spoke of accompanying signs and wonders that verified his call as a minister to the Gentiles (Rom 15:18–19) and proved that he was called by God as an apostle (2 Cor 12:12).

Acts occur primarily through the apostles (2:42; 5:12), especially Peter (5:15–16) and Paul (14:3; 15:12; 19:11–12). Miracles also occur through Stephen (6:8), Philip (8:6,13), and Barnabas (14:3; 15:12), who preached and taught the apostles' message. Signs and wonders verify their leadership and message about the resurrected Jesus (4:33). In Acts every reference to miracles is in the context of the apostolic message of the resurrected Jesus going forth. Proclamation occurs in Acts without a mention of miracles, but miracles are never mentioned apart from God's word and His spokesmen.[48] Signs and wonders cannot be separated from the apostolic message in Acts overall, just as they do not appear separately within the summary narratives.

This fact may shed some light on debates over whether Luke believes signs and wonders should characterize church life for readers and whether churches should expect to see the same thing today. Do signs and wonders stand on their own as aspects of exemplary church life that Luke wants all churches to expect to see? Or do they certify the leadership and doctrine of the apostles, so that the emphasis is not on the miracles but on the apostles' message? Some of the tension between these positions is built into the very fabric of the summary narratives, especially the inseparability of signs and wonders from the apostles. On the one hand, those who think the emphasis should not lie on signs and wonders as normative occurrences in the church should at least acknowledge that they are prominent in Acts, especially in Luke's portraits of exemplary church life. On the other hand, taken together the miracle narratives in Acts and the emphasis on signs and wonders in the summary narratives testify that the apostles and their message have divine approval and should be heeded. The emphasis on signs and wonders through the apostles calls readers to recognize the authority of their doctrine and leadership for the faith and life of the church. Perhaps a balanced approach should confess that God is God. He can suspend His own laws of creation and work any wonder or sign that pleases Him that His name might be glorified. Yet, it should also recognize that the emphasis of signs and wonders in the New Testament is overwhelmingly on the apostles and the gospel they proclaimed as the power of God that saves (Rom 1:16).

---

[48] Acts 2:14,19,22,40–41,43; 4:29–31,33; 5:1–12,17,20; 6:7–8; 7:35,38; 8:4,6,13–14; 14:3; 15:7,12. See Leo O'Reilly, *Word and Sign in the Acts of the Apostles: A Study in Lukan Theology* (Rome: Editrice Pontifica Universita Gregoriana, 1987), 191–92; Wilhelm Mundle, Otfried Hofius, and Colin Brown, "Miracle, Wonder, Sign," in *NIDNTT*, 632.

SUMMARY

The third summary narrative begins on a sober note, following God's judgment against Ananias and Sapphira's duplicity, which brought great fear over the church. Readers begin Acts 5:12–16 with the sense that God is serious about the integrity of His church, and He will take action to protect it. The third portrait also follows an unambiguous message about the special role of the apostle Peter, whose words pronounced the death sentence on Ananias and Sapphira. These events prepare readers to recognize an emphasis in Acts 5:12–16 on the leadership of the apostles as evidenced by the many signs and wonders that were happening through their hands. The repetition of the theme of signs and wonders from the first summary narrative further underscores their role in the Jerusalem church. Peter's healing ministry is singled out for special emphasis in Luke's third portrait of church life. Readers are left with the deep impression as the repetitions of the theme accumulate that the apostles are the believers' connection to the ongoing ministry of Jesus on the earth through the church. Their leadership and teaching, which begins the first summary narrative (Acts 2:42), was and is authoritative for the faith and life of the church. The prevalence of signs and wonders in Acts 5:12–16 also reminds readers that God can perform signs and wonders whenever He is pleased to do so, in order to make His presence and power known.

The church's regular meetings in the temple complex and astonishing numerical growth are also repeated from the first summary narrative, which continues the sense that a great movement began and is continuing in the city of Jerusalem. New material in the third summary narrative includes an acknowledgment that many would not dare join with the other believers because of the risk of persecution. This statement prepares readers to hear more about persecution in coming episodes and warns them that following Jesus might be dangerous. However, those who were afraid to join still praised the believers highly, because they had such respect for the way they lived and loved each other.

CHAPTER SIX

EXEMPLARY LIFE IN THE
GENTILE CHURCHES OF ACTS

T he narrative of the Jerusalem church does not end with Luke's description of exemplary church life in Acts 5:12–16. Three episodes follow that echo important themes introduced in the summary narratives and in surrounding passages.

In the first episode the apostles faced further persecution from the Sanhedrin (Acts 5:17–42) because they would not stop bearing witness to the resurrection of Jesus (5:20–21,25,29–32; cf. Acts 4:33). In contrast to those who did not dare to join them (5:13), the apostles rejoiced that they were counted worthy to be persecuted on behalf of the name of Jesus (5:41). In 5:42 they continued teaching and preaching about Jesus (cf. 2:42; 4:33) every day in the temple (cf. 2:46) and in homes (cf. 2:46). Acts 5:17–42 is striking due to the fact that the plot of Acts moves forward, but as it does, echoes of church life in the summary narratives appear repeatedly that reinforce their message.

In the second episode (Acts 6:1–7) important themes from the summary narratives and surrounding passages are repeated again. In 6:1 the Hellenistic (*Hellēnistōn*) Jews were believers in Jesus who were formerly Gentile converts to Judaism. The Hebraic (*Hebraious*) Jews were believers in Jesus who were Jews by birth. Both groups made up the Jerusalem church, but the Hellenists felt overlooked in the daily distribution of food. The problem threatened the unity of the church emphasized in the summary narratives (4:32). The apostles needed a ministry structure that would help the church care for its widows (6:2a; cf. 4:35) so they could stay focused on preaching and prayer (6:2b,4; cf. 2:42; 4:33). They asked the church to select seven men who were full of the Holy Spirit (6:3,5; cf. 2:4; 4:31). The apostles consecrated the men by praying and laying hands on them (6:6; cf. 5:12), so that the work of distributing contributions and meeting the needs of the widows could continue (cf. 2:45; 4:34–35). The episode concludes in 6:7 with a brief summary statement that shows the ongoing impact of the church's ministry breakthrough on the city of Jerusalem. The preaching flourished (cf. 4:33). The number of disciples multiplied, and a large number of priests became obedient to the faith (*tē pistei*) (cf. 2:47; 5:14).[1] Like the summary statement in 5:42, this episode echoes many important aspects of exemplary church life introduced in the summary narratives. The echoes of the summary narratives in later episodes reinforce Luke's portraits of exemplary church life.

The third episode, the martyrdom of Stephen, also contains echoes of Luke's exemplary portraits in the summary narratives and surrounding passages. Stephen was a man full of grace (Acts 6:8; cf. 4:33) who performed many wonders and signs (6:8; cf. 2:43; 5:12). He was also filled with the Holy Spirit (6:10; 7:55; cf. 2:4; 4:31) as he proclaimed the resurrected and exalted Jesus (7:56; cf. 4:33). Stephen was only one man and not an apostle, but even his positive example as an individual echoes themes in the Luke's portrait of exemplary church life in Jerusalem. The themes introduced in the summary narratives are never far from view as the narrative of Acts moves forward.

These three episodes illustrate one of Luke's favorite rhetorical strategies of repeating themes from the summary narratives in later episodes. Echoes of the summary narratives can be heard throughout Acts in Luke's descriptions of life in newly planted churches among the Gentiles.

---

[1] The "obedience to the faith" of the priests could even be considered an echo of the obedience of the crowd at Pentecost in response to Peter's command to repent and be baptized (Acts 2:38,41).

Parallel Themes and Echo Effect in Acts

Echoes of material introduced earlier in Acts have been given much scholarly attention under the label of parallel themes. Interpreters have focused on echoes of Peter's ministry heard in the ministry of Paul.[2] Prominent Peter-Paul parallels include the following: Signs and wonders were prominent in their ministries (Acts 2:43; 14:4); both healed a man who was lame from birth (3:1–10; 14:8–10); and both issued a rebuke followed by judgment (5:1–11; 13:8–12). A building Peter was in and the prison where Paul was incarcerated were both shaken (4:31; 16:26), and prison chains miraculously fell off each of them (12:7; 16:26). Healings occurred through Peter's shadow and through handkerchiefs and aprons that touched Paul (5:15; 19:12); Peter healed a paralytic and Paul healed a man with fever and dysentery (9:33–35; 28:7–9); and both raised the dead (9:36–41; 20:9–10).[3] The parallels between Peter and Paul are so pervasive in Acts that early historical critics thought Luke invented them to create an illusion of unity in order to cover up a deep division between the apostles. This view has less support as the influence of F. C. Baur and the Tübingen school wanes, and historical questions are less apt to be pitted so quickly against the theological perspective of Acts.[4]

As the literary perspective has taken hold, scholars have focused on connections and parallels within Acts and between Luke and Acts as deliberate rhetorical strategies used by Luke to convey his message. In his two-volume narrative commentary on Luke and Acts, Robert Tannehill studies individual texts as functioning members of a total narrative in order to discern meanings that emerge when one considers how part interacts with related part.[5] He pays special attention to the repetition of key words, phrases, and activities across the text of Acts. Tannehill called these repetitions an "echo effect" in a 1984 essay titled "The Composition of Acts

---

[2] See Susan Marie Praeder, "Jesus-Paul, Peter-Paul, and Jesus-Peter Parallelisms in Luke-Acts," in *SBLSP* 1984, 23–39; A. J. Mattill Jr., "The Jesus-Paul Parallels and the Purpose of Luke-Acts: H. H. Evans Reconsidered," *NovT* 17 (1975): 15–21; Frans Neirynck, "The Miracle Stories in the Acts of the Apostles," in *Les Actes des Apôtres: Traditions, rédaction, théologie*, ed. Jacob Kremer (Louvain, Belgium: Leuven University Press, 1979), 169–213, for surveys of research.

[3] John A. Hardon, "The Miracle Stories in the Acts of the Apostles," *CBQ* 16 (1954): 308–9.

[4] C. Marvin Pate et al., *The Story of Israel: A Biblical Theology* (Downers Grove, IL: InterVarsity, 2004), 180–84.

[5] Robert C. Tannehill, *The Narrative Unity of Luke-Acts: A Literary Interpretation, Volume 1: The Gospel According to Luke* (Minneapolis: Fortress, 1986); *Volume 2: The Acts of the Apostles* (Minneapolis: Fortress, 1990); and William S. Kurz, *Reading Luke-Acts: Dynamics of Biblical Narrative* (Louisville, KY: Westminster/John Knox, 1993), 4–5.

3–5: Narrative Development and Echo Effect."[6] The subtitle of the article, "Narrative Development and Echo Effect," indicates Tannehill's twofold reading strategy. First, readers should trace the narrative development of the plot of Acts forward through a series of causally connected events. Next, Acts should be read retrospectively, listening for enriching echoes of earlier events in subsequent parts of the narrative.[7] When echoes of earlier passages multiply in Acts, a resonance is produced that amplifies Luke's message in them. Luke's complex and subtle strategy of echoing earlier aspects of his narrative later in the story can impact readers (and hearers) significantly.[8] At a basic level, repetition combats the tendency to forget important ideas in a long narrative work like Acts, and it serves as a means for emphasizing important parts of the story. It can have a persuasive effect when positive activity is affirmed, because it fits what readers have already heard and agreed with at earlier points in the narrative. Repetition of earlier material in subsequent episodes involves readers actively in the interpretation of the story by holding their interest and causing characters and events to interact in their minds during the reading process. Repetitive patterns preserve a sense of unity of purpose within Acts too, because as the narrative advances from Jerusalem to the Gentile world it travels to diverse locations and cultures. However, a basic continuity persists throughout. Echoes of earlier themes later in the narrative of Acts also have tremendous potential to shape the moral and spiritual imagination of readers as resonating themes impact their understanding of following Christ in their own ecclesial context.[9]

The most striking illustration of Luke's use of echo effect is his repetition of themes introduced in the summary narratives in subsequent descriptions of Gentile church life in Acts. As the gospel moves into Gentile territories, echoes of exemplary life in the Jerusalem church can be heard repeatedly, especially in the churches planted in Samaria, Antioch, Ephesus, and Troas.[10]

---

[6] Robert C. Tannehill, "The Composition of Acts 3–5: Narrative Development and Echo Effect," in SBLSP, 217–40. This article was reprinted as a chapter in Robert C. Tannehill, *The Shape of Luke's Story: Essays on Luke-Acts* (Eugene, OR: Cascade Books, 2005), 185–219. References are to the 2005 edition.

[7] Tannehill, *Shape of Luke's Story*, 185–86.

[8] The following survey is a synopsis of Tannehill's comments on "echo effect" as a rhetorical strategy in Acts (ibid., 216–19).

[9] Douglas A. Hume, *The Early Christian Community: A Narrative Analysis of Acts 2:41–47 and 4:32–35* (Tübingen, Germany: Mohr Siebeck, 2011), 22, 150–51.

[10] Beverly Roberts Gaventa, *The Acts of the Apostles*, ANTC (Nashville: Abingdon, 2003), 282; Tannehill, *Narrative Unity of Luke-Acts: Acts*, 149.

THE GENTILE CHURCHES OF ACTS

Exemplary Church Life in Samaria (Acts 8:1–25; 9:31)

Many echoes of exemplary life in the summary narratives appear in Luke's description of gospel preaching in Samaria. Christ is first preached there because of the persecution and scattering of the church away from Jerusalem (Acts 8:1–4). The first occurrence in Acts of the word persecution (*diōgmos*) appears in 8:1. Opposition to the church in Jerusalem has moved from a warning (4:21), to a flogging (5:40), to martyrdom (7:58–60), and now a "great persecution."[11] The believers were scattered from Jerusalem throughout Judea and Samaria, preaching the word wherever they went (8:4; cf. 4:33). Philip went to a city in Samaria and proclaimed the Messiah (8:5; cf. 2:31,36; 4:33). Luke does not clarify whether he thinks of the Samaritans as estranged Jews, as half Jew and half Gentile, or fully Gentile.[12] First-century Jews did not think of Samaritans as one of them (Luke 17:18; John 4:9,22; 8:48). What Luke does make clear is that the gospel was making its way beyond the borders of Judea with Samaria as a transitional stage on the way to the ends of the earth (Acts 1:8). From this point on, the gospel begins to know no geographic or ethnic boundaries.[13]

Many in Samaria had probably heard of Jesus' visit to the town of Sychar a few years earlier when a large number of Samaritans believed (John 4:4–30,39–42).[14] Jesus had detractors in Samaria too (Luke 9:52).[15] Rather than a fully developed church, we encounter only the initial reaction

---

[11] John Polhill, *Acts*, NAC (Nashville: Broadman, 1992), 211.

[12] See discussions of options in Christoph W. Stenschke, *Luke's Portrait of Gentiles Prior to Their Coming to Faith* (Tübingen: Mohr Siebeck, 1999), 64–71; Martina Böhm, *Samarien und die Samaritai bei Lukas: Eine Studie zum religionshistorischen und traditionsgeschichtlichen Hintergrund der lukanischen Samarientexte und zu deren topographischer Verhaftung*, WUNT 2/111 (Tübingen: Mohr Siebeck, 1999), 279–308; Jacob Jervell, *Luke and the People of God: A New Look at Luke-Acts* (Minneapolis: Augsburg, 1972), 113–32; and Darrell L. Bock, *Acts*, BECNT (Grand Rapids: Baker Academic, 2007), 324–25.

[13] Pedrito U. Maynard-Reid, "Samaria," in *DLNT*, 1076; Bertram L. Melbourne, "Acts 1:8 Re-Examined: Is Acts 8 Its Fulfillment?" *JRT* 57/58, no. 2/1/2 (2005): 8–9, 15–16.

[14] The Gospel of John does not utilize summarization to advance its narrative as often as Acts and the Synoptic Gospels do. However, two summary statements appear in close proximity in this episode that describe the conversion of large numbers of people. "Now many Samaritans from that town believed in Him because of what the woman said" (John 4:39). "Many more believed because of what He [Jesus] said" (John 4:41). On summarization in John's Gospel, see R. Alan Culpepper, *Anatomy of the Fourth Gospel: A Study in Literary Design* (Philadelphia: Fortress Press, 1983); 70–75.

[15] On the Samaritan view of the arrival of Christianity in their region, see Robert T. Anderson and Terry Giles, *Tradition Kept: The Literature of the Samaritans* (Peabody, MA: Hendrickson, 2005), 252–61. On the Samaritans in the NT, see Morton S. Enslin, "The Samaritan Ministry and

of the Samaritans to the gospel. Crowds gathered, and they listened "with one mind" to Philip's message (Acts 8:6; cf. 2:46; 5:12).[16] Philip's preaching was accompanied by the performance of signs (8:6,13; cf. 2:43; 5:12), exorcisms, and healings (8:7; cf. 5:16). The Samaritans turned to Christ in large numbers (cf. 2:41,47; 5:14) as evidenced not only by many healings, but also by the great joy in the city (8:8; cf. 2:26,28,46). Both men and women believed and were baptized, including a man named Simon who had previously practiced sorcery (8:12–13; cf. 2:38,41; 5:14).

The apostles in Jerusalem heard that Samaria had accepted the word of God. They sent Peter and John who prayed for them to receive the Holy Spirit and laid hands on them (Acts 8:14–17; cf. 2:1–4; 5:12). The visit from two of the most prominent apostles and their endorsement of what they saw demonstrates that a sense of continuity and cooperation existed early on between the church in Jerusalem and the new church in Samaria.[17] When Peter and John returned to Jerusalem, they preached the word of the Lord in many Samaritan villages (8:25; cf. 4:33a).

Another reference to the Samaritan church occurs in the summary statement in Acts 9:31. In it we learn that the church in Samaria had peace after the conversion of Saul. The church was built up and walked in the fear of the Lord (cf. 2:43) and the encouragement of the Holy Spirit (cf. 2:4; 4:31). It also increased in numbers (cf. 2:41,47; 5:14). Acts does not tell readers any more about the church in Samaria after 9:31.[18] However, Luke makes one thing clear. The Samaritans, a people estranged from the Jews for many generations, now were responding to the gospel of Jesus in the same manner as Jews in Jerusalem.[19] The echoes of exemplary life in the Jerusalem church, heard in Samaria, reinforce Luke's message about

---

Mission," *HUCA* 51 (1980): 29–38; and Gerard S. Sloyan, "The Samaritans in the New Testament," *Hor* 10, no. 1 (1983): 7–21.

[16] The word *homothumadon* has already been used by Luke to describe believers being together in the same place (Acts 2:46) as well as believers committing to meet together (5:12). Both senses seem to be implied here (Steve Walton, "Ὁμοθυμαδόν in Acts," *The New Testament in Its First Century Setting: Essays in Context and Background in Honor of B. W. Winter on His 65th Birthday*, ed. P. J. Williams, Andrew D. Clarke, Peter M. Head, and David Instone-Brewer [Grand Rapids: Eerdmans, 2004], 100).

[17] Tannehill, *Narrative Unity of Luke-Acts: Acts*, 104.

[18] Little is known outside of the NT about the fate of the early Christian movement in Samaria. For archeological and epigraphic evidence for early Samaritan Christianity, see Reinhard Pummer, "New Evidence for Samaritan Christianity?" *CBQ* 41 (1979): 98–117.

[19] V. J. Samkutty, *The Samaritan Mission in Acts*, Library of New Testament Studies 328 (New York: T&T Clark, 2006), 36, 51.

church life in the summary narratives. They also prepare readers for more echoes of exemplary life in his portrait of church life in Antioch.

Exemplary Church Life in Antioch (Acts 11:19–30; 13:1–3)

In Acts 11:19–30 we encounter a lengthy description of the newly planted church in Antioch that, like the description of gospel preaching in Samaria, echoes the summary narratives repeatedly. Built on the Orontes River in what is now modern Turkey, the city of Antioch grew in size and influence until it was the third largest city in the Empire behind Rome and Alexandria, with a population of several hundred thousand. Antioch had a diverse population where race, culture, religion, and nationality mixed constantly, making it an ideal city for the beginning of the Gentile movement.[20]

The gospel came to Antioch with the Jewish believers who escaped the persecution in Judea (Acts 11:19; cf. 8:1). The theme of persecution, as much as any other emphasis in Acts, ties Luke's descriptions of church life in Jerusalem, Samaria, and Antioch together. Many of the believers went to Phoenicia, Cyprus, and Antioch and preached only to Jews (11:19). However, in Antioch some declared the "good news about the Lord Jesus" to Hellenists (*Hellēnistas*)[21] (11:20; cf. 4:33). The Greek word for "Hellenists" (ESV, HCSB, NKJV) has also been rendered "Greeks" (NIV, NASB, RSV) and "Gentiles" (GNT, NLT). It is difficult to translate with precision, because it appears in the New Testament only in Acts 6:1; 9:29; and 11:20 and means something different in each context. In 6:1 *Hellēnistas* refers to Hellenistic Jewish Christians. In 9:29 it refers to unbelieving Hellenistic Jews. Here in 11:20 Luke speaks of people who were fully immersed in Hellenism, the Greek culture and way of life, and probably had little formal association with Judaism.[22] His statement

---

[20] Frederick W. Norris, "Antioch of Syria," in *ABD*, 1:265–69; Lee Martin McDonald, "Antioch (Syria)," in *DNTB*, 34–37.

[21] Some uncertainty exists over the exact wording of Acts 11:20. *Hellēnistas* (Ἑλληνιστάς) is supported by B, D, E, P, and Y. *Hellēnas* (Ἕλληνας) is supported by p⁷⁴, ℵ, A, D*. Most scholars prefer the former reading, though the difference in meaning is not significant for Luke's purpose in Acts 11:20. See the discussion in Bruce M. Metzger, *A Textual Commentary on the Greek New Testament* (Stuttgart: United Bible Societies, 1971), 386–89.

[22] Ben Witherington III, *The Acts of the Apostles: A Socio-Rhetorical Commentary* (Grand Rapids: Eerdmans, 1998), 240–47. J. Julius Scott Jr., "The Church's Progress to the Council of Jerusalem according to the Book of Acts," *BBR* 7 (1997): 215 n. 25, is even more precise, identifying the Hellenists of Antioch as members of an urban-centered society that placed a high priority on culture. In his words, these weren't "just any uncircumcised Gentiles, but *urban, cultured* ones." For

demonstrates that a door was thrown open in Antioch. A line was crossed in Caesarea in Cornelius's home when he and his Gentile family believed, but his was one family (10:1–11:18, esp. 11:18). In Antioch, the gospel was preached no longer to Jews only, or even half Jews in Samaria, but now to anyone in the city who would listen. Also, the apostles were not the primary preachers of the gospel. Lay people, the believers scattered in the persecution, founded and initially led the church in Antioch.[23]

Three times in his account Luke refers to large numbers who became believers in Antioch (Acts 11:21,24,26).[24] This echoes the theme of the explosive growth of the mother church in Jerusalem (2:41,47; 4:4; 5:14; 6:1,7). The hand of the Lord was with the preaching of Christ in Antioch (11:21), just as God's hand and power accompanied the testimony of the apostles in Jerusalem (4:30,33).[25] Luke does not attribute the success of the gospel to any responsiveness in Antioch or the skill of the witnesses. All three references to numerical growth credit God's gracious intervention in the city (cf. 2:47a).[26]

When the church in Jerusalem heard about the many conversions in Antioch, they sent Barnabas there, presumably to investigate (Acts 11:22–24; cf. 8:14). The grace of God was evident to Barnabas in Antioch, just as it was in Jerusalem (11:23; cf. 4:33b; 14:26). What Barnabas saw made his heart glad (*ekarē*), like the gladness of the believers in Jerusalem (11:23; cf. 2:46).[27] Barnabas urged them to "remain true to the Lord with a firm resolve of the heart," like the commitment of the church in Jerusalem (11:23; cf. 2:42,46). Barnabas was "a good man, full of the Holy Spirit and of faith" (11:24), like the Seven in Jerusalem who were appointed to oversee the distribution of food (6:3,5) and the believers in the Jerusalem church (2:1–4,38; 4:31). Both churches emphasized teaching and the discipleship of new converts. The apostles were the primary teachers

---

more background on the term Hellenist and who it represents see Greg R. Stanton, "Hellenism," in *DNTB*, 468–70.

[23] Norman E. Thomas, "The Church at Antioch: Crossing Racial, Cultural, and Class Barriers," in *Mission in Acts: Ancient Narratives in Contemporary Context*, ed. Robert L. Gallagher and Paul Hertig (Maryknoll, NY: Orbis Books, 2004), 146–48.

[24] "A large number" (*polus te arithmos*) in 11:21 and "a large crowd" (*ochlos hikanos*) in 11:24,26 (ἱκανός is in the accusative case in Acts 11:26, ἱκανόν).

[25] Luke Timothy Johnson, *The Acts of the Apostles*, SP (Collegeville, MN: Michael Glazier, 1992), 203.

[26] Stenschke, *Luke's Portrait of Gentiles*, 164–65.

[27] Luke used *agalliassei* to indicate the believer's gladness in the Jerusalem church (Acts 2:46) and *ekarē* here, but both terms express the joyful disposition of the believers (BAGD, 3, 873–74).

in Jerusalem, and Saul and Barnabas were the lead teachers in Antioch (11:25–26; cf. 2:42; 5:42; 6:4).

The disciples were called Christians for the first time in Antioch (Acts 11:26). That they were called Christians indicates that the label was first applied by outsiders. Whether the designation is meant pejoratively is not made clear. The term appears only three times in the New Testament, with two of the occurrences in Acts (11:26; 26:28; also 1 Pet 4:16). The more common word for the Jesus movement in Acts is "the Way" (Acts 9:2; 19:9; 22:4; 24:14,22; cf. John 14:6). The designation "Christian" is, however, significant for what happened in Antioch. *Christianios* is a Greek term with a Latin form and a Semitic background. Thus, the word itself encapsulates the cosmopolitan nature of the Gentile mission in Antioch.[28] It also implies that the disciples in Antioch had a connection to Judaism but that they were distinct from it too. The term connected the disciples to Judaism in that although they were ethnically and culturally diverse, they identified in their faith with Jesus, the Jewish Messiah. Yet, it distinguished them from Judaism by suggesting that a separate identity had emerged in Antioch for a movement that formerly attracted only Jews.[29]

Perhaps the most striking parallel between the churches in Jerusalem and Antioch is their generosity. The believers in the Jerusalem church gave freely to help each other (Acts 2:44–45; 4:34–37). In Antioch a prophet named Agabus predicted through the Spirit that a severe famine would cover the entire Roman world. Such a famine occurred during the time of the emperor Claudius (11:27–28), and it affected provinces from Egypt through Syria over a several year period, including the residents of Antioch.[30] However, the Antioch church's first instinct was not self-preservation. Instead, they took up a relief offering to help their brothers in Judea. Everyone voluntarily participated, according to their means (11:29; cf. 2:45; 4:34), and the offering was sent to the elders of the church in Jerusalem (11:30; cf. 4:35a).

The city of Antioch possessed considerable wealth due to an abundance of natural resources and its strategic location on a trade route between

---

[28] Richard I. Pervo, *Acts*, Hermeneia (Minneapolis: Fortress, 2009), 294–95.

[29] Bock, *Acts*, 416; Arthur G. Patzia, *The Emergence of the Church: Context, Growth, Leadership, and Worship* (Downers Grove, IL: IVP Academic, 2001), 101; John E. Stambaugh and David L. Balch, *The New Testament in Its Social Environment* (Philadelphia: Westminster Press, 1986), 148–49.

[30] Bruce W. Winter, "Acts and Food Shortages," in *The Book of Acts in Its Graeco-Roman Setting*, ed. David W. J. Gill and Conrad Gempf (Grand Rapids: Eerdmans, 1994), 65–69.

Asia and the Mediterranean.[31] It is not unreasonable to assume that some members of the church in Antioch were owners of lands and houses like the property owners in the Jerusalem church (Acts 4:34,36–37). Yet, God's grace worked powerfully in the lives of these Gentile Christians, so that they showed the same concern for their Jewish Christian neighbors to the south that God commanded Israel to show to the poor and the foreigners among them (Lev 23:22; 25:35; Deut 15:4).

A second snapshot of church life in Antioch appears in Acts 13:1–3, where several additional echoes of the Jerusalem church can be heard. The church in Antioch contained prophets and teachers, which indicates the importance of teaching to church life (13:1; cf. 2:42).[32] On one occasion the church was ministering to the Lord in worship when the Holy Spirit interrupted their meeting with instructions (13:2). He told them to "set apart for Me Barnabas and Saul for the work that I have called them to" (13:2b). The Holy Spirit demonstrated His sovereignty in Antioch as the initiator of the Gentile mission, just as He gave birth to the church in Jerusalem (cf. 2:1–41). The church did four things in response (13:3). They fasted and prayed (cf. 2:42; 6:6); laid hands on Barnabas and Saul to consecrate them to the Lord (cf. 6:6); and sent them off—and the Gentile mission was launched. Antioch became the first major Hellenistic city in which Christianity gained a foothold.[33] The three major missionary journeys in Acts into Gentile lands were initiated in Antioch (see 13:1–14:28; 15:36–18:22; 18:23–21:19), making it a strategic city in the transition of the Christian faith from a sect within Judaism to good news for the nations.

Luke's description of church life in Antioch is remarkable for the way it echoes Jerusalem church life in the summary narratives. The parallels are all the more striking when one considers how different the cultures of these two churches were. The church in Antioch was made up primarily of Gentiles with little or no exposure to Judaism. The church in Jerusalem was made up exclusively of Jews. Yet, when Luke's descriptions of these two fellowships are compared, similar images emerge.[34] The gospel is preached in power. Large numbers believe. Teaching the word of God is

---

[31] McDonald, "Antioch," 34. The Jewish population of Antioch participated in its growing economy and wealth as well. See Irina Levinskaya, *The Book of Acts in Its Diaspora Setting* (Grand Rapids: Eerdmans, 1996), 127–35; and Stambaugh and Balch, *New Testament in Its Social Environment*, 145–48, for discussion of the Jewish experience in Antioch.

[32] John H. Orme, "Antioquía: Paradigma para la Iglesia y la Misión," *Kairos* 25 (1999): 31–32.

[33] Patzia, *Emergence of the Church*, 99.

[34] Richard P. Thompson, *Keeping the Church in Its Place: The Church as Narrative Character in Acts* (New York: T&T Clark, 2006), 150, 152–53.

foundational to church life. Teaching in the Gentile church is rooted in the teaching about the Jewish Messiah. God's people give sacrificially to meet the needs of others, and so on. The numerous echoes of the summary narratives in Acts 11:19–30 amplify Luke's convictions about what exemplary church life should look like, as expressed in the summary narratives.

Exemplary Church Life in Ephesus (18:19–21,24–26; 19:1–20; 20:17–38)

The next major depiction of Gentile church life occurs in the account of Paul's ministry in Ephesus (Acts 18:19–26; 19:1–20) and Paul's assessment of his Ephesian ministry in a speech he gave in Miletus (20:17–38).

Paul's Ministry in Ephesus. The ministry in Ephesus began when Paul arrived with Priscilla and Aquila (Acts 18:19a). The strategic location of Ephesus at the mouth of the Cayster River and on a major east-west trade route made it a major city in the Roman Empire. Numerous cultures and ethnic groups converged there, as well as many ancient religions, with the Artemis cult as the most famous (19:23–28). Ephesus also had a large and prosperous Jewish community.[35]

Paul first spoke to the Jews in the synagogue. They wanted Paul to spend more time with them, but he had to leave with the promise that he would try to return (Acts 18:19b–21). Paul left Priscilla and Aquila in Ephesus to continue the ministry. They were joined by a Jew from Alexandria named Apollos. It is not made clear whether Paul actually started the church in Ephesus, or if it was founded by Priscilla, Aquila, and Apollos after Paul left.[36] Apollos was known as one who "taught the things about Jesus accurately" but had only heard of John's baptism. Priscilla and Aquila invited Apollos into their home and explained the way of God more adequately to him (18:24–26).

Several echoes of church life in Jerusalem can already be heard in the mission to Ephesus. Paul and his friends focused on teaching from the beginning of their time in Ephesus (cf. Acts 2:42). Paul taught in the synagogue. Priscilla, Aquila, and Apollos continued his teaching ministry. When Apollos needed extra instruction himself, it occurred in Priscilla and Aquila's home (cf. 2:46; 5:42).

---

[35] Lee Martin McDonald, "Ephesus," in *DNTB*, 319; Clinton E. Arnold, "Centers of Christianity," in *DLNT*, 146–47. On what Paul might have seen in Ephesus, see Jerome Murphy O'Connor, *St. Paul's Ephesus: Texts and Archaeology* (Collegeville, MN: Liturgical Press, 2008), 186–200. On the Jewish experience in Ephesus, see Levinskaya, *Acts in Its Diaspora Setting*, 143–48.

[36] McDonald, "Antioch," 319.

Paul returned to Ephesus and found disciples who had experienced the baptism of John, but they did not know about the Holy Spirit (Acts 19:1–3). Debate exists over whether Luke thinks of these disciples as believers. For Darrell Bock, the implication of Luke calling them "believers" in verse 2 is that they were Christians whose instruction was incomplete.[37] However, they still needed Paul to explain that John called people not only to repent but also to believe in the One coming after him (Acts 19:4; cf. Luke 3:1–18; John 1:29–34). It makes more sense to see them as non-Christians who either learned about the baptism of repentance from John (Luke 3:3) or perhaps from some of his followers who left John and made their way to Ephesus before Jesus was revealed to Israel (John 1:29).[38] When Paul explained the gospel, they were (re)baptized, this time in the name of Jesus (Acts 19:5; cf. 2:38,41; 8:12,36–38). Paul laid hands on them, and the Holy Spirit came upon them. They began to speak in other languages (*elaloun glōssais*) and to prophesy (*eprophēteuon*) (19:6), like the Jewish believers in Jerusalem (2:1–4).

The phenomenon in Acts of persons receiving the Holy Spirit, or at least visibly manifesting His presence, after they believed raises questions about the relationship between believing, baptism, laying on hands, and the reception of the Holy Spirit in Acts. No clear pattern can be identified.[39] In Jerusalem on Pentecost Day, repentance, faith, reception of the Holy Spirit, and baptism are grouped together as multiple aspects of conversion, and there appears to be a logical order to them (Acts 2:38,41). In Samaria the Spirit came upon the believers after baptism and after the apostles laid hands on them (8:14–17). In Cornelius's home in Caesarea, the Spirit came down before Peter even finished preaching (!), and certainly before they could profess their faith publicly and be baptized (10:44–47). In Ephesus the Spirit came after baptism and after Paul laid hands on the believers (19:5–6). Elsewhere Scripture affirms that the Holy Spirit precedes conversion as the One who convicts of sin, who gives the new birth, and the only One by whom anyone can confess that Jesus is Lord (John 3:3–6; 16:8–11; 1 Cor 12:3; Gal 3:2–3).

Speaking in tongues appears as evidence of the Spirit's reception by the 120 believers in Jerusalem (Acts 2:1–17), Caesarea (11:15–17; 15:8),

---

[37] Bock, *Acts*, 599. Also, Mikael C. Parsons, *Acts*, Paideia: Commentaries on the New Testament (Grand Rapids: Baker, 2008), 264–65.

[38] Witherington, *Acts*, 569–71; David Peterson, *The Acts of the Apostles*, PNTC (Grand Rapids: Eerdmans, 2009), 530–31; Polhill, *Acts*, 398–99.

[39] Polhill, *Acts*, 400.

and in Ephesus (19:6). However, speaking in tongues is not mentioned in relation to the 3,000 who believed in Jerusalem (2:41) nor in relation to the new believers in Samaria (8:17). Added to all this is the fact that speaking in tongues is not reported in most church planting situations in Acts, and it does not appear in the summary narratives at all. Can an exact pattern be inferred from the data in Acts that readers should expect to see in their own church situation? To attempt this would be to forget the utterly unique circumstances of the first-generation church in Acts. The gospel was moving rapidly from Judaism outward to the nations. It was a time of tremendous upheaval and transition. Believing Jews faced the unrepeatable circumstance of Gentiles, who were formerly outsiders to Israel, for the first time ever being included in God's people apart from becoming Jews. Believing Jews needed confirmation that God had indeed granted repentance to the Gentiles (10:18; 15:7–9). What can be affirmed at a minimum as universal is that the Holy Spirit is Lord over and intimately involved in both conversion and in the movement of the gospel across ethnic and cultural boundaries. Beyond this, Justo González's advice is instructive: "Let us not claim to know more than we really know, nor try to limit and to control the action of the Spirit."[40]

Luke continues his description of the ministry in Ephesus with Paul preaching in the synagogue for three months (Acts 19:8). Paul was eventually rejected by the Jews, and he took the disciples he gained with him and for two years held daily discussions in the lecture hall of Tyrannus (19:9). The word for "lecture hall" (*scholē*) can refer to either a building where public discussions were held or to a school building.[41] It was owned by Tyrannus, who either rented or perhaps even donated its use to the Ephesian church for its larger assemblies. The presumably public meetings held there were combined with instruction in smaller groups in multiple homes throughout Ephesus (20:20). Once again, teaching is a major theme of the ministry in Ephesus (cf. 2:42). Paul's missionary strategy changed during his time in Ephesus too. Instead of an itinerant ministry, Paul poured himself into one city for an extended period of time.[42] For Paul to have invested so much time in one place means he was likely able to teach in depth on a wide range of subjects and Scripture texts. The

---

[40] Justo L. González, *Acts: The Gospel of the Spirit* (Maryknoll, NY: Orbis Books, 2001), 220. Of tremendous help on the relationship between salvation and Spirit baptism is Chad O. Brand, ed., *Perspectives on Spirit Baptism: Five Views* (Nashville: B&H, 2004).

[41] Bock, *Acts*, 601; LSJ, 1747.

[42] Patzia, *Emergence of the Church*, 127.

church of Ephesus was surely blessed during Paul's extended stay.[43] As a result the word of the Lord was heard by Jews and Greeks throughout the province of Asia (19:10), and Ephesus became a great center for church planting in this part of the Roman Empire.[44]

Acts 19:11–19 describes the amazing miracles God performed through Paul.[45] God's power was so great through Paul that even handkerchiefs and aprons that touched him were taken to the sick, and they were cured, and the evil spirits left them (19:11–12; cf. 5:15–16). On one occasion, an evil spirit answered some Jewish exorcists who were trying to drive it out of a man (19:13–17). The demon said that he knew about Jesus and Paul but not them. He gave the exorcists such a beating that everyone in Ephesus heard about it. Great fear fell on the city (19:17; cf. 2:43; 5:11), and the name of the Lord Jesus was magnified (19:17; cf. 2:47). The failed exorcism implicitly affirmed God's presence among the believers whose Lord and His apostle Paul this demon clearly feared.[46] Many repented and believed, and a great turning to God occurred (19:18–19; cf. 2:38–41; 3:19). The result was that the word of the Lord continued to spread widely and grow in power (19:20; cf. 6:7; 9:31; 12:24; 16:5).

Paul's ministry in Ephesus eventually aroused opposition (cf. Acts 4:1–22; 5:17–42). Demetrius the silversmith and other craftsmen were angry over how Paul's preaching had cut into their idol-making business (19:23–27). A riot nearly occurred until the city clerk was able to disperse the crowd (19:28–41). The anger of the craftsmen in Ephesus against Paul's success echoes the rage of the Jewish leaders who persecuted the apostles for preaching the resurrection of Jesus in Jerusalem (cf. 5:33). When the gospel is preached courageously, it will stir opposition among people who do not want to hear it.

Paul's Review of His Ministry in Ephesus (The Miletus Speech). Paul left Ephesus and traveled more (Acts 20:1–16), eventually arriving at Miletus where he called the elders of the church in Ephesus to meet him

---

[43] James D. G. Dunn, *Beginning from Jerusalem*, Christianity in the Making (Grand Rapids: Eerdmans, 2009), 769.

[44] Arnold, "Centers of Christianity," 146–47; Patzia, *Emergence of the Church*, 127–28.

[45] Josep Rius-Camps, "Els tres sumaris dels Fets dels Apòstols (Ac 2,41–47; 4,32–5,16 i 19,11–19)," *RCT* 14 (1989): 243–56, identified a tryptich (three-panel) structure in Acts 19:11–19 that parallels the structure of 4:32–5:16. Both begin and end with a summary (4:32–35; 5:12–16; cf. 19:11–12,18–19), and both contain a concrete illustration of the summaries between them (4:36–5:11; cf. 19:13–17).

[46] Thompson, *Keeping the Church in Its Place*, 214; Dunn, *Beginning from Jerusalem*, 771–73; Stenschke, *Luke's Portrait of Gentiles*, 224–27.

(20:17). When they arrived Paul reviewed his ministry with them in an extended time of teaching (20:18–35; cf. 2:42). Paul did not expect to return to Ephesus, which made his message a sort of farewell speech that has much in common with earlier farewell speeches in the Old and New Testaments.[47] His sermon also has much in common with the art of persuasive speech-making, which used forms and strategies of Greco-Roman rhetoric, although the particular speech form Paul may have utilized is disputed.[48]

Paul exhorted the elders of the Ephesian church to exemplary behavior in light of his personal example and the looming threat of false teachers. Numerous echoes of Jerusalem church life appear in Paul's Miletus sermon.[49] Paul mentioned the persecution he faced (Acts 20:19; cf. 4:1–31; 5:13,17–41). He taught in Ephesus publicly and from house to house (20:20,27,31) in a way similar to how the Jerusalem church met in the temple complex and in each other's homes (2:42,46; 5:42). Teaching "in public" (*dēmosia*) referred to teaching in important open places in Ephesus where political and civic activities might occur. Teaching "from house to house" (*kat' oikous*) refers to private household gatherings across the city of Ephesus.[50] The sense is that Paul was at home teaching about Jesus anywhere in Ephesus, both in significant cultural centers and in the intimate setting of personal residences. Wherever he preached, and whether preaching to Jews or Greeks, he called people to repentance and faith in

---

[47] See, for example, Jacob's blessing on his sons (Genesis 49), Moses' final blessing on Israel (Deuteronomy 33), Joshua's covenant renewal speech at Shechem (Josh 24:1–28), Samuel's farewell speech (1 Samuel 12), and Jesus' teaching at the Last Supper (John 13–17) (Polhill, *Acts*, 422–23).

[48] The two primary positions currently argued are that Paul's Miletus address is an example of either epideictic or deliberative rhetoric. Epideictic rhetoric highlights important beliefs and values embodied by the subject matter of the speech, which the speaker wants to affirm in the minds of hearers. Duane F. Watson, "Paul's Speech to the Ephesian Elders (Acts 20:17–38) Epideictic Rhetoric of Farewell," in *Persuasive Artistry: Studies in New Testament Rhetoric in Honor of George A. Kennedy*, ed. Duane F. Watson (Sheffield, England: Sheffield Academic Press, 1991), 184–208; and George A. Kennedy, *New Testament Interpretation through Rhetorical Criticism* (Chapel Hill: University of North Carolina Press, 1984), 132–33, categorize Paul's sermon as an epideictic farewell speech. Deliberative rhetoric is similar to epideictic, but the emphasis is more on recommending a specific course of action to hearers in light of the speaker's arguments. Witherington, *Acts*, 612–14, sees the speech as an example of deliberative rhetoric. On the distinction, see the entries on "Deliberative Rhetoric" (124), "Epideictic Rhetoric" (162), and "Rhetorical Genres" (418–420) in David E. Aune, *The Westminster Dictionary of New Testament and Early Christian Literature and Rhetoric* (Louisville, KY: Westminster John Knox, 2003).

[49] Beverly R. Gaventa, "Theology and Ecclesiology in the Miletus Speech: Reflections on Content and Context," *NTS* 50 (2004): 43, notes several. See also Thompson, *Keeping the Church in Its Place*, 220–23.

[50] Jerome H. Neyrey, "'Teaching You in Public and from House to House' (Acts 20.20): Unpacking a Cultural Stereotype," *JSNT* 26 (2003): 98, 102.

the Lord Jesus (20:21; cf. 2:38; 3:19). The Holy Spirit ruled over the work in the Ephesian church as He did in Jerusalem, Samaria, and Antioch (20:22–23,28; cf. 2:1–4,38; 4:31; 8:17; 13:2–3).[51] Paul testified to the gospel of God's grace in Ephesus as well (20:24,32; cf. 4:33). In 20:32 Paul reminded the elders that the message of God's grace can build up the church (cf. Eph 4:29) and give her an inheritance among those who are sanctified. This is another way of saying that even though Paul knew he had to leave, the message of grace he preached was lasting and would make them secure. God will never abandon His work or His people.[52]

Paul exhorted the elders to shepherd the church and to be alert for false teachers (Acts 20:28–31), reminding them of how he taught them the whole plan of God (20:27). The best way to accomplish this would be to give close attention to Paul's teaching the way the Jerusalem church devoted themselves to the teachings of the apostles (cf. 2:42). Paul reminded them of God's sovereign initiative, when the Holy Spirit made them overseers of the Ephesian church (20:28). God's initiative is stressed in Jerusalem in the witness of the believers and apostles (cf. 1:8; 2:4,11,17–18) and in the conversion of people to Christ (cf. 2:47). Paul emphasized in Ephesus what Christ accomplished through the cross in the same manner as Peter when he preached the death and resurrection of Jesus (20:28; cf. 2:23; 3:13–16; 4:10–12,33).

Paul pointed out how he provided for his own needs and for the needs of his companions. He set an example for how "we must help the weak," because Jesus said that "it is more blessed to give than to receive" (Acts 20:33–35; cf. 2:44–45; 4:34–35). By closing his record of Paul's address with these words, Luke is able to tie Paul's teaching to both the portrait of the Jerusalem church in the summary narratives and to Jesus' teachings about generosity (Luke 12:33; 14:12–14; 18:22; 19:8; 21:3–4).[53]

After Paul finished teaching, the church prayed together, which was an important practice in the Jerusalem church (Acts 20:36; cf. 2:42; 4:23–31). Finally, their tears and expressions of grief as they parted reveal the

---

[51] Robert Banks, "The Role of Charismatic and Noncharismatic Factors in Determining Paul's Movements in Acts," in Stanton, Barton, and Longenecker, *The Holy Spirit and Christian Origins*, 126–28.

[52] Dean S. Gilliland, "For Missionaries and Leaders: Paul's Farewell to the Ephesian Elders," in Gallagher and Hertig, *Mission in Acts*, 268.

[53] Paul Mumo Kisau, "The Sharing of Goods with the Poor Is a Christian Imperative," *Africa Journal of Evangelical Theology* 19, no. 1 (2000): 31.

loyalty, closeness, and fellowship these believers shared with each other, like the unity that existed in the Jerusalem church (20:37; cf. 4:32).

The echoes of exemplary Jerusalem church life in the description of Gentile church life in Ephesus are so numerous that the attentive reader is led to ask what Luke is trying to accomplish with them. Here is a Gentile church planted in Ephesus that represented the cultural and ethnic diversity of first-century Asia Minor. Yet, nearly everything Luke says about this church, whether through his narrator (Acts 18:19–21,24–26; 19:1–20) or through Paul's speech in Miletus (20:17–38), echoes either directly or indirectly some aspect of Jewish church life in Jerusalem. Two implicit affirmations are unavoidable. First, Luke wants to show that the power of God at work through Paul in the Gentile church of Ephesus was the same power found in Peter and the apostles' ministry in the Jerusalem church. Both the Jewish mission and the Gentile mission are affirmed, because God was present with the power to change lives in both places. Second, Luke does not show the church in Ephesus severing all ties with Jerusalem. Instead, his portrait of church life in Ephesus keeps bringing readers back to his portrait of exemplary church life in Jerusalem in the summary narratives, just as he does in his portraits of church life in Samaria and Antioch.[54] Luke presents his portrait of church life in Ephesus and Paul's review of his ministry there as examples from which readers could learn.[55] However, his description of exemplary church life in Ephesus is amplified all the more by its constant echoes of exemplary church life in Jerusalem. One final example of echo effect in Acts will drive this point home.

Exemplary Church Life in Troas (Acts 20:7–12)

The final portrait of Gentile church life in Acts to consider is Paul's ministry in Troas. The city of Troas is located in what is modern-day Turkey on the coast of the Aegean Sea, ten miles south of the ancient city of Troy. It has been called an artificial city, because it lacked the normal institutions of Greek civic life that could create strong social, political, and religious bonds among its people. It was made up of traders, sojourners, and elements of older communities that had a Roman colony forced

---

[54] Tannehill, *Narrative Unity of Luke-Acts: Acts*, 237–40.

[55] Jan Lambrecht, "Paul's Farewell-Address at Miletus (Acts 20, 17–38)," in Kremer, *Les Actes des Apôtres*, 328–37; Thomas E. Phillips, "Paul as a Role Model in Acts: The 'We' Passages in Acts 16 and Beyond," in *Acts and Ethics*, ed. Thomas E. Phillips, New Testament Monographs (Sheffield, England: Sheffield Academic Press, 2005), 58–61.

upon them, but they were never well integrated.[56] Paul's normal pattern was to seek major urban centers of cultural influence with large Jewish communities as a beachhead for evangelizing Roman provinces, but he did not neglect smaller cities like Troas when the opportunity arose. Paul had already stopped over in Troas earlier, where he had his vision of a man of Macedonia (Acts 16:9). It has been suggested that Paul planted the church in Troas at this time. However, it does not appear that he stayed long enough in Troas his first time through to accomplish this, unless his mention of finding an open door for the gospel in Troas in 2 Cor 2:12 is a reference to his visit in Acts 16:8–11.[57] On this occasion he went through Troas to avoid capture by the Jews (Acts 20:3–6). The summary of church life in Troas is shorter than the portraits of Gentile church life in Antioch and Ephesus. Yet, Luke's account of the church at worship echoes several major themes from the summary narratives.

The believers in Troas gathered on the first day of the week (Acts 20:7). The phrase "first day of the week" (*en tē mia tōn sabbatōn*) means the "first day after the Sabbath." It is unclear whether this refers to our Saturday or Sunday evening, because Luke does not clarify whether he is following the Jewish or the Roman method for reckoning the start of a day. Jews began their day at sundown and the Romans at midnight. The church meeting happened at night. So, if Luke follows the Jewish way of reckoning time, the church met on Saturday evening, the beginning of the first day after the Sabbath. If he followed the Roman reckoning, the church met on Sunday evening.[58] Either way, in Troas the first indication appears that Christians had begun to assemble for worship on a day other than the Jewish Sabbath. It is logical to suppose that many Jewish Christians continued to honor their ancient tradition regarding the Sabbath. However, the Christian movement eventually established the first day of the week (1 Cor 16:2) as the "Lord's day" (Rev 1:10), because Jesus' resurrection occurred then (Luke 24:1).[59] As to when this transition occurred, and whether one day is indicated as more sacred than another for Christian worship, the New Testament gives

---

[56] Colin J. Hemer, "Alexandria Troas," *TynBul* 26 (1975): 92, 95. Also see Hemer's entry on Troas in *NBD*[3], 1211–12.

[57] Paul also mentions visiting Troas again and leaving his cloak and important documents there with Carpus (2 Tim 4:13). This visit probably occurred at a time after Paul's appeal to Caesar was resolved (i.e., beyond the close of Acts), when Paul presumably was able to continue his missionary work.

[58] Witherington, *Acts*, 606.

[59] See *Did.* 14.1; and Ignatius, *Magn.* 9.1; *Barn.* 15.9; and Justin, *1 Apol.* 67, for postapostolic Christian references to Sunday as the Lord's Day. Also see Pliny, *Ep.* 10.96.7.

more description than prescription and instead leaves the matter to the consciences of individual believers (Rom 14:5–6).[60]

The church in Troas met "to break bread" (*klasai arton*, Acts 20:7; cf. 2:42,46). The context does not clarify whether Luke means that the church shared the Lord's Supper that night, or if he means they shared a meal together, or both.[61] Luke may be assuming that his readers would know what he means. The phrase probably includes both practices, since the early church often shared the Lord's Supper together as a part of fellowship meals (cf. Acts 2:42,46; 1 Cor 11:20–34).[62] The church apparently held its regular Sunday meetings in the evenings, which would not have seemed out of the ordinary in the first-century Roman world. The ancient world did not have weekends, so Sunday may have been a work day for Gentile believers, like any other day.[63] Because Paul had to leave the next day, he taught until midnight. There were many lamps in the room (Acts 20:8). A sense of foreboding is built here as the scene is set up. The room was crowded, the many torches likely consumed much of the oxygen in the room, and the hour was late. A young man named Eutychus was seated in a window sill, sinking into a deep sleep, as Paul "kept on speaking" (*dialegomenou tou epi pleion*, 20:9a).[64] One cannot help but hear Luke, who

---

[60] Further discussion of the issues surrounding the development of Sunday as the Christian day of worship can be found in Jon C. Laansma, "Lord's Day," in *DLNT*, 679–86, esp. 680–81; and D. A. Carson, ed., *From Sabbath to Lord's Day: A Biblical, Historical and Theological Investigation* (Eugene, OR: Wipf and Stock, 2000). For a helpful treatment of biblical and practical issues concerning how Christians should relate to the Sabbath today, see *Perspectives on the Sabbath: Four Views*, ed. Christopher John Donato (Nashville: B&H Academic, 2011).

[61] I. Howard Marshall, *The Acts of the Apostles*, New Testament Guides (Sheffield, UK: Sheffield Academic Press, 2001), 325; F. Scott Spencer, *Journeying through Acts: A Literary-Cultural Reading* (Peabody, MA: Hendrickson, 2004), 202; and Joseph A. Fitzmyer, *The Acts of the Apostles: A New Translation with Introduction and Commentary*, AB (New York: Doubleday, 1998), 669, see "to break bread" as a reference to the Lord's Supper. Peterson, *Acts*, 557; Bock, *Acts*, 619; C. K. Barrett, *Acts 15–28*, ICC (New York: T&T Clark, 1998), 950; and Robert W. Wall, "The Acts of the Apostles," in *NIB*, 277, see the phrase as a reference to a fellowship meal.

[62] The view of Witherington, *Acts*, 606; F. F. Bruce, *The Book of the Acts*, NICNT, rev. ed. (Grand Rapids: Eerdmans, 1988), 384; and Polhill, *Acts*, 418.

[63] J. Bradley Chance, *Acts*, SHBC (Macon, GA: Smyth & Helwys, 2007), 366.

[64] Andrew Arterbury, "The Downfall of Eutychus: How Ancient Understandings of Sleep Illuminate Acts 20:7–12," in *Contemporary Studies in Acts*, ed. Thomas E. Phillips (Macon, GA: Mercer University Press, 2009), 201–21 (following the Venerable Bede's eighth-century commentary on this text), has proposed the intriguing theory that Luke also intended for readers to understand the sleep of Eutychus metaphorically as a reference to spiritual slothfulness and inattentiveness. Sleep is used in this way in the NT (Rom 13:11; Eph 5:14; 1 Thess 5:6), and Jesus' disciples nearly missed moments of tremendous importance because of sleepiness (Luke 9:32; 22:39–46). It would be reading more into the text than Luke made clear to conclude that this was Luke's intention. Nevertheless, the analogy certainly points to poignant lessons about watchfulness.

witnessed the incident, gently ribbing his good friend Paul for "going long" that night.[65] Everything changed in an instant when Eutychus finally fell asleep and tumbled out of the window to his death (20:9b). The text indicates that Eutychus fell "from the third floor" (*apo tou tristegou*), which may indicate something about the socioeconomic status of the church in Troas. The better homes of antiquity were more likely to be one story. The poor in cities like Troas often lived in multifamily tenement buildings that could be several floors high.[66]

Paul raced downstairs and threw himself on the young man, and God raised him from the dead (Acts 20:10). The scene harkens back to Peter raising Tabitha earlier in Acts (Acts 9:38–41) and Jesus raising the son of the widow of Nain (Luke 7:11–17). The parallels to Elijah raising the son of the widow of Zarephath (1 Kgs 17:17–24) and Elisha raising the son of the Shunammite woman (2 Kgs 4:18–37) are especially striking, because in each circumstance the prophet physically laid upon the body before they were raised (2 Kgs 2:43; 5:15–16; 20:10). Perhaps Paul remembered what the prophets did in similar situations and simply imitated their actions. After Eutychus came back to life, Paul went back upstairs, "broke bread and ate" (*klasas ton arton kai geusamenos*) with the believers (Acts 20:11; cf. 2:46), and kept talking until dawn. Now, in Eutychus, they had a dramatic personal illustration of the message of the death and resurrection of Jesus in the Lord's Supper. The second reference to breaking bread in the Troas summary refers to a shared meal. One might reasonably conclude from Acts 20:7–12 that sharing meals, including the Lord's Supper, and being taught were central elements in church life in Troas (cf. Luke 10:38–42).

The summary of church life in Troas is brief. Nevertheless, it echoes several important themes of church life in the summary narratives, like a commitment to regular meetings, communion, teaching, miracles, and shared meals. These echoes would be very difficult for the attentive readers or hearers to miss. Like Luke's descriptions of church life in Samaria, Antioch, and Ephesus, his portrait of church life in Troas has much to teach readers. Yet, the lessons are amplified all the more by the subtle but powerful way they echo exemplary church life in the summary narratives.

---

[65] The NIV reads this nuance into the phrase by saying, "Paul talked on and on." See the NLT too.
[66] Barrett, *Acts 15–28*, 954; Marshall, *Acts*, 326.

SUMMARY

In this chapter I took cues from Tannehill's twofold strategy for analyzing the presence of echo effect in Acts. He applies his theory profitably to Acts 3–5.[67] I applied it to echoes of the summary narratives in Luke's descriptions of exemplary life in the Gentile churches of Acts. When Acts is read in a forward direction, echoes of the summary narratives can already be clearly heard. However, when Acts is read retrospectively with close attention given to these echoes, the results are dramatic. Many more examples could have been included beyond Samaria, Antioch, Ephesus, and Troas.[68] However, these four demonstrate that Luke has an agenda in writing Acts that goes beyond merely tracing the development of the Gentile movement. Luke also wants to offer readers a portrait of what life together could be like in the local church.

As the gospel was preached and churches were planted on the way to the ends of the earth (Acts 1:8), echoes of the summary narratives can be heard repeatedly in Luke's descriptions of the new congregations. Persecution often drove the gospel to new locations and occurred regularly in the cities where the apostles preached. The gospel of the resurrected Jesus was preached first to Samaritans and soon to anyone who would listen. The Gentiles repented of sin and believed. They were baptized, and new churches emerged. Numerical growth occurred regularly as multitudes of new believers swelled the ranks of the Gentile churches. They devoted themselves to being taught by the apostles. The apostles' message was often confirmed by signs and wonders, and the apostles on occasion saw the Holy Spirit's work among the Gentiles confirmed when they spoke in tongues. The believers in the new churches met in public places that could accommodate large groups. They also regularly shared meals and the Lord's Supper together in their homes. The Gentile churches were

---

[67] Tannehill, "Composition of Acts 3–5"; Tannehill, *The Shape of Luke's Story*, 185–219.

[68] Gospel preaching in Iconium and Philippi could have been added to the survey. Paul and his associates preached in Iconium, and a great number of Jews and Greeks believed (Acts 14:1; cf. 5:14; 11:21,24). They preached boldly (14:3; cf. 4:31) and relied on the Lord who gave evidence of His grace by granting signs and wonders through them (14:3; cf. 2:43; 4:33; 5:12). Even persecution played an important role in driving Paul and his friends out of the city of Iconium, where they evangelized the countryside (14:4–7; cf. 8:1–4; 11:19–21). When Paul preached in Philippi, he found a place of prayer and spoke to the women there about Jesus (16:13; cf. 2:42; 4:33; 5:14). God opened Lydia's heart, and she responded to Paul's message and was saved (16:14; cf. 2:47a). Lydia was baptized and invited Paul and his friends to her home (16:15,40; cf. 2:38,41; 2:46). Paul also preached Christ to a Philippian jailor and his family (16:30–32; cf. 4:33). The jailor and his family believed and were baptized, and they shared a meal together in his home (16:33–34; cf. 2:38,41,46).

characterized by unity, joy, gladness, boldness, resolve, prayer, encouragement, closeness, the fear of the Lord, the presence of grace from God, and by a deep generosity toward fellow believers. They were committed to helping the weak and the poor. The voluntary gift of the church in Antioch to the church in Jerusalem is especially striking in this regard. The church in Antioch was made up primarily of Gentiles, but their behavior echoed the exemplary generosity of the mother church in Jerusalem. The Holy Spirit oversaw the work of church planting and intervened often to guide the believers. These are the main echoes.

Every time an echo of the summary narratives is heard in descriptions of exemplary life in the Gentile churches, the message of the summary narratives is amplified all the more with three results. First, the descriptions reinforce the rhetorical force of Luke's portraits of exemplary life in the summary narratives. Second, they show the Gentile churches honoring their Jewish roots when life in their churches bears remarkable resemblance to church life in Jerusalem. Third, an implicit message is sent to readers and hearers of Acts that Luke's portraits of exemplary church life in the summary narratives ought to be taken seriously by them too.

CHAPTER SEVEN

A THEOLOGY OF CHURCH LIFE IN ACTS

C hapters 3 through 5 pursued a close reading of Luke's portraits of Jerusalem church life in the summary narratives. The goal was to understand what exemplary church life looks like from Luke's perspective in the summary narratives. The 24 statements below reiterate the findings of chapters 3 through 5 (all citations from Acts).

1. The believers committed themselves to the apostles' teaching (2:42).
2. The believers committed themselves to the fellowship (2:42).
3. The believers committed to breaking bread together (2:42).
4. The believers committed themselves to prayer (2:42).
5. The believers experienced the fear of the Lord (2:43).
6. God performed many wonders and signs through the apostles (2:43).
7. The believers shared in each other's lives (2:44).
8. The believers practiced radical generosity in giving to meet needs (2:45).

9. The believers devoted themselves to gathering daily in the temple complex (2:46).
10. The believers devoted themselves to the practice of hospitality in their homes (2:46).
11. The believers were continually praising God (2:47).
12. The believers cared for the people of Jerusalem (2:47).
13. People were saved and added to the fellowship daily (2:47).
14. The community of believers was knit together in unity (4:32).
15. The believers made their belongings available to other believers in need (4:32).
16. The apostles bore powerful witness to the resurrection of the Lord Jesus (4:33).
17. Great grace rested on all the believers (4:33).
18. The believers gave generously to help fellow believers in need (4:34–35).
19. God performed many signs and wonders through the apostles among the people (5:12a).
20. The believers committed to meeting together regularly (5:12b).
21. The potential cost of joining the church caused many to stay away (5:13a).
22. The people of Jerusalem spoke well of the church in their city (5:13b).
23. More and more believers were being added to the Lord (5:14).
24. The believers brought multitudes who were sick and tormented by unclean spirits to the apostles, and they were healed (5:15–16).

Chapter 6 surveyed the church-planting movements in Samaria, Antioch, Ephesus, and Troas, looking for aspects of church life already introduced in the summary narratives. The echoes of the summary narratives in the descriptions of Gentile church life amplify their rhetorical effect and drive home their message for readers. Chapter 7 will draw together the insights gained from the study of exemplary church life in Acts and articulate a Lukan theology of church life with the summary narratives as the foundation.

ARTICULATING A THEOLOGY OF
CHURCH LIFE IN ACTS

A brief review of the theoretical foundation for this study is necessary, before turning to Luke's theology of church life. I pursued the study of the summary narratives out of a desire to reassert Luke's voice in contemporary conversations about the faithful formation of churches. Chapter 1 showed how the historical-critical method undermined confidence in their historical reliability and cut them off from their literary context within the overall narrative of Acts. The result was an underemphasis on their contribution to the theological vision of Acts. Because the summary narratives focus on church life in Jerusalem, Luke's theology of church life in Acts suffered most.

Under the historical-critical paradigm, even the parallels between Peter and Paul have been seen as part of Luke's agenda to create a sense of rapprochement between the Jewish and Gentile factions of the early church, at the expense of history. However, when the narrative/rhetorical perspective was applied and the repetition of key words, phrases, and activities related to church life were observed across the entire text of Acts, a different picture emerged. We saw how Luke repeatedly echoes features of his portraits of exemplary life in the summary narratives in his descriptions of the Gentile churches of Acts.

The result of Luke's rhetorical strategy is a subtle but powerful echo effect that causes Luke's convictions about church life in the summary narratives to resonate in the ecclesial imagination of readers. Luke's portraits of exemplary life invite readers to consider what God might want to do in their own churches. This is why, when believers today look for Scriptures that will help them wrestle with God's will for church life, they keep instinctively turning to various verses in the summary narratives for guidance. I have demonstrated through narrative and rhetorical analysis that when we do this, we do exactly what Luke hopes will happen. My desire through this study, however, is that believers and churches will go beyond merely accessing one or a few verses from the summary narratives. To be faithful to Luke's intentions, they also need to be considered in their entirety as a resource for thinking about and living faithfully as the church today. Attending to the theology of church life in Acts is to make the turn toward biblical theology and the theological interpretation of Scripture.

BIBLICAL THEOLOGY AND
CHURCH LIFE IN ACTS

Biblical theology is a descriptive discipline that seeks to articulate what biblical authors believed and taught in the context of their own particular setting.[1] It works inductively from the data of Scripture to describe what the Bible teaches, prior to the development of confessions, creeds, or other dogmatic statements of faith.[2] The scope of biblical theology can be as wide as the Old or New Testaments, or even the entire Bible. Or it can be as narrow as the body of writings of a single author (Paul's letters for example), a single Bible book, or even a theme within a book, which I have done with the theme of church life in Acts.[3]

Applied to church life in Acts, biblical theology seeks to express Luke's beliefs about life together in the community of believers in Jesus. Biblical theology asks, What did Luke think church life should look like? My study of exemplary life in the Jerusalem church and its echoes in Luke's descriptions of church life in Samaria, Antioch, Ephesus, and Troas, though primarily exegetical in orientation, sought to answer this question. Luke describes a church that began in Jerusalem and was flung by persecution (Acts 8:4; 11:20–21; 14:5–6) and the call of the Holy Spirit (8:29; 13:2–4) throughout the Roman Empire as Jesus' witnesses to the ends of the earth.

The church went through many changes as it moved away from Jerusalem. Though it remained connected to and respectful of its roots in the faith and Scriptures of Israel, it also changed as Gentiles began to hear the gospel and believe (Acts 10:1–11:18). Circumcision was no longer required, because Gentile believers did not have to become Jews in order to follow Jesus (15:1–35). Leadership evolved from the twelve apostles

---

[1] Robert W. Yarbrough, "Biblical Theology," in *Evangelical Dictionary of Biblical Theology*, ed. Walter A. Elwell (Grand Rapids: Baker, 1996), 61. On the work of moving from exegesis to theology, see I. Howard Marshall, *Beyond the Bible: Moving from Scripture to Theology* (Grand Rapids: Baker Academic, 2004); and Gary T. Meadors, *Four Views on Moving beyond the Bible to Theology* (Grand Rapids: Zondervan, 2009).

[2] Graeme Goldsworthy, "Biblical Theology and Hermeneutics," *Southern Baptist Journal of Theology* 10, no. 2 (2006): 4; D. A. Carson, "New Testament Theology," in *DLNT*, 799.

[3] The best single volume on the theology of Acts is I. Howard Marshall and David Peterson, eds., *Witness to the Gospel: The Theology of Acts* (Grand Rapids: Eerdmans, 1998). Several of the essays deal with aspects of church life and occasionally mention verses from the summary narratives (especially David Seccombe on the new people of God, David Peterson and Brad Blue on worship in the early church, and Brian Capper on reciprocity). However, none of the writers attempt a comprehensive survey of church life in Acts.

(2:42; 4:35; 5:12) to the addition of the Seven who oversaw mercy ministries in Jerusalem (6:1–7). Later in Acts we hear less from the Twelve, but Christian prophets appear (11:27; 13:1; 15:32; 21:9), and elders are appointed to shepherd the churches (11:30; 14:23; 15:2–6; 20:17). The church evolved from meeting every day (2:46) to meeting on the first day of the week in honor of the resurrection of Jesus (20:7). Yet, in spite of the changes, an enduring continuity in church life can be seen as well, especially in the echoes of the summary narratives in Luke's descriptions of Gentile church life in Acts. This continuity within a rapidly changing social, cultural, and religious context provides the foundation upon which a theology of church life in Acts can be built.

THEOLOGICAL INTERPRETATION AND CHURCH LIFE IN ACTS

The theological interpretation of Scripture is driven by the quest to live faithfully before the triune God.[4] Whereas biblical theology is more descriptive, theological interpretation is more prescriptive and reads Scripture in light of the gospel and the call to follow Jesus today. It asks what the Bible teaches about the person and character of God and His relationship to the world. Theological interpretation also asks what the Bible teaches about the world in its relationship to God and our place in it.[5]

Applied to church life in Acts, theological interpretation seeks to articulate how believers are called to live before God today as His gathered people in the world and as His witnesses to the resurrection of Jesus to the ends of the earth. Theological interpretation asks, What should church life look like today? Steve Walton's chapter on the message of Acts in *Theological Interpretation of the New Testament* helpfully sets up the

---

[4] Steven E. Fowl, "The New Testament, Theology, and Ethics," in *Hearing the New Testament: Strategies for Interpretation*, ed. Joel B. Green (Grand Rapids: Eerdmans, 2010), 401.

[5] William P. Brown, "Theological Interpretation: A Proposal," in *Method Matters: Essays on the Interpretation of the Hebrew Bible in Honor of David L. Petersen*, ed. Joel M. LeMon and Kent Harold Richards (Atlanta: Society of Biblical Literature, 2009), 390. For introductions to the theological interpretation of Scripture, see Daniel J. Treier, *Introducing Theological Interpretation of Scripture: Recovering a Christian Practice* (Grand Rapids: Baker Academic, 2008); and Kevin J. Vanhoozer, "Introduction: What Is the Theological Interpretation of the Bible?" in *Theological Interpretation of the New Testament*, ed. Kevin J. Vanhoozer, Daniel J. Treier, and N. T. Wright (Grand Rapids: Baker Academic, 2008), 13–26. An appreciative survey that also identifies some pitfalls of the movement can be found in Gregg R. Allison, "Theological Interpretation of Scripture: An Introduction and Preliminary Evaluation," *Southern Baptist Journal of Theology* 14, no. 2 (2010): 28–36. Especially helpful is Allison's extensive bibliography on the field (33–34 n. 5).

answer to this question. Walton acknowledges that the theme of "salvation" is commonly accepted as the theological center of Acts.[6] He works toward this theme but begins a few steps before it with what Acts teaches about the purpose and character of God in three statements. First, God is a *purposeful* God. The books of Luke and Acts present the coming of the Messiah and the spread of His gospel as the fulfillment of God's saving purpose, announced by the prophets and Jesus (Luke 4:18–19; cf. Isa 61:1–2) and proclaimed by the apostles (Acts 2:14–36; cf. Pss 16:8–11; 110:1; Joel 2:28–32).[7] Second, God is a *missionary* God (Acts 1:8) who pursues reaching the Jewish people first (2:22,37–41; 3:19,26; 4:12; 5:42) and then the Gentiles (8:26; 9:15; 13:46–47; 14:28; 26:23). Third, God is a *saving* God who offers salvation through Jesus to all who repent and believe (2:40; 4:12; 11:14; 15:11; 16:31).[8] Walton's perspective rightly points readers toward God's character and purpose in the salvation He brought into the world through Jesus. He also notes that when people are saved, they are added to the believing community, but he does not make this a major emphasis in his perspective on salvation. Yet, salvation and commitment to the fellowship of believers have been shown to be inseparable in Acts.[9] Thus, a fourth statement should be added to Walton's proposal. God is a *community-making* God. When God saves people, He adds them to the community of believers called the church that He created and continues to grow (2:41,47; 9:31).[10] A theology of church life in Acts must begin here with the origin of the church in the plan and purpose of a community-making God.

---

[6] Steve Walton, "Acts," in Vanhoozer, Treier, and Wright, *Theological Interpretation of the New Testament*, 76. Also I. Howard Marshall, *Luke: Historian and Theologian* (Grand Rapids: Zondervan, 1989), 92–102, esp. 92–93; and ibid., *The Acts of the Apostles*, New Testament Guides (Sheffield, UK: Sheffield Academic Press, 2001), 43–46.

[7] Stephen E. Porter, "Scripture Justifies Mission: The Use of the Old Testament in Luke-Acts," in *Hearing the Old Testament in the New Testament*, ed. Stephen E. Porter (Grand Rapids: Eerdmans, 2006), 104–26, esp. 124–25.

[8] Walton, "Acts," 76–77.

[9] See chap. 3 on Acts 2:41,47 and chap. 5 on Acts 5:14.

[10] Robert Wall does something similar in his commentary introduction on reading Acts as theology. He outlines a "master" story in Acts of God bringing salvation to the world. His first three elements are similar to Walton's, but Wall adds a fourth: "Those who repent and belong to the Lord Jesus Christ receive the Holy Spirit and are initiated into a community of goods." See Robert W. Wall, "The Acts of the Apostles," in *NIB*, 22. I would quibble with making only the community of goods the point, but not with seeing an important purpose of God in salvation as that of creating a community out of those who have repented and belong to the Lord Jesus Christ.

A THEOLOGY OF CHURCH LIFE IN ACTS

I offer here a theology of church life in Acts in three movements: the church's origin, character, and mission. All three components are rooted in the summary narratives and the descriptions of Gentile church life in Acts, but they also branch out to consider other Bible authors, wherever they speak on the community-making activity of God.

The Origin of the Church

The church's origin is in God. Before the creation of the world the church was part of the plan of the triune God to raise up a people He would redeem through Jesus Christ and seal with the promised Holy Spirit (Eph 1:4–14). The Holy Spirit is the key person in the Godhead in relation to the origin of the church in Acts. The Spirit of God was present at creation (Gen 1:2). On occasion the Spirit came upon individual judges, kings, and prophets who were sent by God to help His people (Judg 6:34; 1 Sam 16:13; Ezek 11:5). God also anointed Jesus with the Holy Spirit and power for His Messianic ministry (Luke 4:18; Acts 10:38). However, on Pentecost everything changed when God poured out His Spirit upon every believer in Jesus (Acts 2:1–4). Peter preached the gospel in the Spirit's power. Three thousand repented and believed, and they were baptized. The new believers received the Holy Spirit as Peter promised (Acts 2:38–41), and the church was born. The church that resulted on Pentecost Day in Acts 2:42–47 was the direct result of the action of the Holy Spirit empowering the proclamation of the gospel and filling those who believed in Jesus for salvation.

What believers in Jesus must understand, as those who join and participate in the life of the church, and especially those who lead, is that the church does not arise from the minds and hearts of people. The church exists because a sovereign God purposed to bless the nations of the earth (Acts 3:25). He does this through the Spirit-empowered witness of people He saves and adds to the church He is building (Acts 1:8; 2:41,47; 5:14; Matt 16:18). Exemplary church life must challenge any anthropocentric thinking that subtly influences the church to think and act in man-centered ways. A radically God-centered approach to church life is needed that will cause our planning, worshipping, and living as the church to be shaped by the God-centered pattern we see in the book of Acts.

Throughout Acts an emphasis is maintained on God's prior purpose and action to bring salvation to the ends of the earth and gather believers into churches. Consider the following examples. The Holy Spirit fills His people for bold witness (Acts 4:31; 6:10; 7:55). He sends persons in specific directions (8:29,39; 11:12; 13:2–4) and sometimes stops them from going in the wrong direction (6:7–10).[11] Angels regularly intervene to deliver and give instructions (5:19–20; 12:7–8). The Holy Spirit guides decision making and even appoints overseers for the church (15:28; 20:28). The Holy Spirit encourages the church along the way too (9:31). The Lord appeared to Paul in a vision at night in Corinth and told him to keep speaking, because He had many people in that city (18:9–11). The Lord also told Paul twice in night visions that he would speak before Caesar in Rome (23:11; 27:24). Witness to Christ and the creation of churches do not happen because the people of God simply decide it should. God goes ahead of His people and prepares the way for us to follow Him into the community-making work He is doing in the world. This realization should humble believers and cause us to praise His grace and goodness (2:47; 4:33; 14:3; 15:11; cf. Eph 1:6) that saves us and brings us into the church He is building.

It should be noted here that the emphasis on God's sovereignty in raising up the church in Acts in no way diminishes the need of individuals to repent and believe or the duty of believers and churches to act decisively to take the gospel to the ends of the earth. The call to repent and believe the good news about Jesus goes to anyone who will listen (Acts 3:19; 16:31; 17:30). Persons must be willing to come to Christ in repentance and faith and be baptized in obedience to Christ's command through His apostles (2:38). The response of persons who willingly listen, repent, believe, and are baptized fairly dominates the narrative of Acts.[12]

In Acts we also see churches and church leaders making decisions and taking deliberate prayerful action to advance the witness to Christ. Consider these examples. The believers took action to replace Judas (Acts 1:21–22), distribute alms (4:35), resolve conflict (6:1–6), and protect Saul

---

[11] In the unique circumstances experienced by the first generation of Jewish believers in Jesus, the Holy Spirit also verified God's saving purpose toward the Gentiles, when He came upon them, in the presence of Jewish believers, as He had come upon Jewish believers at Pentecost (Acts 8:15–17; 10:44–46; 19:6).

[12] Acts 2:41; 4:4; 5:14; 6:7; 8:12–13,36–37 (though most early witnesses omit Acts 8:37, including p[45], ℵ, A, B, C); 9:18,35,42; 10:47–48; 11:21,24; 13:12,48; 14:1; 16:14–15,33; 17:4,12,34; 18:8; 19:5,18; 28:24.

from a plot to kill him (9:23–24). The church in Antioch decided to take up an offering for famine relief in Judea (11:29–30). Paul had to take evasive action to flee persecution in Iconium (14:5–7). The council in Jerusalem required church leaders to debate different viewpoints as they came to grips with the movement of the gospel to the Gentiles (15:2,5–21). When they resolved the dispute, they wisely decided to send a delegation to the Gentile churches along with a letter of encouragement (15:22–29). Paul made a strategic decision to visit the churches where he and Barnabas had preached to see how they were doing (15:36). He also circumcised Timothy in an effort to accommodate the consciences of Jews in the cities where they would be traveling (16:3). Paul skillfully shaped his preaching in Greece, even utilizing Greek philosophers and poets like Epimenides, Cleanthes, and Aratus to drive home his arguments within the Athenian context.[13] He knew when to stop witnessing to blasphemers (18:6), and he knew how to divide a room full of his enemies, in order to divert hostility away from himself (23:6–10). Paul even had an ace up his sleeve, Roman citizenship, which he used to appeal charges against him to Caesar in order to avoid the threat of assassination in Jerusalem (25:9–12). In Rome he was kept in chains under house arrest while he waited for his appeal hearing to occur. He was not free to move about the city (28:16,20), but Paul did not let chains stop him. He held church in his own rented house for two years, welcoming visitors, preaching the kingdom of God and teaching about Jesus boldly and without hindrance (28:30–31).

The point of these examples is to demonstrate how Acts also shows believers acting deliberately and decisively, even shrewdly, as they faced challenges and had to figure out solutions that would enable them to keep advancing the gospel. Churches today should not hesitate to think strategically about how to reach their communities for Christ. God's command to "seek the welfare of the city" is a call to deliberate planning and action to be a blessing to others (Jer 29:7; Gen 12:2; Isa 32:8).[14] Nevertheless, the exemplary church worships, lives, plans, and acts with a deep humility that acknowledges that the church's story began with the prior purpose of God to redeem a people through Christ for His glory. The work of the church is God's work that we engage as those He has saved and included in His mission to take the name of Jesus to the ends of the earth through us.

---

[13] Darrell L. Bock, *Acts*, BECNT (Grand Rapids: Baker Academic, 2007), 568; John Polhill, *Acts*, NAC (Nashville: Broadman, 1992), 375–76.

[14] See also Ps 20:4; Prov 12:5; 15:22; 16:1,3; 19:21; 20:18; 21:5.

The Character of an Exemplary Church

With a proper humility that flows from seeing the church's origin in God, believers and churches should ask what kind of church the Holy Spirit desires to create. What should exemplary church life look like today? The twenty features of an exemplary church below are based on the exegetical study of the summary narratives with several modifications. A few statements that cover the same ground due to repetition have been combined, and every statement is worded as a general principle to facilitate analysis and reflection on church life today.

(1) An exemplary church calls people to repent and believe in the Lord Jesus Christ, demonstrated by baptism (Acts 2:37–41). Some interpreters begin Luke's description of Jerusalem church life with the initial response to Peter's preaching in Acts 2:37.[15] Peter's sermon pierced his hearers' hearts, and they asked what they should do. Peter commanded them all to repent (2:38). He pleaded with them to save themselves from this corrupt generation (2:40). His call to repentance was the first command to the people who would become the church described in 2:42–47.[16] Peter's call to repentance was the same as that of John the Baptist who called people to turn away from evil deeds like selfishness, dishonesty, extortion, and lying about others (Luke 3:10–14). He also called the people to be baptized as an expression of the kind of repentance that leads to forgiveness and the reception of the Holy Spirit (Acts 2:38; cf. Luke 3:3; Acts 13:24; 19:4).

Peter's call has two applications for church life today. First, Peter did not knock down all the barriers that might keep people from professing faith and joining with the 120 disciples. If anything, he made things harder by confronting their complicity in the death of Jesus twice in his sermon (Acts 2:23,36). This was not an anti-Semitic statement. Peter was a Jew telling his own people they were wrong about Jesus. God raised Jesus from the dead and exalted Him to His right hand as both Lord and Messiah (2:24,32–33,36). They needed to change their minds about Him. True repentance flows out of a heart that has been pierced by the realization of the sinfulness of sin and is possessed with the urgent desire to get right with God (Acts 2:37; Rom 7:13; 2 Cor 7:10–11a). Only those who truly repent are able to believe in Jesus Christ for salvation.

---

[15] Luke Timothy Johnson, *The Acts of the Apostles*, SP (Collegeville, MN: Michael Glazier, 1992), 56; F. Scott Spencer, *Journeying through Acts: A Literary-Cultural Reading* (Peabody, MA: Hendrickson, 2004), 49.

[16] Or the second command if one includes Peter's exhortation to the crowd to listen carefully to his words, before he preached his Pentecost sermon (Acts 2:14).

Second, Peter stressed the importance of baptism as an expression of true repentance. Too often Baptists and other evangelicals, in a sincere effort to emphasize that Jesus alone—not baptism—saves, end up minimizing the role of baptism as the gospel sign of true repentance. It is correct to say that baptism does not save a person. However, Luke might hear how we articulate this conviction and reply, "But has a person really repented if they will not be baptized? Did they really believe if they will not obey Jesus?"[17] Luke shows those who repented in Acts being baptized.[18] The call to be baptized is God's gift to the church for helping seekers examine themselves (2 Cor 13:5) and sort out whether they have obeyed God's command to repent and believe in Jesus (Acts 17:30; 1 John 2:3). The exemplary church must have integrity in its call to repentance and faith in Jesus to those who profess faith and desire to join.

(2) An exemplary church deliberately assimilates new believers (Acts 2:41–42). Acts 2:42 describes four intentional and serious commitments made by the new believers. They devoted themselves to the apostles' teaching, to the fellowship, to the breaking of bread, and to prayer. Because Luke utilizes all four rhetorical features of summarization in 2:42, the activity is meant to be understood as a part of his description of exemplary church life. However, because the proper subject of 2:42 is the new believers in 2:41, the verse places a special emphasis on the activities of new converts too. Throughout Acts we see new believers engaging in these activities, especially being taught the word of God.[19]

Genuine conversion will show itself in a commitment to these activities, and an exemplary church makes sure they happen. An exemplary church does not lead persons to profess faith in Christ and stop there. If the pattern in Acts is our guide, then intentional assimilation into the local church and the life of a Christ-follower cannot be left to chance. The exemplary church makes sure new converts are instructed in the faith, connected to the fellowship, breaking bread with the church, and learning to pray with other believers. The exemplary church does not lead people to Christ and then hope that assimilation happens. New believers are assimilated intentionally.

(3) An exemplary church submits itself to the authority of Scripture (Acts 2:42). The church in Jerusalem had the apostles among them, but

---

[17] See Matt 28:19.
[18] See Acts 2:41; 8:12,36–38; 9:18; 10:47–48; 16:15,33; 18:8; 19:5; 22:16.
[19] See Acts 11:26; 13:12; 14:21–22; 18:11,25–26; 19:9–10; 20:18–20.

not their writings. At this stage of church life in Acts, none of the New Testament documents had been written. The apostles' teaching referred to a set of core beliefs about Jesus that the early church learned from the apostles. Elements of this core can be identified within the New Testament (1 Cor 11:23–26; 15:3–5). As copies of the writings of the apostles circulated (Col 4:16), they eventually began to be recognized as authoritative Scripture (2 Pet 3:15–16). Subsequent generations of churches do not have the apostles among them, but we have their writings. The apostles are the church's connection to the ministry and teachings of Jesus as well as eyewitnesses to His resurrection (Acts 1:21–22; cf. Luke 23:11). Their Spirit-inspired memory preserved the teachings of Jesus, which they learned as His disciples.

At the beginning of Acts, Luke tells Theophilus that his first volume was about what Jesus began to do and teach (Acts 1:1), which implies that Jesus continued teaching through His apostles. The apostles taught about the resurrection of the dead through Jesus (Acts 4:2) and the good news that Jesus is the Messiah (5:42). They taught the "message of the Lord" and the "word of God" (15:35; 18:11). The speeches of Acts are filled with expositions of Old Testament Scripture, interpreted in light of Jesus the Messiah and applied to the spiritual needs of hearers.

Acts concludes with Paul "proclaiming the kingdom of God and teaching the things concerning the Lord Jesus Christ" (Acts 28:31), which connects the ending of Acts back to the beginning and Luke's reference in 1:1 to Jesus' ongoing teaching through the apostles.[20] The final word in the Greek text of Acts is *akōlutōs*, which means "without hindrance."[21] Luke ends his two-volume work with a rhetorical marker that indicated that no barrier, not even chains and imprisonment (Acts 28:20; 2 Tim 2:9), can keep the teaching about the reign of God and salvation through Jesus from going forth. In this sense "without hindrance" sums up the progress of the teaching about Jesus in Luke and Acts and its prospects for success in the future.[22] The open-ended conclusion of Acts invites readers into the

---

[20] Mikael C. Parsons, *Acts*, Paideia: Commentaries on the New Testament (Grand Rapids: Baker, 2008), 366.

[21] BAGD, 34; LSJ, 59.

[22] It was for this reason that Frank Stagg in his introduction to Acts famously called *akōlutōs* an "epitome in an adverb" (Frank Stagg, *The Book of Acts: The Early Struggle for an Unhindered Gospel* [Nashville: Broadman, 1955], 1). Also see Richard I. Pervo, *Acts*, Hermeneia (Minneapolis: Fortress, 2009), 687–88. The abrupt ending of Acts has led to speculation as to why Luke did not tell readers how Paul's legal problems were resolved. Some have suggested that Luke intended to write a third volume but never got around to it, or that he wrote Acts as a legal brief for Paul's defense but

ongoing story of the spread of the gospel, as the message about Jesus was taught from house to house, from city to city, and from nation to nation, to the ends of the earth (Acts 1:8).

In light of the central importance of teaching in Luke–Acts, it can hardly be overstated that the first commitment of the new believers was to the teaching of the apostles (Acts 2:42). This was no accident. Luke wants to make clear that the apostles' teaching, preserved in their writings, should undergird the beliefs, practices, and the mission of the church until Jesus returns (1:8–11).

In the church today we think of the apostles' teaching as the collection of twenty-seven authoritative books written by the apostles and a few close associates, which we call the New Testament. We would also include the thirty-nine books of the Old Testament, which the apostles and Jesus acknowledged as authoritative. The sixty-six books of the Old and New Testaments are the church's standard for faith and life. Brian Harper and Paul Metzger have argued that we need to submit to the authority of Scripture so we can understand God rightly and avoid the human tendency to redefine God on our own terms. We need to hear Scripture read and taught, because we are in constant need of its message of grace. We also need the prophetic element of Scripture to be spoken into our lives and churches, so we will know what pleases God and what a Christ-honoring community of faith looks like.[23] The Jerusalem church's devotion to the teaching of the apostles calls churches everywhere to form their ministries around the apostles' teaching too.

(4) Believers in an exemplary church commit themselves to the fellowship (Acts 2:42). Before the first summary of church life begins, Luke notes that the 3,000 who believed on Pentecost were "added to them," meaning added to the 120 (Acts 1:15; 2:41). At the conclusion to the first summary narrative Luke indicates that those being saved were also "added to them." A boundary existed between believers in the church and those

---

did not know the outcome of Paul's appeal before it was needed. Neither of these views is satisfying compared to seeing Luke deliberately making the unhindered gospel the point of Acts, and not Paul's fate before Caesar. More discussion of these issues can be found in William F. Brosend II, "The Means of Absent Ends," in *History, Literature, and Society in the Book of Acts*, ed. Ben Witherington III (New York: Cambridge University Press, 1996), 348–62, esp. 362; and Daniel Marguerat, "The End of Acts (28.16–31) and the Rhetoric of Silence," in *Rhetoric and the New Testament: Essays from the 1992 Heidelberg Conference*, ed. Stephen E. Porter (Sheffield: Sheffield Academic, 1993), 74–89, esp. 87–88.

[23] Brad Harper and Paul Lewis Metzger, *Exploring Ecclesiology: An Evangelical and Ecumenical Introduction* (Grand Rapids: Brazos Press, 2009), 164.

who did not believe on the outside. Believing in Jesus for salvation in Acts was accompanied by joining the fellowship of others who believed.

Words like "fellowship" and "community" are tossed about as buzzwords today, but they are packed with theological and spiritual significance for the life of the church. The church's fellowship is first with the triune God (1 Cor 1:9; 2 Cor 13:13; 1 John 1:3). He redeems us through the atoning work of His Son Jesus Christ and makes us alive by the Holy Spirit who brings us into God's family. The word *fellowship* (Acts 2:42) encompasses all of the relationships in the community of believers. As individuals we have fellowship with God through Jesus Christ. We have fellowship with other believers in the church as brothers and sisters in Christ. The church herself is a body of believers that relates to God through her connection to Jesus as the church's head. Local churches even have fellowship with one another, like the fellowship between the church in Antioch and the church in Jerusalem (Acts 11:27–30; 15:1–35).What fellowship looks like is fleshed out further in the summary narratives, but one thing is made clear at the outset. A commitment to follow Jesus includes a commitment to His people.

(5) An exemplary church regularly takes the Lord's Supper and centers its life on the gospel it represents (Acts 2:42). The "breaking of bread" is Luke's shorthand for the early church's fellowship meal in which they also took the Lord's Supper (Acts 2:42; 20:7). This meal was modeled on the Passover meal Jesus celebrated with His disciples before His suffering. The bread Jesus broke symbolizes His body that was broken for sin. The cup represents the new covenant in Jesus' blood that was poured out for sinners (Luke 22:14–20; 1 Cor 11:23–26). The new believers in Jerusalem immediately began to participate in the Lord's Supper as a part of their assimilation into the life of the church. The gospel preached through the Lord's Supper was at the heart of the apostles' preaching, and it was at the center of the life of the church in Acts.

The Lord's Supper declares the gospel to the church today. Through the Lord's Supper the church proclaims that Jesus is the Lamb of God who takes away the sin of the world (John 1:29; 1 Cor 5:7). In the Lord's Supper, believers express their common faith in the one true God and their common life in Jesus His Son.[24] Participating in the Lord's Supper provides believers with a regular reminder that their life is in the broken body and shed blood of Jesus Christ (John 6:53–58). We do not preach the gos-

---

[24] Geoffrey Wainwright, "Lord's Supper, Love Feast," in *DLNT*, 687.

pel to people until they become believers and then stop preaching it. The church needs to turn again and again to the good news of the finished work of Jesus on the cross and His victory over sin and death. An exemplary church regularly takes the Lord's Supper, because it seeks to build itself on everything the gospel signifies for the life we have in Christ.

(6) An exemplary church commits to praying together (Acts 2:42). The new believers in Jerusalem were immediately included in times of corporate prayer. Having a private prayer life was important to Jesus (Luke 5:16; 6:12; 9:28–29), and it was important for individual believers in Acts (Acts 9:11; 10:9,30). However, Acts places a special emphasis on believers praying together too (1:12–14; 2:42). They met as a church to pray at appointed hours (3:1; 16:16), during times of great need (4:23–30; 12:5,12; 16:25), before significant ministry activities (9:40; 28:8), and to consecrate persons for special assignments (1:24; 6:6; 13:3; 14:23). Prayer was so important to the apostles that when the demands of ministry threatened their devotion to prayer, they brought the problem to the church and made major adjustments in their ministries in order to prioritize prayer again (6:4). In an exemplary church, prayer is a high priority in the life of the leaders, and prayer together plays a vital role in the life and ministry of the church.

(7) An exemplary church maintains reverence and the fear of the Lord (Acts 2:43a). The fear of the Lord can signify amazement, reverence, and awe at what God is doing, or terror at His judgments. Both kinds of fear are present in Acts. The church was seized with great fear after the deaths of Ananias and Sapphira (Acts 5:5,11). The city of Ephesus became afraid after a demon acknowledged his awareness of Jesus and Paul before he trounced a team of Jewish exorcists (19:17). The fear of the Lord described in the summaries (2:43; 9:31) describes a lasting reverence for God that acknowledges His presence and power among His people. When people recognize God's sovereignty through His actions that are beyond anyone's ability to predict or control, they humble themselves and confess that He reigns and does as He pleases. The church that fears God does not allow its spiritual senses to become dulled by worries, riches, and the pleasures of life (Luke 8:13–14; Rev 3:10). Instead, it deliberately cultivates an attitude of reverence, awe, and the fear of the Lord out of the knowledge that He holds everything in His hands, including His people.

(8) An exemplary church believes God can perform any miracle that pleases Him in order to verify His gospel or certify His messenger (Acts 2:43b; 4:33; 5:12a,15–16). When considering the place of signs and

wonders in the summary narratives, the question of their role today arises immediately. Signs and wonders feature prominently in the summary narratives, with a special emphasis on Peter's healing ministry and authority over unclean spirits (Acts 2:43; 5:12a,15–16). If the "great power" that accompanied the apostles' witness (4:33) is understood as a reference to the miraculous too, then it could be said that signs and wonders are a dominant feature of the summary narratives. Does Luke believe that all churches should expect to see signs and wonders like he described them in the summary narratives? Those who answer yes point out how prominent they are not just in the summaries but throughout Acts (6:8; 8:6; 14:3; 19:11). Those who emphasize that their primary role in Acts is limited to certifying the apostles and their message point out that signs and wonders are mentioned only in association with God's word going forth from an apostle or someone bringing the message of the apostles.

Our study of the summary narratives yielded several insights into this question. First, some of the tension in modern debates seems to be built into the very fabric of the summary narratives. Signs and wonders do dominate the summary narratives. However, they are tightly connected to the ministry and witness of the apostles and seem calculated to certify their leadership and preaching in the early church. Second, God is the one performing the miracles through His apostles. The apostles are agents of God's power, but the prerogative belongs to God. Third, the phrase "signs and wonders" points to a specific time when God certified His spokesmen Moses and Aaron to Pharaoh and to Israel (Exod 4:1–8,30; 7:3). Miracles are reported throughout the Bible (e.g., especially with Elijah and Elisha in 1 Kgs 18:16–46 and 2 Kgs 2:19–25). However, they are concentrated during times of increased revelation, when God began something new and sent a representative to lead His people through the changes. Massive changes in the way God dealt with Israel accompanied the coming of Jesus as Messiah. Signs and wonders certified His ministry and the witness of His apostles (Acts 2:19,22,43; 4:33; 5:12,15–16). The early church recognized "signs and wonders" as signs of a genuine apostle (2 Cor 12:12; Heb 2:4).

The miracle of speaking in other languages also played a verifying role in Acts. It certified the salvation of the Gentiles to the Jewish Christian leadership in Jerusalem (Acts 10:46–48; 11:15–18; 15:12), and it certified the conversion of Gentiles in Ephesus to the apostle Paul (19:6).

The best way to navigate this issue is to acknowledge two realities. First, we should remember that God is God. The laws of creation belong to Him. He can and does suspend them any time He is pleased to perform miracles that will bring glory to His name and gospel. Second, the focus of the miraculous in Acts is overwhelmingly on certifying God's apostles and their gospel as the power of God that saves (Rom 1:16). If any church's focus is on the apostles' writings and message, then they are honoring the primary purpose of God for signs and wonders in Acts.

(9) Believers in an exemplary church meet together regularly and share in each other's lives (Acts 2:44). The Jerusalem church was "together," and they had "everything in common." Luke's statement includes both the objective idea of being physically present before God and to each other and the more subjective idea of sharing in each other's lives. When church members disperse during the week, they continue to be the church. However, the church should recognize the special importance of regularly gathering for worship, the ordinances, teaching, service, and other activities that characterize the corporate life of God's people. The activity of gathering as a part of regular associations in the world is such a normal part of life that it can tempt churches to take their gatherings for granted. However, if Jesus said that He is present whenever two or more gather in His name (Matt 18:20), then something special happens when the church meets. God is present in the church's worship and in Spirit-led interaction between believers as they minister God's grace to each other (Eph 4:29; 1 Pet 4:10).

Holding "everything in common" is not a reference to a form of Christian communism that included property sharing. A figurative sense is implied where believers recognize that they belong to God and to each other. Believing in Jesus for salvation and sharing in each other's lives are inseparable in Luke's theology of church life. Luke alludes to the popular Greek proverb, "Friends have all things in common." However, in doing so he also made clear that the experience of forgiveness and filling with the Holy Spirit are what makes such friendships possible. When believers share their lives with fellow believers, they learn each other's stories and discover how to stir one another to love and good deeds (Heb 10:24–25). The church is not merely an aggregation of individual believers in Jesus. The Holy Spirit forms Christians into a community of believers who follow Jesus together. The exemplary church makes sure this is happening.

(10) In an exemplary church the believers give generously to meet each other's needs (Acts 2:44–45; 4:32b,34–35). Luke shows a people in Jerusalem whose grip on possessions was radically transformed by Jesus Christ. The believers did not formally renounce all property and live communally. Rather, they regularly sold their property and possessions and gave them generously to anyone who had a need (Acts 2:44–45; 4:34–35). People with many possessions and those with few all participated. Luke makes his point about the giving of the believers emphatic by repeating material from the first summary narrative (2:45) in the second (4:34–35) with one slight modification. In 2:45 the believers took the initiative to share with each other directly. In 4:34–35 the church had become so large that believers were selling lands or houses and simply laying the proceeds at the apostles' feet. By Acts 6 a ministry structure was needed that would free up the apostles to focus on the word and prayer (6:1–7).

The believers' generosity led to an astonishing result. The needs of the poor were met. Luke's language skillfully weaves the Mosaic commands about the Sabbath year with the highest ideals of the Greek friendship tradition. The Sabbath commands called for God's people to help each other through hard times, so that there would be no poor in Israel (Deut 15:4). Yet, the Lord complained through the prophets that Israel often failed to care for the poor, the orphan, and the widow (Isa 3:14–15; Jer 2:34; Amos 2:7; 5:11–12). The Greek friendship tradition aspired to a high level of mutual concern, but such thinking was never more than a reference to ancient utopian ideals. Yet, when the Holy Spirit arrived, the believers in Jerusalem began to do exactly what the Sabbath laws required and what Greek idealists aspired to but could never achieve. Great grace from God overflowed in their lives (Acts 4:33) and transformed them into gracious givers (4:34–35). The result was that there was not a needy person among them (4:34).

The churches in Antioch and Ephesus followed the example of the church in Jerusalem. The church in Antioch was so transformed by the grace they experienced in Christ (Acts 11:23) that when they heard a prophecy about a coming famine, they took up a collection for their brothers in Jerusalem (11:29–30). The church in Ephesus learned from Paul about generosity and how believers must help the weak, remembering that it is more blessed to give than to receive (20:33–35).

Except for the emphasis on signs and wonders, no subject receives as much attention in the summary narratives as the believers' generosity toward people in need. Luke makes clear that the exemplary church engages the problem of poverty. The church possesses the twin resources of the life-changing power of the gospel and material resources among its members, so that everyone in the fellowship can be helped. The summary narratives do not commend or exclude any particular social policy or government role in alleviating poverty in society. Luke's focus is more local, on how the church helped fellow believers in need. The call to neighbor love (Gal 5:14) includes a call to work for the good of all people too, but there is a special emphasis in the summary narratives on those who "belong to the household of faith" (Gal 6:10). Both can be done, because believers in an exemplary church know that God can use them in a powerful way to help the poor, if they will engage the issue.

(11) An exemplary church gathers regularly for worship (Acts 2:46; 5:12b). The believers "devoted themselves" (2:46) by "common consent" (5:12b) to meeting together in the temple complex. The church made a decision together that they would regularly gather the entire fellowship together. In a large public space such as Solomon's Colonnade the church could worship together, hear the apostles teach (5:42), and share the experience of being a part of a movement. An exemplary church commits itself to a time and place where it can gather together to worship God.

The summary narratives do not exhaust the biblical idea of worship. Other Scriptures and the practices of the church throughout Christian history are needed to reflect on and develop more fully the practice of Christian worship. Luke does not do this in his exemplary portraits. Instead, he emphasizes a lifestyle of worship that pervades everything that happened in lives of believers. Worship occurred when the church met together, but it did not stop when the believers parted ways. Evidence of whether a church worships God can certainly be seen in her corporate worship services. However, the summary narratives indicate that perhaps the truest evidence of the depth and reality of the church's corporate worship can be seen in the believers' lives after the meeting ends. Do we walk consistently with an attitude of reverence and praise? Are we conscious of the great grace we have from God? Do we maintain the gratitude we experience in worship when we remember the body and blood of Jesus at the Lord's Table? A church that consciously pursues these things will surely experience dynamic worship when God's people come together corporately.

(12) In an exemplary church the believers share meals regularly in each other's homes (Acts 2:46). In addition to large group meetings in the

temple complex, the believers also "broke bread from house to house." Chapter 3 argued for a close relationship between the Lord's Supper and the shared meal in the early church (Acts 2:42,46).[25] Sharing a meal allows believers to experience the welcome and hospitality of God. The Lord Jesus enjoyed sharing meals with others (Luke 5:30; 7:34; 15:2; John 2:1–11) and often accepted dinner invitations (Luke 7:36; 14:1). He encouraged His disciples to accept the hospitality of those they stayed with as they ministered, eating whatever was set before them (Luke 10:7–8). Jesus fed 5,000 from five loaves of bread and two fish and made sure everyone was filled (9:12–17). He looked forward to eating the Passover meal with His disciples (22:15). Jesus even used the image of a great banquet to describe God's welcome of the poor, the crippled, the blind, and the lame into His kingdom (14:15–24). In a sense for believers, to share a meal together is to experience a foretaste of heaven.

The early church regularly shared meals together. Luke's stress on the believer's "gladness and simplicity of heart" (Acts 2:46) tells us that the early church genuinely enjoyed each other's company and accepted one another as friends. One can imagine the early church lingering over conversations into the evening as they shared their joys and struggles, worshiped and prayed together, and carried each other's burdens (1 Cor 12:26; Gal 6:2). The exemplary church does not view shared meals in a merely utilitarian way. Shared meals allow believers in Jesus to share deeply in each other's lives.

(13) An exemplary church cares for its city (Acts 2:47). The church in Jerusalem literally had "grace" (*charis*) toward the people of Jerusalem, which means they loved their city. They had a heart of compassion for her inhabitants and wanted their neighbors to experience the kindness of God in Christ. The Bible speaks of God as a city dweller and the pilgrimage of His people as a journey toward "the city of the living God (the heavenly Jerusalem)" (Heb 12:22). The city of God is an apt picture of the Father's home, a place of perfect safety, sharing, justice, and joy.[26] Believers in Jesus know this and look forward to it. However, in a fallen world the city is a place of brokenness, where there is often danger, selfishness, injustice, and tears. Luke tells us that the prophetess Anna was one of many who

[25] Also see chap. 6 on Acts 20:7–12, where the meeting on the first day of the week to break bread refers to the Lord's Supper (v. 7), and the resumption of bread breaking after Eutychus's resurrection included a shared meal (v. 11).

[26] Dennis E. Johnson, *The Message of Acts in the History of Redemption* (Phillipsburg, NJ: P&R, 1997), 70–71.

looked forward to the redemption of Jerusalem (Luke 2:38). Jesus wept over the city and longed to gather her children, even though they were not willing (13:34; 19:41). After His resurrection Jesus wanted the gospel preached in Jerusalem first (24:47).

In an exemplary church, God's people have God's heart of compassion for the city. They are not satisfied simply to be an island cut off from the community. Instead, her members look with compassion upon the brokenness around them and set out to be a balm to hurting people.

(14) An exemplary church expects to see people saved (Acts 2:47; 4:33; 5:14). People were coming to faith in Christ every day in Jerusalem (2:47). So many men and women were becoming believers that the steady stream took on the feel of a great movement (5:14). The emphasis in 2:47 is on both the sovereignty of God in salvation and the sense of expectation that an exemplary church will see people regularly saved. The mystery in the twin affirmations of God's sovereignty and human responsibility has been addressed in the discussion of the origin of the church above. Throughout Acts an emphasis is maintained on God's sovereign purpose and action to bring salvation to the ends of the earth and gather believers into local churches. At the same time Acts shows the apostles witnessing boldly and moving out deliberately to advance the gospel. In the summary narratives the same mystery is affirmed without explanation. The apostles kept bearing witness to the resurrection of Jesus (4:33), and the Lord kept adding to their number those who were being saved (2:47; 5:14).

An important lesson can be drawn from the summary narratives for exemplary churches today. Wrestling with the relationship between God's sovereignty and human duty can be healthy for a church that wants to understand the word of God rightly (2 Tim 2:15). However, some aspects of this mystery are not fully explained in Scripture. There are secret things that belong to the Lord alone, and it is to His glory when He conceals them (Deut 29:29; Prov 25:2). His judgments are unsearchable, His ways are untraceable, and no one has ever known His mind fully (Rom 11:33–34). This mystery calls the church to humility before God. On the other hand, it does not excuse the church from obedience to Christ's command to go and make disciples of all nations (Matt 28:19). We should agree with Scripture when it tells us that people will not believe unless we go to them with the gospel (Rom 10:14–15) and plead with them to repent and be saved (Acts 3:19; 17:30). The message we preach is the means by which God saves those who believe (1 Cor 1:21). Yet, we should also humbly confess with

Scripture that God draws and opens the heart of sinners to hear and believe the gospel (John 6:44; Acts 16:14). The church that accepts this mystery without having to understand it fully will have a high view of God, and it will be possessed with an urgency that compels it to take the gospel to the ends of the earth by any means available.

(15) An exemplary church protects the unity it has from God (Acts 4:32). The church in Jerusalem was made up of a "multitude" of believers, and yet Luke tells us they were of "one heart and soul" (Acts 4:32). The popularity of the idea of unity in heart and soul among ancient writers reveals how the desire for harmony in relationships is a universal human longing. Communities and nations occasionally sees flashes of unity when they come together in a great project or face a common threat, but lasting unity is impossible to achieve in a fallen world. However, the church needs to remember that Jesus asked His Father to make the church one (John 17:20–23), and the Holy Spirit carried out Jesus' request (Acts 4:31–32). Perfect unity may not be fully experienced until the remaining effects of the fall are finally gone. However, the church should pursue unity (Eph 4:3; Phil 2:2), believing God gives it as a gift so that His people may glorify Him with a united mind and voice (Rom 15:5–6).

(16) An exemplary church testifies boldly to the resurrection of Jesus (Acts 4:33a). Jesus promised His disciples power for witness (Luke 24:47–49; Acts 1:8). When power came, the apostles began to witness boldly to the resurrection of Jesus (Acts 2:24,32; 3:15; 4:2) and were arrested and threatened by the Jewish leaders (4:3,18,21). Instead of retreating in fear, they cried out to God for boldness, and God granted their request (4:29–31), but the attacks did not stop. The apostles were soon thrown in jail again (5:18), but they kept preaching the resurrection of Jesus (5:30–32). Next they were flogged, but they kept on preaching (5:40–42). Even after the death of Stephen and the scattering of the church in the great persecution, the believers proclaimed Christ wherever they went (8:1–4; 11:19–20). Throughout Acts we see followers of Jesus proclaiming Christ boldly, being challenged and persecuted, but not backing down. When a person or a church encounters the risen Christ, they cannot help but be bold. When people are convinced that Jesus is alive and exalted to God's right hand and coming again, they know they have nothing to lose that really matters. Persecution will not be able to stop them from declaring the name of Jesus to others. A church that knows Jesus will witness boldly to His resurrection, and their witness will be accompanied by great power (4:33).

(17) An exemplary church lives in the grace of God (Acts 4:33b). God's grace was upon Jesus as He grew up and during His public ministry (Luke 2:40; John 1:14). In Acts the essence of the apostles' preaching was a message about God's grace (Acts 14:3). God saves sinners by grace, and sinners are able to believe by the grace that comes from God (Acts 15:11; 18:27). To be saved by grace is to realize that though no good work can ever make a sinner righteous before God (Rom 3:19–20), God justifies sinners freely by His grace (Rom 3:24). To believe by grace is to experience the kindness of God that overcomes our resistance and leads us to repentance (Rom 2:4; Jer 31:3). The sense of Acts 4:33 is that a profound awareness of the favor and kindness of God rested upon the entire church in Jerusalem. The atmosphere was thick with grace. In such a fellowship, there is great power to lead people to repentance, to be reconciled to others, to experience healing, and so on. An exemplary church is determined to know and live in the grace of God and to give His grace to others (2 Cor 8:1–7; 9:1; 1 Pet 4:10).

(18) The risk of persecution will keep some from joining an exemplary church (Acts 5:13a). Many people in Jerusalem were afraid to join the church due to the risk of persecution. The call to follow Jesus and be associated with His apostles and other believers potentially had real consequences (Luke 9:23; Acts 5:40; 7:58–8:3; 12:2), which is why Jesus insisted that people count the cost before they became His disciples (Luke 14:25–33). The proclamation that salvation was only available in Jesus (Acts 4:12) put the apostles in the crosshairs of the Sanhedrin. The gospel confronts a person's pride, and if people do not want to hear the message, they will turn on the messenger. Luke wanted readers to know that professing Jesus as Messiah and joining the church can be costly. Association with the church in Jerusalem was costly enough to keep some people from joining. Such a statement seems strange in a portrait of positive activity. However, it needs to be acknowledged that if a bold witness and a godly life will likely lead to persecution (2 Tim 3:12), then an exemplary church will not be surprised when it comes. It will also recognize that some will not want to join, because they have counted the cost and found it to be too high.

(19) An exemplary church will earn the respect of its community (Acts 5:13b). Even though many people in Jerusalem stayed away from the church due to the fear of persecution, they still respected the believers. The religious leaders were filled with jealousy toward the church (5:17) but not their neighbors. They spoke highly of the believers (5:13b).

When the church has integrity and is authentically present to the world, people who do not know Jesus will observe God's presence in the lives of His people and respect them. The world sees their courage and boldness (Acts 4:31; 5:13). It sees the way they care for each other (Acts 2:44–45; 4:32,34–35) and is convinced that they are Jesus' disciples (John 13:34–35). They see the good works of believers and are led to give glory to God (Matt 5:16). They see the unity of the church and are convinced that the Father sent the Son (John 17:20–21). They see the good conduct of believers, and the ignorant talk of foolish people is silenced (1 Pet 2:15). When the church tolerates rebellion and compromise, it gives people a reason to blaspheme God's name (Rom 2:24). However, when believers aspire by grace to live up to their calling of being the presence of Christ in the world, God makes them influential and causes people to respect them. This respect is often the first step people take toward considering the gospel.

(20) An exemplary church respects other believers and churches in matters of difference in race and culture (Acts 2:5,9–11; 4:32). The final feature of an exemplary church's character is hinted at in the summary narratives but developed more fully in the relationship between the Jerusalem church and the Gentile churches of Acts. Acts 4:32 indicates that the Jewish church in Jerusalem was of "one heart and soul." However, this unity would be tested regularly as the gospel moved toward the Gentiles. Luke shows how God's people must learn to respect each other in matters of difference in race and culture, as the following examples show.

First, the Jerusalem church already possessed considerable racial and cultural diversity. God-fearing Jews "from every nation under heaven" made a pilgrimage to Jerusalem for the feast of Pentecost (Acts 2:5). Parthians, Medes, Elamites, Mesopotamians, Judeans, Cappadocians, people from Pontus, Asians, Phrygians, Pamphylians, Egyptians, Libyans, Romans, Cretans, and Arabs were among the Jews who heard Peter preach and surely among the 3,000 who believed (2:9–11,41). The Jewish church in Jerusalem, from its inception, experienced the diversity of the nations in its midst.

Second, the rift between the Hellenistic and the Hebraic Jewish widows shows that this diversity in the Jerusalem church was not always easy to navigate (Acts 6:1–7). It is often noted by commentators that the Seven who were selected to oversee all ministry to widows had Greek names (6:5) and were likely from the Hellenistic wing of the church.[27] If this is true, then the Hebraic Jews, who would have been considered insiders and

---

[27] C. K. Barrett, *Acts 1–14*, ICC (New York: T&T Clark, 1994), 314–15; Bock, *Acts*, 261; F. F.

closest to the apostles and their families, showed remarkable deference to the Hellenistic families who felt overlooked.

Third, when the Samaritans accepted the word of God, the Jerusalem church sent Peter and John to them who prayed that they might receive the Holy Spirit. That God waited until the apostles from Jerusalem arrived to give the Holy Spirit shows His concern that the two groups recognize and affirm His hand on each of them (Acts 8:14–17).

Fourth, the same thing happened with the conversion of the Gentile Cornelius's household. The Jewish leadership of the Jerusalem church struggled with Peter's entrance into the home of an uncircumcised man, until Peter told them how he saw the Holy Spirit come on them (Acts 10:44–48; 11:1–3,15–16). He asked them, "How could I possibly hinder God?" On hearing this, the Jewish church glorified God, saying that God had granted repentance to the Gentiles (11:17–18).

Fifth, when the Jerusalem church heard about the great number of Greeks turning to the Lord in Antioch, they sent Barnabas to them. When he saw the evidence of God's grace, he was glad and stayed on for a long time to teach them (Acts 11:21–23,26). The church in Antioch showed deference and respect for the Jewish church through the famine relief offering they collected for their brothers in Judea (11:29–30).

Sixth, when the dispute over the salvation of Gentiles who had not been circumcised was resolved, respect and deference went both ways (Acts 15:1–29). The Jewish church in Jerusalem affirmed unequivocally that Gentiles did not have to become Jews in order to be saved (15:19). However, they also asked the believers in Antioch to abstain from several practices that were associated with paganism, which would help the consciences of Jews (15:20–21).[28] The result of the Council in Jerusalem was that the Jewish church in Jerusalem respected and affirmed God's work among the Gentiles, and the Gentile church in Antioch deferred to the consciences of the Jewish believers in Jerusalem. All the churches were strengthened in the faith and grew daily in numbers (16:5).

Seventh, perhaps the most poignant example of Luke's desire to show mutual respect between Jewish and Gentile believers is the numerous echoes of life in the Jerusalem church in his descriptions of Gentile churches. Every time Luke shows a Gentile church imitating behaviors

---

Bruce, *The Acts of the Apostles: The Greek Text with Introduction and Commentary* (Grand Rapids: Eerdmans, 1990), 183; Polhill, *Acts*, 181.

[28] See the helpful discussions in Ben Witherington III, *The Acts of the Apostles: A Socio-Rhetorical Commentary* (Grand Rapids: Eerdmans, 1998), 461–70; and Bock, *Acts*, 505–6.

first introduced in the summary narratives, the effect is an implicit affirmation of their Jewish roots by the Gentiles.

The many examples in Acts of Jewish and Gentile believers learning to respect each other serve as a case study for dealing with differences in race and culture among Christians. Acts acknowledges that genuine differences can exist that are not always easy to sort out or set aside. Yet, the call to respect each other and overcome differences is not optional, for in Christ there is neither Jew nor Gentile (Gal 3:28). By his death Jesus tore down the dividing wall of hostility between Jew and Gentile that He might reconcile the two and bring us all near to Him through the blood of Christ (Eph 2:13–16). An exemplary church looks outside of itself and beyond the people who are like them to see the church composed of people from every culture, tribe, and nation (Rev 4:9).

The Mission of the Church

Jesus assigned the mission of the church to His disciples when He told them they would be His witnesses in the power of the Holy Spirit to the ends of the earth (Acts 1:8). I have argued that the call to go and tell others about Jesus cannot be separated from the call to gather new converts into churches. The mission in Acts is about going and gathering, not just going and telling.[29] The 120 believers who prayed and waited in the upper room (Luke 24:49; Acts 1:8,12–14) for power (Acts 2:1–4) became the church (Acts 2:42–47; 4:32–35; 5:12–16) before they were thrust into their mission. Everywhere the believers went proclaiming the gospel and leading people to faith in Jesus, they left churches in their wake. The church that was planted in Antioch became a missionary-sending church that quickly surpassed her parent church in Jerusalem in missional living. Without the church new believers will struggle to grow. They need to be taught. They need a fellowship they can connect with, take the Lord's Supper with, and pray with (2:42). They need a group of friends with whom they can share their lives. In short, they need the experience of church life that the summary narratives describe that will mature and equip them as they take the gospel to the ends of the earth.

---

[29] Edmund P. Clowney, *The Church* (Downers Grove, IL: InterVarsity, 1995), 159–60.

CHAPTER EIGHT

DIRECTIONS FOR APPLICATION

T his study of church life in Acts grew out of a deep love for the local church and the desire to see her strengthened. Luke's voice has been underemphasized in conversations about the formation of churches that are faithful to the New Testament pattern. My friends in the restorationist movements look to Acts for help on how to pattern their churches, and I am grateful for their efforts, even if I might not approach church life in exactly the same way they do. Yet, Luke has definite convictions about the church that can be articulated in a theology of church life that transcends the generation in which the church was birthed and is relevant to twenty-first-century living. I demonstrated that the historical-critical approach to Acts casts a shadow over the summary narratives by undermining confidence in their historicity and cutting them off from their larger literary and theological context in Acts. The commentary survey showed how this neglect has caused interpreters to pay insufficient attention to church life in Acts as an important theme. Moreover, when church life in Acts is studied, the summary narratives often are not accessed in their entirety as a resource for Luke's thinking. I have shown that Acts 2:42–47; 4:32–35; and 5:12–16 should be considered the starting point for Luke's theology of church life.

Other reasons for their neglect could have been considered. For instance, Paul's letters were written specifically to churches or leaders of churches. This gives his letters a pastoral character, which makes it easier to look to Paul for wisdom on the church. Acts is usually treated as a historical account that serves as a resource for information about the early church—and it is no less than that. However, Acts is also an invaluable theological resource for reflection on church life. Luke and Paul traveled together and partnered in the work of church planting as the "we" passages of Acts show. Paul's letters represent his best, Spirit-led, thinking on the church. Yet Luke clearly was thinking hard about the church as he labored with Paul, and he embedded his convictions within the fabric of his historical account.

Another reason we miss Luke's emphasis on church life is our tendency to read Acts from a modernist historical perspective that does not adequately consider the rhetorical character of Acts. Luke's education included training in how to write history, but he clearly was steeped in the oral and rhetorical culture of the first century that taught him how to speak and write persuasively. Acts was meant to be read out loud in a meeting of the church, rather than read silently. The speeches of Acts show the influence of Luke's rhetorical training, but the narrative sections do too. The summary narratives are a skillful use of the narrative technique of summarization, modified to suit Luke's own rhetorical purposes, to set forth his descriptions of life in the Jerusalem church in exemplary fashion for readers. The attentive listener in the first century would have caught many of the rhetorical clues discussed in chapter 2, which modern readers often miss. However, we still turn instinctively to verses in them when we want help on the church, because they present an exemplary picture of church life. Luke wants the summary narratives to do just that in the minds of his hearers and readers. His descriptions of exemplary life in the Gentile churches of Acts echo the summary narratives and reinforce their message. Luke shows Gentile believers and churches responding to Jesus in the same way as the Jerusalem church. This continuity in church life is all the more remarkable when one considers that the Jerusalem church was born in a thoroughly Jewish culture, and the Gentile churches arose out of a Hellenistic culture. Yet, they both worshipped and served the same Jesus who is the Savior for all nations.

How might this book be of service to the church today? I have four suggestions. First, we should approach Acts the way Luke intended. Acts should be read publicly. Paul exhorted the young pastor Timothy to give attention to the public reading of Scripture (1 Tim 4:13). He also gave instructions to the church in Colossae about reading his letter aloud there (Col 4:16). Paul and Luke wrote in a day when the oral reading of texts was the way most people learned their content. The oral performance of great texts was important in the Roman Empire so people could learn their history and heritage. The oral performance of the Scriptures in the worship of the church was important so that believers could learn their story as the people of God and be formed by it. Acts was written with listeners in mind, not just readers. Luke writes to inform, but he also writes to shape the moral and spiritual imaginations of his audience so they will see themselves as a part of the story God was writing (see Acts 1:1; 28:31).[1] Read Acts out loud within a group of believers in Jesus. Listen for the plot and discuss the big picture ideas about the church together as the church (19:9–10). Resist the temptation to study the summary narratives in isolation from their relationship to the overall narrative of Acts, especially the mission of witness to Jesus to the ends of the earth (1:8). Focus, instead, on how going and "telling" and going and "gathering" complement each other in the story of the expansion of the church. More importantly, consider how church life in your own congregation might be shaped fruitfully toward mission by Luke's exemplary portraits in Acts.

Second, after reading Acts as a whole and hearing it performed orally, study it closely. Give special attention to the exemplary character of the believers in the Jerusalem church. Remember that Luke employs a rhetorical device known as the exemplum in order to highlight their positive qualities in a persuasive way for readers. Luke does not ignore the church's problems in surrounding episodes, but he deliberately highlights her best

---

[1] Doug Hume's recent work on Acts 2:41–47 and 4:32–35 is of tremendous help here. Hume, interacting with my doctoral work and others, recommends the application of narrative ethics as a way of cultivating the interpreter's "narrative literary and narrative theological sensibilities." He does this in order to get at the "morally performative potential" of the summary narratives and shows how they allow members of a specific reading community to be engaged by God. Hume is especially interested in how the summary narratives engage the Greco-Roman idea of friendship in terms of God's community-making activity among the believers in Jerusalem, in particular around the ideas of sharing possessions, hospitality, and bold witness. See Douglas A. Hume, *The Early Christian Community: A Narrative Analysis of Acts 2:41–47 and 4:32–35* (Tübingen, Germany: Mohr Siebeck, 2011), 42–43.

qualities in the summary narratives so that they will have an impact on readers. The twenty qualities that describe the character of an exemplary church in chapter 7 are somewhat arbitrary. The list could be shortened or lengthened, and hopefully it will be improved upon by students of the church in Acts who read this book. My purpose in compiling such a list was to make it easier to bring the results of my exegesis to readers. But there is a danger in list-making that readers will do the same kind of atomizing of the summary narratives that I have accused historical critics of doing. Luke wants us to hear the summary narratives above all as a whole and as part of the overall narrative fabric of Acts. Nevertheless, reading them closely in order to understand the various commitments the believers made can provide a fruitful pathway for applying Luke's teaching to church life today.

Third, after reading Acts closely with attention to Luke's convictions about church life, read it alongside other New Testament writings on the church. What emphases in Acts stand out that need to be reasserted today in our quest to be faithful to the New Testament pattern? What would Luke add to the conversation on the church that needs to be said today? Several distinctive Lukan emphases have impacted me during this study. First, it has been driven home that to be the church is to be on God's mission. Missiology cannot be separated from ecclesiology because they run together in Acts. Every local church should see itself as a Great Commission people, called and empowered by God to take the gospel to its city and to the ends of the earth. Second, to be the church is to proclaim the welcome of God. The breaking of bread in Acts uniquely expresses God's hospitality because it refers both to shared meals and the Lord's Supper. The message of Jesus' death for sin is at the heart of the Lord's Supper. However, Luke sets this message within a context of friends who truly loved one another's company. They ate together with glad and sincere hearts as they followed a Savior who genuinely enjoys the friendship of His people. God calls sinners to come to Him through Christ and experience His welcome. Third, an exemplary church radically reorients itself toward worldly possessions. The summary narratives depict a fellowship that was shot through with compassion for people in need. They gave extravagantly. Everyone participated. And there were no poor among them. God's people have in the gospel of Jesus Christ and the church He is building a powerful resource with which to engage the poverty and brokenness of our world, especially our cities. These and other emphases in

Acts challenge me to listen more carefully to Luke's voice on church life and adjust my thinking and habits accordingly.

Finally, I offer an encouragement to writers of commentaries on Acts, especially works written with the church in mind. Remember that high on Luke's list of reasons for writing Acts is a desire to communicate his convictions about what life together could be like in the church of the risen Jesus. Recent scholarship has given this aspect of Acts less attention than it deserves. More attention should be paid in future commentaries to the role the summary narratives play in the theology of church life in Acts. My prayer is that this study will provoke a greater love for the church of the risen Jesus and a desire to see her become everything God intends for her to be. If that happens, the effort will have been worth it.

BIBLIOGRAPHY

Allison, G. R. "Theological Interpretation of Scripture: An Introduction and Preliminary Evaluation." *The Southern Baptist Journal of Theology* 14, no. 2 (2010): 28–36.

Alter, R. *The Art of Biblical Narrative.* New York: Basic Books, 1981.

———. *The Pleasures of Reading in an Ideological Age.* New York: Simon and Schuster, 1989.

Andersen, T. D. "The Meaning of ΕΧΟΝΤΕΣ ΧΑΡΙΝ ΠΡΟΣ in Acts 2:47." *NTS* 34, no. 4 (1988): 604–10.

Andrews, M. E. "Tendenz Versus Interpretation: F. C. Baur's Criticisms of Luke." *JBL* 58, no. 3 (1939): 263–76.

Anthony, P. "What Are They Saying about Luke-Acts?" *ScrB* 40, no. 1 (January 2010): 10–21.

Arieti, J. A. *Longinus.* Lewiston, NY: Edwin Mellen Press, 1985.

Arnold, C. E. "Centers of Christianity." In *DLNT*, edited by R. P. Martin and P. H. Davids, 144–52. Downers Grove, IL: InterVarsity, 1997.

Arrington, F. L. *The Acts of the Apostles.* Peabody, MA: Hendrickson, 1988.

Arterbury, A. "The Ancient Custom of Hospitality, The Greek Novels and Acts 10:1–11:18." *PRSt* 29, no. 1 (2002): 53–72.

———. "The Downfall of Eutychus: How Ancient Understandings of Sleep Illuminate Acts 20:7–12." In *Contemporary Studies in Acts*, edited by T. E. Phillips, 201–21. Macon, GA: Mercer University Press, 2009.

Ascough, R. S. "Narrative Technique and Generic Designation: Crowd Scenes in Luke-Acts." *CBQ* 58, no. 1 (1996): 69–81.

Atkins, J. W. H. *Literary Criticism in Antiquity.* Cambridge: Cambridge University Press, 1934.

Aune, D. E. *The New Testament in Its Literary Environment.* Philadelphia: Westminster, 1987.

———. *The Westminster Dictionary of New Testament and Early Christian Literature and Rhetoric*, 173. Louisville: Westminster John Knox, 2003.

Bailey, J. L. "Genre Analysis." In *Hearing the New Testament: Strategies for Interpretation*, edited by J. B. Green, 140–65. Grand Rapids: Eerdmans, 2010.

Baird, W. *From Deism to Tübingen*. Vol. 1 of *History of New Testament Research*. Minneapolis: Augsburg Fortress, 1992.

Baker, D. L. *Tight Fists or Open Hands? Wealth and Poverty in Old Testament Law*. Grand Rapids: Eerdmans, 2009.

Bal, M. *Narratology: Introduction to the Theory of Narrative*. Toronto: University of Toronto Press, 1997.

Balch, D. "The Genre of Luke-Acts: Individual Biography, Adventure Novel, or Political History." *SwJT* 33, no. 1 (1990): 5–19.

Banks, R. "The Role of Charismatic and Noncharismatic Factors in Determining Paul's Movements in Acts." In *The Holy Spirit and Christian Origins: Essays in Honor of James D. G. Dunn*, edited by G. N. Stanton, S. C. Barton, and B. W. Longenecker, 117–30. Grand Rapids: Eerdmans, 2004.

Bar-Efrat, S. *Narrative Art in the Bible*. Sheffield: Almond, 1989.

Barr, J. *The Bible in the Modern World*. Philadelphia: Trinity, 1987.

Barrett, C. K. *Acts 1–14*. ICC. New York: T&T Clark, 1994.

———. *Acts 15–28*. ICC. New York: T&T Clark, 1998.

Bartchy, S. S. "Divine Power, Community Formation, and Leadership in the Acts of the Apostles." In *Community Formation in the Early Church and in the Church Today*, edited by R. N. Longenecker, 89–104. Peabody, MA: Hendrickson, 2002.

———. "Narrative Criticism." In *DLNT*, edited by R. P. Martin and P. H. Davids, 787–92. Downers Grove, IL: InterVarsity, 1997.

Bartholomew, C. G., and R. Holt. "Prayer in/and the Drama of Redemption in Luke." In *Reading Luke: Interpretation, Reflection, and Formation*, edited by C. G. Bartholomew, J. B. Green, and A. C. Thiselton, 350–75. Grand Rapids: Zondervan, 2006.

Barton, S. C. "The Communal Dimension of Earliest Christianity: A Critical Survey of the Field." *JTS* 43, no. 2 (October 1992): 399–427.

Bauckham, R. "The Early Jerusalem Church, Qumran, and the Essenes." In *The Dead Sea Scrolls as Background to Postbiblical Judaism and Early Christianity*, edited by J. R. Davila, 63–89. Leiden: Brill, 2003.

————. "For Whom Were the Gospels Written?" In *The Gospel for All Christians*, edited by R. Bauckham, 9–48. Grand Rapids: Eerdmans, 1998.

————. *Jesus and the Eyewitnesses: The Gospels as Eyewitness Testimony.* Grand Rapids: Eerdmans, 2006.

Bauer, D. *The Structure of Matthew's Gospel: A Study in Literary Design.* Sheffield: Almond, 1988.

Bauer, W., W. F. Arndt, F. W. Gingrich, and F. Danker. *BAGD.* Chicago: University of Chicago Press, 1979.

Bayer, H. "The Preaching of Peter in Acts." In *Witness to the Gospel: The Theology of Acts*, edited by I. H. Marshall and D. Peterson, 257–74. Grand Rapids: Eerdmans, 1998.

Beardslee, W. A. *Literary Criticism of the New Testament.* Philadelphia: Fortress, 1969.

Beasley-Murray, G. R. *Baptism in the New Testament.* Grand Rapids: Eerdmans, 1962.

Beck, J. A. *God as Storyteller: Seeking Meaning in Biblical Narrative.* St. Louis: Chalice, 2008.

Benoit, P. "Remarques sur les Sommaries des Actes II, IV, et V." In *Exégèse et Théologie*, vol. 2, 181–92. Paris: Les Editions du Cerf, 1961.

Bieder, W. "Der Petruschatten, Apg. 5:15." *TZ* 16 (1960): 407–9.

Blass, F., A. Debrunner, and R. W. Funk. *BDF.* Chicago: University of Chicago Press, 1961.

Blevins, W. L. "The Early Church: Acts 1–5." *RevExp* 71, no. 4 (1974): 462–74.

Blocher, H. "Biblical Narrative and Historical Reference." In *Issues in Faith and History*, edited by N. M. de S. Cameron, 102–22. Edinburgh: Rutherford House, 1989.

Blomberg, C. L. "Form Criticism." In *DJG*, edited by J. Green and S. McKnight, 243–50. Downers Grove, IL: InterVarsity, 1992.

Blue, B. B. "Acts and the House Church." In *The Book of Acts in Its Greco-Roman Setting*, edited by D. W. J. Gill and C. Gempf, 119–222. Grand Rapids: Eerdmans, 1994.

————. "Architecture, Early Church." In *DLNT*, edited by R. P. Martin and P. H. Davids, 91–95. Downers Grove, IL: InterVarsity, 1997.

————. "The Influence of Jewish Worship on Luke's Presentation of the Early Church." In *Witness to the Gospel: The Theology of Acts*, edited by I. H. Marshall and D. Peterson, 473–97. Grand Rapids: Eerdmans, 1998.

Bock, D. L. *Acts*. BECNT. Grand Rapids: Baker Academic, 2007.

Bockmuehl, M. *Seeing the Word: Refocusing New Testament Study*. Grand Rapids: Baker Academic, 2006.

Böhm, M. *Samarien und die Samaritai bei lukas: Eine Studie zum religionshistorischen und traditionsgeschichtlichen Hintergrund der lukanischen Samarientexte und zu deren topographischer Verhaftung*. Tübingen: Mohr Siebeck, 1999.

Bonheim, H. *The Narrative Modes*. Cambridge: D. S. Brewer, 1982.

Bonnah, G. K. A. *The Holy Spirit: A Narrative Factor in the Acts of the Apostles*. Stuttgart: Katholisches Bibelwerk, 2007.

Booth, W. C. *The Rhetoric of Fiction*. Chicago: University of Chicago Press, 1961.

Bori, P. C. *Chiesa Primitiva: L'immagine della communità delle origini-Atti 2,42–47; 4,32–37-nella storia della chiesa antica*. Brescia, Italy: Paideia Editrice, 1974.

Bornhäußer, D. K. *Studien zur Apostelgeschichte*. Gütersloh: Bertelsmann, 1934.

Brand, C. O., ed. *Perspectives on Spirit Baptism: Five Views*. Nashville: B&H, 2004.

Brawley, R. L. *Centering on God: Method and Message in Luke-Acts*. Louisville: Westminster John Knox, 1990.

———. "Social Identity and the Aim of Accomplished Life in Acts 2." In *Acts and Ethics*, edited by T. E. Phillips, 16–33. Sheffield: Sheffield Academic, 2005.

Bray, G. *Biblical Interpretation: Past and Present*. Downers Grove, IL: InterVarsity, 1996.

Brehm, A. "The Significance of the Summaries for Interpreting Acts." *SwJT* 33, no. 1 (Fall 1990): 29–40.

Brock, R. "Authorial Voice and Narrative Management in Herodotus." In *Herodotus and His World*, edited by P. Derow and R. Parker, 3–16. Oxford: Oxford University Press, 2003.

Brooks, J. *Mark*. NAC. Nashville: B&H, 1991.

Brosend, W. F., II. "The Means of Absent Ends." In *History, Literature, and Society in the Book of Acts*, edited by B. Witherington, 348–62. New York: Cambridge University Press, 1996.

Brown, J. K. "Genre Criticism and the Bible." In *Words and the Word: Explorations in Biblical and Literary Theory*, edited by D. G. Firth and J. A. Grant, 111–50. Downers Grove, IL: InterVarsity, 2008.

Brown, W. P. "Theological Interpretation: A Proposal." In *Method Matters: Essays on the Interpretation of the Hebrew Bible in Honor of David L. Petersen*, edited by J. M. LeMon and K. H. Richards, 387–405. Atlanta: Society of Biblical Literature, 2009.

Bruce, F. F. *The Acts of the Apostles: The Greek Text with Introduction and Commentary*. Grand Rapids: Eerdmans, 1990.

———. *The Book of Acts*. NICNT. Rev. ed. Grand Rapids: Eerdmans, 1988.

———. "The Church of Jerusalem in the Acts of the Apostles." *BJRL* 67 (Spring 1985): 641–61.

———. "The History of New Testament Study." In *New Testament Interpretation: Essays on Principles and Methods*, edited by I. H. Marshall, 21–59. Grand Rapids: Eerdmans, 1977.

———. *A Mind for What Matters: Collected Essays of F. F. Bruce*. Grand Rapids: Eerdmans, 1990.

Buckwalter, H. D. "Luke as Writer of Sacred History." *EvJ* 14, no. 2 (1996): 86–99.

Cadbury, H. J. "Acts of the Apostles." In *Interpreters Dictionary of the Bible*, edited by G. A. Buttrick, 21–42. Nashville: Abingdon, 1962.

———. *The Making of Luke-Acts*. New York: Macmillan, 1927.

———. *The Style and Literary Method of Luke*. Cambridge, MA: Harvard University Press, 1920.

———. "The Summaries in Acts." In *The Beginnings of Christianity*, vol. 5, edited by F. J. Foakes-Jackson and K. Lake, 392–402. London: MacMillan, 1933.

Campbell, W. S. "The Narrator as 'He,' 'Me,' and 'We': Grammatical Person in Ancient Histories and in the Acts of the Apostles." *JBL* 129, no. 2 (2010): 385–407.

Capper, B. J. "Holy Community of Life and Property Amongst the Poor: A Response to Steve Walton." *EvQ* 80, no. 2 (2008): 113–27.

———. "The Palestinian Cultural Context of Earliest Christian Community of Goods." In *The Book of Acts in Its Palestinian Setting*, edited by R. Bauckham, 323–56. Grand Rapids: Eerdmans, 1995.

Carr, A. "The Fellowship (Κοινωνία) of Acts II.42 and Cognate Words." *The Expositor* 29, no. 8 (1913): 458–64.

Carson, D. A. "New Testament Theology." In *DLNT*, edited by R. P. Martin and P. H. Davids, 796–814. Downers Grove, IL: InterVarsity, 1997.

———. "Redaction Criticism: On the Legitimacy and Illegitimacy of a Literary Tool." In *Scripture and Truth*, edited by D. A. Carson and J. D. Woodbridge, 119–42. Grand Rapids: Zondervan, 1983.

———, ed. *From Sabbath to Lord's Day: A Biblical, Historical and Theological Investigation.* Eugene, OR: Wipf and Stock, 2000.

Cerfaux, L. "La Composition de la première partie du Livre des Actes." *ETL* 13 (1936): 667–91.

———. "La première communauté chrétienne à Jérusalem." *ETL* 16 (1939): 5–31.

Chambers, A. "An Evaluation of Characteristic Activity in a Model Church as Set Forth by the Summary Narratives of Acts." Ph.D. diss., Southwestern Baptist Theological Seminary, 1994.

———"The Promise and Peril of Postmodernism for Ministry Today." *Intégrité* (Fall 2003): 53–69.

Chance, J. B. *Acts*. SHBC. Macon, GA: Smyth & Helwys, 2007.

———. *Jerusalem, the Temple, and the New Age in Luke-Acts.* Macon, GA: Mercer University Press, 1988.

Chatman, S. *Story and Discourse: Narrative Structure in Fiction and Film.* Ithaca, NY: Cornell University Press, 1978.

Cheetham, F. P. "Acts ii.47: ἔχοντες χαρίν πρὸς ὅλον τὸν λαόν." *ExpTim* 74, no. 7 (1963): 214–15.

Clark, A. "The Role of the Apostles." In *Witness to the Gospel: The Theology of Acts*, edited by I. H. Marshall and D. Peterson, 169–90. Grand Rapids: Eerdmans, 1998.

Classen, C. J. "Rhetoric and Literary Criticism: Their Nature and Their Functions in Antiquity." *Mnemosyne* 48, no. 5 (1995): 513–35.

Clowney, E. P. *The Church*. Downers Grove, IL: InterVarsity, 1995.

Co, M. A. *The Composite Summaries in Acts 2–5: A Study of Luke's Use of Summary as a Narrative Technique.* Louvain, Belgium: Louvain University Press, 1990.

———. "The Major Summaries in Acts." *ETL* 68, no. 1 (1992): 49–81.

Coats, G. W. "On Narrative Criticism." *Semeia* 3 (1975): 137–41.

Cobley, P. "Narratology." In *The Johns Hopkins Guide to Literary Theory and Criticism*, edited by M. Groden, M. Kreiswirth, and I. Szeman, 677–82. Baltimore, MD: Johns Hopkins University Press, 2005.

Conzelmann, H. *Acts of the Apostles*. Translated by J. Limburg. Hermeneia. Philadelphia: Fortress, 1987.

Conzelmann, H., and A. Lindemann. *Interpreting the New Testament: An Introduction to the Principles and Methods of N.T. Exegesis*. Translated by S. S. Schatzmann. Peabody, MA: Hendrickson, 1988.

Coste, D. *Narrative as Communication*. Minneapolis: University of Minnesota Press, 1989.

Cranford, L. L. "Modern New Testament Interpretation." In *Biblical Hermeneutics: A Comprehensive Guide to Interpreting Scripture*, edited by B. Corley, S. Lemke, and G. Lovejoy, 116–32. Nashville: B&H, 1996.

Creech, R. R. "The Most Excellent Narratee: The Significance of Theophilus in Luke-Acts." In *With Steadfast Purpose*, edited by N. H. Keathley, 107–26. Waco, TX: Baylor University Press, 1990.

Culler, J. *Structuralist Poetics: Structuralism, Linguistics, and the Study of Literature*. Ithaca, NY: Cornell University Press, 1975.

Culpepper, R. A. *Anatomy of the Fourth Gospel: A Study in Literary Design*. Philadelphia: Fortress, 1983.

Culy, M. M., and M. C. Parsons. *Acts: A Handbook on the Greek Text*. Waco, TX: Baylor University Press, 2003.

Damon, C. "Rhetoric and Historiography." In *A Companion to Roman Rhetoric*, edited by W. Dominik and J. Hall, 439–50. Oxford: Blackwell, 2007.

Darr, J. A. "Narrator as Character: Mapping a Reader-Oriented Approach to Narration in Luke-Acts." *Semeia* 63 (1993): 43–60.

Davids, P. H. "Miracles in Acts." In *DLNT*, edited by R. P. Martin and P. H. Davids, 746–52. Downers Grove, IL: InterVarsity, 1997.

Davies, W. D. *The People and the Land*. Berkley, CA: University of California Press, 1974.

De Jong, I. J. F. "Aristotle on the Homeric Narrator." *CQ* 55, no. 2 (2005): 616–21.

De Jong, I. J. F., and R. Nünlist, eds. *Time in Ancient Greek Literature*. Leiden: Brill, 2007.

Demoen, K. "A Paradigm for the Analysis of Paradigms: The Rhetorical Exemplum in Ancient and Imperial Greek Theory." *Rhetorica* 15, no. 2 (Spring 1997): 125–58.

Derow, P. "Historical Explanation: Polybius and His Predecessors." In *Greek Historiography*, edited by S. Hornblower, 73–90. Oxford: Clarendon, 1994.

De Zwaan, J. "Was the Book of Acts a Posthumous Edition?" *HTR* 17 (1924): 95–153.

Dibelius, M. "Stilkritisches zur Apostelgeschichte." In *Aufsätze zur Apostelgeschichte*, edited by H. Greeven, 9–28. Göttingen: Vandenhoecht & Ruprecht, 1951.

———. *Studies in the Acts of the Apostles*. Translated by M. Ling, 1–25. New York: Charles Scribner's Sons, 1956.

Dockery, D. S. *Christian Scripture: An Evangelical Perspective on Inspiration, Authority, and Interpretation*. Nashville: B&H, 1995.

———. "The Theology of Acts." *CTR* 5, no. 1 (1990): 43–55.

Donato, C. J., ed. *Perspectives on the Sabbath: Four Views*. Nashville: B&H Academic, 2011.

Dowd, W. "Breaking Bread: Acts 2:46." *CBQ* 1, no. 2 (1939): 358–62.

Dunn, J. D. G. *The Acts of the Apostles*. Valley Forge: Trinity Press International, 1996.

———. *Baptism in the Holy Spirit*. Philadelphia: Westminster, 1970.

———. *Beginning from Jerusalem*. Christianity in the Making. Grand Rapids: Eerdmans, 2009.

Dupertuis, R. R. "The Summaries of Acts 2, 4, and 5 and Plato's Republic." In *Ancient Fiction: The Matrix of Early Christian and Jewish Narrative*, edited by J. Brant, C. Hedrick, and C. Shea, 275–95. Atlanta: Society of Biblical Literature, 2005.

Dupont, J. "Community of Goods in the Early Church." In *The Salvation of the Gentiles: Essays on the Acts of the Apostles*. Translated by J. R. Keating, 85–102. New York: Paulist, 1979.

Egger, W. *Frohbotschaft und Lehre: Die Sammelberichte des Werkens Jesu im Markusevangelium*. Frankfurt: Joseph Knecht, 1976.

Elliott, J. H. "Temple Versus Household in Luke-Acts: A Contrast in Social Institutions." In *The Social World of Luke-Acts*, edited by J. H. Neyrey, 211–40. Peabody, MA: Hendrickson, 1991.

Ellis, E. E. "Historical-Literary Criticism after 200 Years: Origins, Aberrations, Contributions, Limitations." In *The Proceedings of the Conference on Biblical Inerrancy*, 411–21. Nashville: Broadman, 1987.

Else, G. "Imitation in the Fifth Century." *CP* 53 (1958): 73–90.

Enslin, M. S. "The Samaritan Ministry and Mission." *HUCA* 51 (1980): 29–38.

Ferguson, E. "'When You Come Together': Epi To Auto in Early Christian Literature." *ResQ* 16 (1973): 202–8.

Filson, F. V. *Three Crucial Decades*. Richmond: John Knox, 1963.

Finger, R. H. "Cultural Attitudes in Western Christianity Toward the Community of Goods in Acts 2 and 4." *Mennonite Quarterly Review* 78 (2004): 235–70.

———. *Of Widows and Meals: Communal Meals in the Acts of the Apostles*. Grand Rapids: Eerdmans, 2007.

Finkel, A. "Prayer in Jewish Life of the First Century as Background to Early Christianity." In *Into God's Presence: Prayer in the New Testament*, edited by R. N. Longenecker, 43–65. Grand Rapids: Eerdmans, 2001.

Fiore, B. *The Function of Personal Example in the Socratic and Pastoral Epistles*. Rome: Biblical Institute, 1986.

Fitzmyer, J. *The Acts of the Apostles*. Anchor Bible. New York: Doubleday, 1998.

———. "Jewish Christianity in Light of the Qumran Scrolls." In *Studies in Luke-Acts*, edited by L. E. Keck and J. L. Martyn, 233–57. Philadelphia: Fortress, 1966.

Fleming, J. D. "The Very Idea of a Progymnasmata." *Rhetoric Review* 22, no. 2 (2003): 105–20.

Fowl, S. E. "The New Testament, Theology, and Ethics." In *Hearing the New Testament: Strategies for Interpretation*, edited by J. B. Green, 397–413. Grand Rapids: Eerdmans, 2010.

Fox, M. "Dionysius, Lucian, and the Prejudice Against Rhetoric in History." *JRS* 91 (2001): 76–93.

Funk, R. W. *The Poetics of Biblical Narrative*. Sonoma, CA: Polebridge, 1988.

Gasque, W. W. *A History of the Interpretation of the Acts of the Apostles*. Peabody, MA: Hendrickson, 1989.

Gaventa, B. R. *The Acts of the Apostles*. ANTC. Nashville: Abingdon, 2003.

———. "Initiatives Divine and Human in the Lukan Story World." In *The Holy Spirit and Christian Origins: Essays in Honor of James D. G. Dunn*, edited by G. N. Stanton, B. W. Longenecker, and S. Barton, 79–89. Grand Rapids: Eerdmans, 2004.

————. "Theology and Ecclesiology in the Miletus Speech: Reflections on Content and Context." *NTS* 50 (2004): 36–52.

————. "'You Will Be My Witnesses': Aspects of Mission in the Acts of the Apostles." *Missiology: An International Review* 10, no. 4 (October 1982): 413–25.

Gehring, R. W. *House Church and Mission: The Importance of Household Structures in Early Christianity.* Peabody, MA: Hendrickson, 2004.

Genette, G. *Fiction and Diction.* Ithaca, NY: Cornell University Press, 1993.

————. *Narrative Discourse: An Essay in Method.* Translated by J. E. Lewin. Ithaca, NY: Cornell University Press, 1980.

Gerhardsson, B. "Einige Bemerkungen zu Apg 4,32." *ST* 24 (1970): 142–49.

Getz, G. *A Biblical Theology of Possessions.* Chicago: Moody, 1990.

Gibson, C. A. "Learning Greek History in the Ancient Classroom: The Evidence of the Treatises on Progymnasmata." *CP* 99, no. 2 (2004): 103–29.

Giles, K. *What on Earth Is the Church? An Exploration in New Testament Theology.* Downers Grove, IL: InterVarsity, 1995.

Giles, T. *Tradition Kept: The Literature of the Samaritans.* Peabody, MA: Hendrickson, 2005.

Gilliland, D. S. "For Missionaries and Leaders: Paul's Farewell to the Ephesian Elders." In *Mission in Acts: Ancient Narratives in Contemporary Context,* edited by R. L. Gallagher and P. Hertig, 257–73. Maryknoll, NY: Orbis, 2004.

Goldingay, J. "How Far Do Readers Make Sense? Interpreting Biblical Narratives." *Them* 18, no. 2 (1993): 5–10.

Goldsworthy, G. "Biblical Theology and Hermeneutics." *Southern Baptist Journal of Theology* 10, no. 2 (2006): 4–18.

González, J. L. *Acts: The Gospel of the Spirit.* Maryknoll, NY: Orbis, 2001.

————. *Faith and Wealth: A History of Early Christian Ideas on the Origin, Significance, and Use of Money.* San Francisco: Harper and Row, 1990.

Gooding, D. *True to the Faith: A Fresh Approach to the Acts of the Apostles.* London: Hodder & Stoughton, 1990.

Gould, J. "Herodotus and Religion." In *Greek Historiography,* edited by S. Hornblower, 91–105. Oxford: Clarendon, 1996.

Green, J. B. "God as Saviour in the Acts of the Apostles." In *Witness to the Gospel: The Theology of Acts*, edited by I. H. Marshall and D. Peterson, 83–106. Grand Rapids: Eerdmans, 1998.

———. "Narrative and New Testament Interpretation: Reflections on the State of the Art." *LTQ* 39, no. 3 (2004): 153–66.

———. "Persevering Together in Prayer: The Significance of Prayer in the Acts of the Apostles." In *Into God's Presence: Prayer in the New Testament*, edited by R. N. Longenecker, 183–202. Grand Rapids: Eerdmans, 2001.

Green, M. *Evangelism in the Early Church*. Grand Rapids: Eerdmans, 1970.

Gribble, D. "Narrator Interventions in Thucydides." *JHS* 118 (1998): 41–67.

Grundmann, W. "μέγας, ετ αλ." In *TDNT*, vol. 4, translated and edited by G. W. Bromiley, 529–44. Grand Rapids: Eerdmans, 1964.

Guthrie, D. *New Testament Theology*. Downers Grove, IL: InterVarsity, 1981.

Haenchen, E. *The Acts of the Apostles*. Translated by R. Wilson. Philadelphia: Westminster, 1971.

Halliwell, S. "The Theory and Practice of Narrative in Plato." In *Narratology and Interpretation: The Content of Narrative Form in Ancient Literature*, edited by J. Grethlein and A. Rengakos, 15–41. Berlin: Walter de Gruyter, 2009.

Hamblin, R. L. "Miracles in the Book of Acts." *SwJT* 17, no. 1 (Fall 1974): 19–34.

Hamel, G. H. *Poverty and Charity in Roman Palestine, First Three Centuries C. E.* Berkley: University of California Press, 1989.

Hamm, D. "The Mission Has a Church: Spirit, World, and Church in Luke-Acts." In *The Spirit in the Church and the World*, edited by B. E. Hinze, 68–80. New York: Orbis, 2004.

Hardon, J. A. "The Miracle Stories in the Acts of the Apostles." *CBQ* 16, no. 3 (1954): 303–18.

Harper, B., and P. L. Metzger. *Exploring Ecclesiology: An Evangelical and Ecumenical Introduction*. Grand Rapids: Brazos, 2009.

Harrington, D. J. *Interpreting the New Testament: A Practical Guide*. Wilmington, DE: Michael Glazier, 1979.

Harris, W. V. *Interpretive Acts in Search of Meaning*. Oxford: Clarendon, 1988.

Harrison, E. F. *Acts: The Expanding Church*. Chicago: Moody, 1975.

Harrison, T. "'Prophecy in Reverse'? Herodotus and the Origins of History." In *Herodotus and His World*, edited by P. Derow and R. Parker, 237–56. Oxford: Oxford University Press, 2003.

Harvey, J. D. "Orality and Its Implications for Biblical Studies: Recapturing an Ancient Paradigm." *JETS* 45, no. 1 (2002): 99–109.

Haulotte, E. "La vie en communion, phase ultime de la Pentecôte, Acts 2,42–47." *Foi et Vie* 80, no. 1 (1981): 69–75.

Hays, J. D., C. M. Pate, E. R. Richards, W. D. Tucker, P. Vang, and S. Duvall. *The Story of Israel: A Biblical Theology*. Downers Grove, IL: InterVarsity, 2004.

Heath, M. "Theon and the History of the Progymnasmata." *GRBS* 43 (2002–03): 129–60.

Hedrick, C. "Realism in Western Narrative and the Gospel of Mark: A Prolegomenon." *JBL* 126, no. 2 (2007): 345–59.

Heil, J. P. *The Meal Scenes in Luke-Acts: An Audience-Oriented Approach*. Atlanta: Society of Biblical Literature, 1999.

Hemer, C. J. "Alexandria Troas." *TynBul* 26 (1975): 79–112.

———. *The Book of Acts in the Setting of Hellenistic History*. Tübingen: J. C. B. Mohr, 1989.

Henderson, I. H. "Quintilian and the Progymnasmata." *Antike und Abendland* 37 (1991): 82–99.

Hengel, M. "Tasks of New Testament Scholarship." *Bulletin for Biblical Research* 6 (1996): 67–86.

Hertig, P., and R. L. Gallagher. "Introduction: Background to Acts." In *Mission in Acts: Ancient Narratives in Contemporary Context*, edited by R. L. Gallagher and P. Hertig, 1–17. Maryknoll, NY: Orbis, 2004.

Hillman, T. P. "Authorial Statements, Narrative, and Character in Plutarch's Agesilaus-Pompeius." *GRBS* 35, no. 3 (1994): 255–80.

Hornblower, S. "Narratology and Narrative Techniques in Thucydides." In *Greek Historiography*, edited by S. Hornblower, 131–66. Oxford: Clarendon, 1996.

Hume, D. A. *The Early Christian Community: A Narrative Analysis of Acts 2:41–47 and 4:32–35*. Tübingen, Germany: Mohr Siebeck, 2011.

Inch, M. "Manifestation of the Spirit." In *The Living and Active Word of God: Studies in Honor of Samuel J. Schultz*, edited by M. Inch and R. Youngblood, 149–55. Winona Lake, IN: Eisenbrauns, 1983.

Jensen, I. L. *Independent Bible Study*. Chicago: Moody, 1963.

Jeremias, J. *The Eucharistic Words of Jesus*. Translated by N. Perrin. New York: Charles Scribner's Sons, 1966.

———. *Jerusalem in the Time of Jesus*. Translated by F. H. and C. H. Cave. Philadelphia: Fortress, 1967.

———. "Untersuchungen zum Quellenproblem der Apostelgeschichte." *ZTK* 36 (1937): 206–21.

Jervell, J. "The Future of the Past: Luke's Vision of Salvation History and Its Bearing on His Writing of History." In *History, Literature, and Society in the Book of Acts*, edited by B. Witherington, 104–26. New York: Cambridge University Press, 1996.

———. *Luke and the People of God: A New Look at Luke-Acts*. Minneapolis: Augsburg, 1972.

Johnson, D. E. *The Message of Acts in the History of Redemption*. Phillipsburg, NJ: P&R, 1997.

Johnson, L. T. *The Acts of the Apostles*. SP. Collegeville, MN: Michael Glazier, 1992.

———. *The Literary Function of Possessions in Luke-Acts*. Atlanta: Scholars, 1977.

———. "Luke-Acts." In *ABD*, edited by D. N. Freedman, 403–20. New York: Doubleday, 1992.

Joubert, S. J. "Die gesigpunt van die verteller en die funksie van die Jerusalemgemeente binne die 'opsommings' in Handelinge." *SK* 10 (1989): 21–35.

Joyce, P. "The Individual and the Community." In *Beginning Old Testament Study*, edited by J. Rogerson, J. Barton, D. J. A. Clines, and P. Joyce, 77–93. Philadelphia: Westminster, 1982.

Jüngst, J. *Die Quellen der Apostelgeschichte*. Gotha: Friedrich Andreas Perthes, 1895.

Kea, P. "Source Theories for the Acts of the Apostles." *Forum* 4, no. 1 (Spring 2001): 7–26.

Kearns, M. *Rhetorical Narratology*. Lincoln, NE: University of Nebraska Press, 1999.

Keegan, T. J. *Interpreting the Bible*. Mahwah, NJ: Paulist, 1985.

Kennedy, G. A. *New Testament Interpretation Through Rhetorical Criticism*. Chapel Hill: University of North Carolina Press, 1984.

———. *Quintilian*. New York: Twayne Publishers, 1969.

Kingsbury, J. D. *Matthew as Story*. Philadelphia: Fortress, 1988.

Kisirinya, S. K. "Re-Interpreting the Major Summaries (Acts 2:42–46; 4:43–35; 5:12–16)." *African Christian Studies* 18, no. 1 (2002): 67–74.

Kistemaker, S. J. "The Speeches in Acts." *CTR* 5, no. 1 (1990): 31–41.

Kodell, J. "The Word of God Grew: The Ecclesial Tendency of ΛΟΓΟΣ in Acts 1,7 [Sic Read 6,7]; 12,24; 19,20." *Bib* 55, no. 4 (1974): 505–19.

Koenig, J. *New Testament Hospitality: Partnership with Strangers as Promise and Mission.* Philadelphia: Fortress, 1985.

Krentz, E. *The Historical-Critical Method.* Philadelphia: Fortress, 1975.

Krieger, M. *A Window to Criticism: Shakespeare's Sonnets and Modern Poetics.* Princeton: Princeton University Press, 1964.

Krodel, G. A. *Acts.* Proclamation Commentaries. Philadelphia: Fortress, 1981.

Kurz, W. S. *Reading Luke-Acts: Dynamics of Biblical Narrative.* Louisville, KY: Westminster John Knox, 1993.

Laansma, J. C. "Lord's Day." In *DLNT*, edited by R. P. Martin and P. H. Davids, 679–86. Downers Grove, IL: InterVarsity, 1997.

Lach, J. "Katechese über die Kirche von Jerusalem in der Apostelgeschichte (2,42–47; 4,32–35; 5,12–16)." *ColT* 52, no. Supplement (1982): 141–53.

Ladd, G. E. *A Theology of the New Testament.* Grand Rapids: Eerdmans, 1974.

Lambrecht, J. "Paul's Farewell-Address at Miletus (Acts 20, 17–38)." In *Les Actes des Apôtres: Traditions, rédaction, théologie*, edited by J. Kremer, 307–37. Louvain: Louvain University Press, 1979.

Lampe, G. W. H. "Miracles in the Acts of the Apostles." In *Miracles: Cambridge Studies in Their Philosophy and History*, edited by C. F. D. Moule, 165–78. London: A. R. Mowbrays, 1965.

Lang, F. G. "Kompositionalyse des Markusevangeliums." *ZTK* 74 (1977): 1–24.

Larkin, W. J. *Acts.* CBC. Carol Stream, IL: Tyndale House, 2006.

Laughery, G. J. "Ricoeur on History, Fiction, and Biblical Hermeneutics." In *Behind the Text: History and Biblical Interpretation*, edited by C. Bartholomew, C. S. Evans, and M. Rae, 338–73. Grand Rapids: Zondervan, 2003.

Lawson, S. J. "The Priority of Biblical Preaching: An Expository Study of Acts 2:42–47." *BSac* 158 (April–June 2001): 198–217.

Levinskaya, I. *The Book of Acts in Its Diaspora Setting*. Grand Rapids: Eerdmans, 1996.

Levinson, B. M. "The Right Chorale: From the Poetics to the Hermeneutics of the Hebrew Bible." In *"Not in Heaven": Coherence and Complexity in Biblical Narrative*, edited by J. P. Rosenblatt and J. C. Sitterson, 129–53. Bloomington: Indiana University Press, 1991.

Liddell, H. G., and R. S. Scott. *LSJ*. Edited by H. S. Jones. Oxford: Clarendon, 1968.

Liederbach, M., and A. L. Reid. *The Convergent Church: Missional Worshipers in an Emerging Culture*. Grand Rapids: Kregel, 2009.

Liefeld, W. *New Testament Exposition*. Grand Rapids: Zondervan, 1984.

Lightfoot, J. *A Commentary on the New Testament from the Talmud and Hebraica*. Vol. 4: *Acts–1 Corinthians*. Peabody, MA: Hendrickson, 1979, orig. 1859.

Lightfoot, J. B. "Acts of the Apostles." In *Smith's Dictionary of the Bible*. Vol. 1, edited by H. B. Hackett, 25–43. Boston: Houghton Mifflin & Co., 1892.

———. "Discoveries Illustrating the Acts of the Apostles." In *Essays on Supernatural Religion*, 291–302. Cambridge: Cambridge University Press, 1889.

Lindemann, A. "The Beginnings of Christian Common Life in Jerusalem According to the Summaries in the Acts of the Apostles (Acts 2:42–47; 4:32–37; 5:12–16)." In *Common Life in the Early Church*, edited by J. Hills, 202–18. Harrisburg, PA: Trinity, 1998.

Liu, P. "Did the Lucan Jesus Desire Voluntary Poverty of His Followers?" *EvQ* 64, no. 4 (1992): 291–317.

Loney, A. C. "Narrative Structure and Verbal Aspect Choice in Luke." *Filología Neotestamentica* 18 (2005): 3–31.

Long, B. O. "Framing Repetitions in Biblical Historiography." *JBL* 106, no. 3 (1987): 385–99.

Long, V. P. "The Art of Biblical History." In *Foundations of Contemporary Interpretation*, edited by M. Silva, 281–429. Grand Rapids: Zondervan, 1996.

Longenecker, B. W. "Rome's Victory and God's Honour: The Jerusalem Temple and the Spirit of God in Lukan Theodicy." In *The Holy Spirit and Christian Origins: Essays in Honor of James*

D. G. Dunn, edited by G. N. Stanton, S. C. Barton, and B. W. Longenecker, 90–102. Grand Rapids: Eerdmans, 2004.

Longenecker, R. N. *The Acts of the Apostles*. EBC, vol. 10. Rev. ed., ed. T. Longman and D. E. Garland. Grand Rapids: Zondervan, 2007.

Longman, T. *Literary Approaches to Biblical Interpretation*. Grand Rapids: Zondervan, 1987.

Löschnigg, M. "Narratological Categories and the (Non-) Distinction Between Factual and Fictional Narratives." *Groupe de Recherches Anglo-Américaines de Tours* 21 (1999): 31–48.

Lüdemann, G. *The Acts of the Apostles: What Really Happened in the Earliest Days of the Church?* Amherst, NY: Prometheus, 2005.

MacMullen, R. *The Second Church: Popular Christianity A.D. 200–400*. Atlanta: Society of Biblical Literature, 2009.

Malas, W. H. "The Literary Structure of Acts: A Narratological Investigation into Its Arrangement, Plot, and Primary Themes." Ph.D. diss., Union Theological Seminary and Presbyterian School of Christian Education, 2001.

Malherbe, A. J. *Moral Exhortation: A Greco-Roman Sourcebook*. Philadelphia: Westminster, 1986.

———. *Social Aspects of Early Christianity*. Baton Rouge: LSU Press, 1977.

Malina, B. J., and J. H. Neyrey. "First-Century Personality: Dyadic, not Individual." In *The Social World of Luke-Acts*, edited by J. H. Neyrey, 67–96. Peabody, MA: Hendrickson, 1991.

Malina, B. J., and J. J. Pilch. *Social-Science Commentary on the Book of Acts*. Minneapolis: Fortress, 2008.

Marguerat, D. "The End of Acts (28.16–31) and the Rhetoric of Silence." In *Rhetoric and the New Testament: Essays from the 1992 Heidelberg Conference*, edited by S. E. Porter, 74–89. Sheffield: Sheffield Academic, 1993.

———. *The First Christian Historian: Writing the Acts of the Apostles*. Translated by K. McKinney, G. J. Laughery, and R. Bauckham. New York: Cambridge University Press, 2002.

———. "Luc-Actes entre Jérusalem et Rome: Un Procédé Lucanien de Double Signification." *NTS* 45, no. 1 (1999): 70–87.

Marshall, I. H. *Acts*. TNTC. Grand Rapids: Eerdmans, 1980.

———. "Acts in Current Study." *ExpTim* 115, no. 2 (2003): 49–52.

————. *The Acts of the Apostles*. New Testament Guides. Sheffield: Sheffield Academic, 2001.

————. *Beyond the Bible: Moving from Scripture to Theology*. Grand Rapids: Baker Academic, 2004.

————. "Historical Criticism." In *New Testament Interpretation: Essays on Principles and Method*, edited by I. H. Marshall, 126–38. Grand Rapids: Eerdmans, 1977.

————. *Luke: Historian and Theologian*. Grand Rapids: Zondervan, 1989.

————. *New Testament Theology: Many Witnesses, One Gospel*. Downers Grove, IL: InterVarsity, 2004.

Marshall, I. H., A. R. Millard, J. I. Packer, and D. J. Wiseman, eds. *New Bible Dictionary*. Downers Grove, IL: InterVarsity, 1996.

Marshall, I. H., and D. Peterson, eds. *Witness to the Gospel: The Theology of Acts*. Grand Rapids: Eerdmans, 1998.

Martin, F. "Monastic Community and the Summary Statements in Acts." In *Contemplative Studies: An Interdisciplinary Symposium*, edited by M. B. Pennington, 13–46. Washington, DC: Consortium, 1972.

Mattill, A. J. "The Jesus-Paul Parallels and the Purpose of Luke-Acts: H. H. Evans Reconsidered." *NovT* 17 (1975): 15–46.

Maxwell, K. R. "The Role of the Audience in Ancient Narrative: Acts as a Case Study." *ResQ* 48, no. 3 (2006): 171–80.

Maynard-Reid, P. U. "Samaria." In *DLNT*, edited by R. P. Martin and P. H. Davids, 1075–77. Downers Grove, IL: InterVarsity, 1997.

McCoy, W. J. "In the Shadow of Thucydides." In *History, Literature, and Society in the Book of Acts*, edited by B. Witherington, 3–32. New York: Cambridge University Press, 1996.

McDonald, A. H. "Herodotus on the Miraculous." In *Miracles: Cambridge Studies on Their Philosophy and History*, edited by C. F. D. Moule, 83–91. London: A. R. Mowbrays, 1965.

McDonald, L. M. "Antioch (Syria)." In *DNTB*, edited by C. A. Evans and S. E. Porter, 34–37. Downers Grove, IL: InterVarsity, 2000.

————. "Ephesus." In *DNTB*, edited by C. A. Evans and S. E. Porter, 318–21. Downers Grove, IL: InterVarsity, 2000.

McGee, D. B. "Sharing Possessions: A Study in Biblical Ethics." In *With Steadfast Purpose*, edited by N. H. Keathley, 163–78. Waco, TX: Baylor University Press, 1990.

McGuire, M. "The Rhetoric of Narrative: A Hermeneutic, Critical Theory." In *Narrative Thought and Narrative Language*, edited by B. K.

Britton and A. D. Pellegrini, 219–36. Hillsdale, NJ: Lawrence Erblaum Associates, 1989.

McIntyre, L. B. "Baptism and Forgiveness in Acts 2:38." *BSac* 153 (January–March 1996): 53–62.

McKeon, R. "Literary Criticism and the Concept of Imitation in Antiquity." In *Critics and Criticism: Ancient and Modern*, edited by R. S. Crane, 147–75. Chicago: University of Chicago, 1952.

McKnight, E. V. *The Bible and the Reader: An Introduction to Literary Criticism*. Philadelphia: Fortress, 1985.

————. "Literary Criticism." In *DJG*, edited by J. Green and S. McKnight, 473–81. Downers Grove, IL: InterVarsity, 1992.

Meadors, G. T. *Four Views on Moving Beyond the Bible to Theology*. Grand Rapids: Zondervan, 2009.

Mealand, D. L. "Community of Goods and Utopian Allusions in Acts II–IV." *JTS* 28, no. 1 (1977): 96–99.

Melbourne, B. L. "Acts 1:8 Re-Examined: Is Acts 8 Its Fulfillment?" *JRT* 57/58, no. 2/1/2 (2005): 1–18.

Menzies, R. P. *Empowered for Witness: The Spirit in Luke-Acts*. Sheffield: Sheffield Academic, 1994.

Metzger, B. M. *A Textual Commentary on the Greek New Testament*. Stuttgart: United Bible Societies, 1971.

Meyer, B. J. F., and G. E. Rice. "The Interaction of Reader Strategies and the Organization of Text." *Text* 2 (1982): 155–92.

Michiels, R. "The Model of Church in the First Christian Community of Jerusalem: Ideal and Reality." *Louvain Studies* 10 (1985): 303–23.

Minear, P. S. *Images of the Church in the New Testament*. Philadelphia: Westminster, 1960.

Miranda, J. P. *Communism in the Bible*. Translated by R. R. Barr. Maryknoll, NY: Orbis, 1982.

Mitchell, A. C. "The Social Function of Friendship in Acts 2:44–47 and 4:32–37." *JBL* 111, no. 2 (1992): 255–72.

Morton, A. Q., and G. H. C. MacGregor. *The Structure of Luke and Acts*. New York: Harper and Row, 1964.

Mowery, R. L. "Direct Statements Concerning God's Activity in Acts." In *1990 SBL Seminar Papers*, edited by D. J. Lull, 196–211. Atlanta: Scholars, 1990.

Moxnes, H. "The Social Context of Luke's Community." *Int* 48, no. 4 (1994): 379–89.

Mumo Kisau, P. "The Sharing of Goods with the Poor Is a Christian Imperative." *Africa Journal of Evangelical Theology* 19, no. 1 (2000): 25–36.

Munck, J. *The Acts of the Apostles*. AB. Garden City, NY: Doubleday, 1967.

Mundle, W., O. Hofius, and C. Brown. "Miracle, Sign, Wonder." In *Dictionary of New Testament Theology*, vol. 2, edited by C. Brown, 621–35. Grand Rapids: Zondervan, 1976.

Myllykoski, M. "Being There: The Function of the Supernatural in Acts 1–12." In *Wonders Never Cease: The Purpose of Narrating Miracle Stories in the New Testament and Its Religious Environment*, edited by C. Brown. M. Labahn and B. J. L. Peerbolte, 146–79. New York: T&T Clark, 2006.

Neil, W. *The Acts of the Apostles*. Grand Rapids: Eerdmans, 1973.

Neill, S., and T. Wright. *The Interpretation of the New Testament from 1861–1986*. New York: Oxford University Press, 1988.

Neirynck, F. "The Miracle Stories in the Acts of the Apostles." In *Les Actes des Apôtres: Traditions, rédaction, théologie*, edited by J. Kremer, 169–213. Louvain, Belgium: Leuven University Press, 1979.

Nelson, W. *Fact or Fiction: The Dilemma of the Renaissance Storyteller*. Cambridge: Harvard University Press, 1973.

Neyrey, J. H. "'Teaching You in Public and from House to House' (Acts 20.20): Unpacking a Cultural Stereotype." *JSNT* 26, no. 1 (2003): 69–102.

Nida, E., J. P. Louw, A. H. Snyman, and J. v. W. Cronje. *Style and Discourse: With Special Reference to the Text of the Greek New Testament*. Cape Town, South Africa: Bible Society, 1983.

Noorda, S. J. "Scene and Summary: A Proposal for Reading Acts 4, 32–5, 16." In *Les Actes des Apôtres: traditions, redaction et théologie*, edited by C. Brown. J. Kremer, 475–83. Louvain: Louvain University Press, 1979.

Norris, F. W. "Antioch of Syria." In *ABD*, edited by D. N. Freedman, 265–69. New York: Doubleday, 1992.

O'Brien, P. T. "Mission, Witness, and the Coming of the Spirit." *BBR* 9 (1999): 203–14.

———. "Prayer in Luke-Acts." *TynBul* 24 (1973): 111–27.

O'Connor, J. R. *St. Paul's Ephesus: Texts and Archeology*. Collegeville, MN: Liturgical, 2008.

O'Day, G. R. "Acts." In *The Women's Bible Commentary*, edited by C. A. Newsom and S. H. Ringe, 305–12. Louisville: Westminster John Knox, 1992.

O'Reilly, L. *Word and Sign in the Acts of the Apostles: A Study in Lukan Theology*. Rome: Editrice Pontifica Universita Gregoriana, 1987.

Öhler, M. "Die Jerusalemer Urgemeinde im Spiegel des antiken Vereinswesens." *NTS* 51, no. 3 (2005): 393–415.

Olsen, G. W. "The Image of the First Community of Christians at Jerusalem in the Time of Lanfranc and Anselm." In *Les Mutations Socio-Culturelles Au Tourant Des XI-XII Siècles*, edited by R. Foreville, 341–53. Paris: Éditions du Centre National de la Recherche Scientifique, 1984.

Onega, S., J. Angel, and G. Landa. "Introduction." In *Narratology: An Introduction*, edited by S. Onega, J. Angel, and G. Landa, 1–41. New York: Longman Group Ltd., 1996.

Orme, J. H. "Antioquía: Paradigma para la Iglesia y la Misión." *Kairos* 25 (1999): 29–36.

Osborne, G. R. *The Hermeneutical Spiral: A Comprehensive Introduction to Biblical Interpretation*. Downers Grove, IL: InterVarsity, 1991.

———. "Literary Theory and Biblical Interpretation." In *Words and the Word: Explorations in Biblical and Literary Theory*, edited by D. G. Firth and J. A. Grant, 17–50. Downers Grove, IL: InterVarsity, 2008.

———. "Redaction Criticism." In *DJG*, edited by J. B. Green, S. McKnight, 662–69. Downers Grove, IL: InterVarsity, 1992.

Ott, W. *Gebet und Heil: Die Bedeutung der Gebetspäranese in der lukanischen Theologie*, 125–29. Münich: n.p., 1965.

Panikulam, G. *Koinōnia in the New Testament: A Dynamic Expression of the Christian Life*. Rome: Biblical Institute, 1979.

Parker, J. *The Concept of Apokatastasis in Acts: A Study in Primitive Christian Theology*. Austin, TX: Scholars, 1978.

Parsons, M. C. *Acts*. Paideia: Commentaries on the New Testament. Grand Rapids: Baker, 2008.

———. "Christian Origins and Narrative Openings: The Sense of a Beginning in Acts 1–5." *RevExp* 87 (1990): 403–22.

————. "Luke and the Progymnasmata: A Preliminary Investigation into the Preliminary Exercises." In *Contextualizing Acts: Lukan Narrative and Greco-Roman Discourse*, edited by T. C. Penner and C. V. Stichele, 43–63. Atlanta: Society of Biblical Literature, 2003.

Patzia, A. G. *The Emergence of the Church: Context, Growth, Leadership, & Worship*. Downers Grove, IL: IVP Academic, 2001.

Pearson, B. W. R. "New Testament Literary Criticism." In *Handbook to Exegesis of the New Testament*, edited by S. E. Porter, 241–66. Leiden: Brill Academic, 2002.

Pelikan, J. *Acts*. BTCB. Grand Rapids: Brazos, 2005.

Penner, T. "Reconfiguring the Rhetorical Study of Acts: Reflections on the Method in and Learning of a Progymnastic Poetics." *PRSt* 30, no. 4 (2003): 425–39.

Perkins, P. "Crisis in Jerusalem: Narrative Criticism in NTS." *TS* 50 (1989): 296–313.

Pervo, R. I. *Acts*. Hermeneia. Minneapolis: Fortress, 2009.

Pesch, R. *Die Apostelgeschichte, Apg. 1–12*. Köln: Benzinger, 1986.

Peterson, D. *The Acts of the Apostles*. PNTC. Grand Rapids: Eerdmans, 2009.

————. "Luke's Theological Enterprise: Integration and Intent." In *Witness to the Gospel: The Theology of Acts*, edited by I. H. Marshall and D. Peterson, 521–44. Grand Rapids: Eerdmans, 1998.

Phillips, T. E. "Paul as a Role Model in Acts: The 'We' Passages in Acts 16 and Beyond." In *Acts and Ethics*, edited by T. E. Phillips, 64–78. Sheffield: Sheffield Academic, 2005.

————. "Reading Recent Readings of Issues of Wealth and Poverty in Luke and Acts." In *Acts Within Diverse Frames of Reference*, 78–117. Macon, GA: Mercer University Press, 2009.

Plymale, S. F. "Luke's Theology of Prayer." In *SBL 1990 Seminar Papers*, edited by D. L. Lull. Atlanta: Scholars, 1990.

Polhill, J. *Acts*. NAC. Nashville: B&H, 1992.

Poorthuis, M., and J. Schwartz, eds. *Saints and Role Models in Judaism and Christianity*. Leiden, Netherlands: Brill, 2004.

Porter, S. E. "Greek Grammar and Syntax." In *The Face of NTS: A Survey of Recent Research*, edited by S. McKnight and G. R. Osborne, 76–103. Grand Rapids: Baker, 2004.

———. "Literary Approaches to the New Testament: From Formalism
    to Deconstruction and Back." In *Approaches to New Testament
    Study*, edited by S. E. Porter and D. Tombs, 77–128. Sheffield:
    Sheffield Academic, 1995.

———. "Scripture Justifies Mission: The Use of the Old Testament in
    Luke-Acts." In *Hearing the Old Testament in the New Testament*,
    edited by S. E. Porter, 104–26. Grand Rapids: Eerdmans, 2006.

Powell, M. A. *The Bible and Modern Literary Criticism: A Critical
    Assessment*. New York: Greenwood, 1992.

———. "Narrative Criticism." In *Hearing the New Testament: Strategies
    for Interpretation*, edited by J. B. Greed. Grand Rapids: Eerdmans,
    2010.

———. "Toward a Narrative-Critical Understanding of Luke." *Int* 48,
    no. 4 (1994): 341–46.

———. *What Are They Saying About Acts?* New York: Paulist, 1991.

———. *What Is Narrative Criticism?* Minneapolis: Fortress, 1990.

Praeder, S. M. "Jesus-Paul, Peter-Paul, and Jesus-Peter Parallelisms
    in Luke-Acts." In *Society of Biblical Literature 1984 Seminar
    Papers*, 23–39. Chico, CA: Scholars, 1984.

Price, B. J. "Paradeigma and Exemplum in Ancient Rhetorical Theory."
    Ph.D. diss., University of California, 1975.

Prieur, J. M. "Actes 2, 42 et le Culte Réformé." *Foi et Vie* 94, no. 2
    (1995): 61–72.

Prince, G. *A Dictionary of Narratology*. Lincoln: University of Nebraska
    Press, 1987.

———. "Introduction to the Study of the Narratee." In *Narratology: An
    Introduction*, edited by S. Onega, J. Angel, and G. Landa, 190–
    202. New York: Longman Group Ltd., 1996.

———. *Narratology: The Form and Functioning of Narrative*. Berlin:
    Walter de Gruyter, 1982.

———. "Surveying Narratology." In *What Is Narratology?: Questions
    and Answers Regarding the Status of a Theory*, edited by T. Kindt
    and H. H. Müller, 1–16. Berlin: Walter de Gruyter, 2003.

Pummer, R. "New Evidence for Samaritan Christianity?" *CBQ* 41, no. 1
    (1979): 98–117.

Rabinowitz, P. J. *Before Reading: Narrative Conventions and the Politics
    of Reading*. Ithaca, NY: Cornell University Press, 1987.

Rah, S. C. *The Next Evangelicalism: Freeing the Church from Western Cultural Captivity*. Downers Grove, IL: InterVarsity, 2009.

Rapske, B. "Opposition to the Plan of God and Persecution." In *Witness to the Gospel: The Theology of Acts*, edited by I. H. Marshall and D. Peterson, 235–56. Grand Rapids: Eerdmans, 1998.

Reed, A. Y. "The Construction and Subversion of Patriarchal Perfection: Abraham and Exemplarity in Philo, Josephus, and the Testament of Abraham." *JSJ* 40 (2009): 185–212.

Reinhardt, W. "The Population Size of Jerusalem and the Numerical Growth of the Jerusalem Church." In *The Book of Acts in Its Palestinian Setting*, edited by R. Bauckham, 237–65. Grand Rapids: Eerdmans, 1995.

Resseguie, J. L. *Narrative Criticism of the New Testament*. Grand Rapids: Baker Academic, 2005.

Reumann, J. "One Lord, One Faith, One God, but Many House Churches." In *Common Life in the Early Church*, edited by J. V. Hill, 106–17. Harrisburg, PA: Trinity, 1998.

Rhoads, D. "Narrative Criticism and the Gospel of Mark." *JAAR* 50 (1982): 411–34.

———. "Narrative Criticism: Practices and Prospects." In *Characterization in the Gospels: Reconceiving Narrative Criticism*, edited by D. Rhoads and K. Syreeni, 264–85. Sheffield: Sheffield Academic, 1999.

Rhoads, D., and D. Michie. *Mark as Story: An Introduction to the Narrative of a Gospel*. Philadelphia: Fortress, 1982.

Richardson, S. *The Homeric Narrator*. Nashville: Vanderbilt University Press, 1990.

Ricoeur, P. "The Time of Narrating (Erzählzeit) and Narrated Time (Erzählt)." In *Narratology: An Introduction*, edited by S. Onega, J. Angel, and G. Landa, 129–42. New York: Longman Group Ltd., 1996.

Rimmon-Kenan, S. *Narrative Fiction: Contemporary Poetics*. New York: Methuen & Co., 1983.

Rius-Camps, J. "Els tres sumaris dels Fets dels Apòstols (Ac 2,41–47; 4,32–5,16 i 19,11–19)." *Revista catalana de teología* 14 (1989): 243–56.

————. "Las variantes de la Recensión Occidental de los Hechos de los
    Apóstoles (VI: Hch 2,41–47)." *Filología Neotestamentaria* 8
    (1995): 199–208.
Robbins, V. K. "The Claims of the Prologues and Greco-Roman Rhetoric:
    The Prefaces to Luke and Acts in Light of Greco-Roman Rhetorical
    Strategies." In *Jesus and the Heritage of Israel: Luke's Narrative
    Claim upon Israel's Legacy*, edited by D. P. Moessner, 63–83.
    Harrisburg, PA: Trinity, 1999.
————. *Exploring the Texture of Texts: A Guide to Socio-Rhetorical
    Interpretation*. Valley Forge: Trinity, 1996.
————. *The Tapestry of Early Christian Discourse: Rhetoric, Society, and
    Ideology*. London: Routledge, 1996.
Robertson, A. T. "Acts of the Apostles." In *The International Standard
    Bible Encyclopedia*. Vol. 1, edited by J. Orr, 39–48. Chicago: The
    Howard-Severance Company, 1915.
————. *A Grammar of the Greek New Testament in the Light of Historical
    Research*. Nashville: Broadman, 1934.
Roller, M. B. "Exemplarity in Roman Culture: The Examples of Horatio
    Cocles and Cloelia." *CP* 99, no. 1 (2004): 1–56.
Rosner, B. S. "The Progress of the Word." In *Witness to the Gospel: The
    Theology of Acts*, edited by I. H. Marshall and D. Peterson, 215–
    33. Grand Rapids: William B. Eerdmans, 1998.
Russell, D. A. *Criticism in Antiquity*. Berkley: University of California
    Press, 1981.
Ryken, L. *Windows to the World: Literature in Christian Perspective*.
    Grand Rapids: Zondervan, 1985.
Samkutty, V. J. *The Samaritan Mission in Acts*. New York: T&T Clark,
    2006.
Satterthwaite, P. E. "Acts Against the Background of Classical Rhetoric."
    In *The Book of Acts in Its Ancient Literary Setting*, edited by B. W.
    Winter and A. D. Clarke, 337–79. Grand Rapids: Eerdmans, 1993.
Schaberg, J. "Luke." In *The Women's Bible Commentary*, edited by C. A.
    Newsom and S. H. Ringe, 275–92. Louisville: Westminster John
    Knox, 1992.
Schildgen, B. D. *Crisis and Continuity: Time in the Gospel of Mark*.
    Sheffield: Sheffield Academic, 1998.
Schmeling, G. "The Spectrum of Narrative: Authority of the Author." In
    Ancient Fiction and Early Christian Narrative, edited by R. F.

Hock, J. B. Chance, and J. Perkins, 19–29. Atlanta: Scholars, 1998.

Schmidt, D. D. "The Jesus Tradition in the Common Life of Early Christian Communities." In *Common Life in the Early Church*, edited by J. V. Hill. Harrisburg: Trinity, 1998.

Schneider, G. *Die Apostelgeschichte*. Vol. 1 of *Herder's Theologischer Kommentar zum Neuen Testament*. Freiburg: Herder, 1980.

Scholes, R., J. Phelan, and R. Kellogg. *The Nature of Narrative*. New York: Oxford University Press, 2006.

Schwartz, D. R. "Non-Joining Sympathizers [Acts 5.13–15]." *Bib* 64 (1983): 550–55.

Scott, J. J. "The Church's Progress to the Council of Jerusalem According to the Book of Acts." *BBR* 7 (1997): 205–24.

Seccombe, D. P. "The New People of God." In *Witness to the Gospel: The Theology of Acts*, edited by I. H. Marshall and D. Peterson, 349–72. Grand Rapids: Eerdmans, 1998.

———. *Possessions and the Poor in Luke-Acts*. Linz: Fuchs, 1982.

Sheeley, S. M. "Getting Into the Act(s): Narrative Presence in the 'We' Sections." *PRSt* 26, no. 2 (1999): 203–20.

———. "Narrative Asides and Narrative Authority in Luke-Acts." *BTB* 18 (1988): 102–7.

———. "The Narrator in the Gospels: Developing a Model." *PRSt* 16 (1989): 213–23.

Shipp, B. "George Kennedy's Influence on Rhetorical Interpretation of the Acts of the Apostles." In *Words Well Spoken: George Kennedy's Rhetoric of the New Testament*, edited by C. C. Black and D. F. Watson, 107–23. Waco, TX: Baylor University Press, 2008.

———. *Paul the Reluctant Witness: Power and Weakness in Luke's Portrayal*. Eugene, OR: Cascade, 2005.

Sloan, R. B. "'Signs and Wonders': A Rhetorical Clue to the Pentecost Discourse." In *With Steadfast Purpose*, edited by N. H. Keathley, 145–62. Waco, TX: Baylor University Press, 1990.

Sloyan, G. S. "The Samaritans in the New Testament." *Hor* 10, no. 1 (1983): 7–21.

Soards, M. L. *The Speeches in Acts: Their Content, Context, and Concerns*. Louisville: Westminster/John Knox, 1994.

Southwell, A. "German and British Approaches to Acts Research: A Comparative Study of F. C. Baur, Ernst Troeltsch, and William Ramsay." Th.M. thesis, Covenant Theological Seminary, 1994.

Spencer, F. S. *Journeying Through Acts: A Literary-Cultural Reading.* Peabody, MA: Hendrickson, 2004.

Squires, J. T. "The Plan of God." In *Witness to the Gospel: The Theology of Acts*, edited by I. H. Marshall and D. Peterson, 19–39. Grand Rapids: Eerdmans, 1998.

Stagg, F. *The Book of Acts: The Early Struggle for an Unhindered Gospel.* Nashville: Broadman, 1955.

Stambaugh, J. E., and D. L. Balch. *The New Testament in Its Social Environment.* Philadelphia: Westminster, 1986.

Stamps, D. L. "Rhetorical and Narratological Criticism." In *Handbook to Exegesis of the New Testament*, edited by S. E. Porter, 219–39. Leiden: Brill Academic, 2002.

Stanton, G. R. "Hellenism." In *DNTB*, edited by C. A. Evans and S. E. Porter, 464–73. Downers Grove, IL: InterVarsity, 2000.

Stein, R. H. "Baptism in Luke-Acts." In *Believer's Baptism: Sign of the New Covenant in Christ*, edited by T. R. Schreiner, S. D. Wright. Nashville: B&H Academic, 2006.

———. "The Benefits of an Author-Oriented Approach to Hermeneutics." *JETS* 44, no. 3 (2001): 451–66.

———. *Gospels and Tradition: Studies on the Redaction of the Synoptic Gospels.* Grand Rapids: Baker, 1991.

Stenschke, C. W. *Luke's Portrait of Gentiles Prior to Their Coming to Faith.* Tübingen: Mohr Siebeck, 1999.

Sterling, G. E. "Athletes of Virtue: An Analysis of the Summaries in Acts (2:41–47; 4:32–35; 5:12–16)." *Journal of Biblical Studies* 113, no. 4 (1994): 679–96.

Sternberg, M. *The Poetics of Biblical Narrative: Ideological Literature and the Drama of Reading.* Bloomington: Indiana University Press, 1985.

Strathman, H. "μάρτυς, ετ αλ." In *TDNT*. Vol. 4, edited by G. Kittel and G. Friederich, 474–514. Translated by G. W. Bromiley. Grand Rapids: Eerdmans, 1942.

Taeger, J. W. *Der Mensch und sein Heil: Studien zum Bild des Menschen und zur Sicht der Bekehrung bei Lukas.* Gütersloh: Gütersloher Verlagshaus Gerd Mohn, 1982.

Talbert, C. H. "Luke-Acts." In *The New Testament and Its Modern Interpreters*, edited by E. J. Epp and G. W. MacRae, 297–320. Philadelphia: Fortress, 1989.

———. "The Place of the Resurrection in the Theology of Luke." *Int* 46, no. 1 (1992): 19–30.

———. *Reading Acts: A Literary and Theological Commentary on the Acts of the Apostles*. New York: The Crossroads Publishing Co., 1997.

———. *Reading Luke-Acts in the Mediterranean Milieu*. Leiden: Brill Academic, 2003.

Tannehill, R. C. "The Composition of Acts 3–5: Narrative Development and Echo Effect." In *Society of Biblical Literature 1984 Seminar Papers*, edited by K. H. Richards, 217–40. Chico, CA: Scholars, 1984.

———. "Do the Ethics of Acts Include the Ethical Teaching in Luke?" In *Acts and Ethics*, edited by T. E. Phillips, 109–22. Sheffield: Sheffield Academic, 2005.

———. *The Narrative Unity of Luke-Acts: A Literary Interpretation: Volume 1: The Gospel According to Luke*. Philadelphia and Minneapolis: Fortress, 1986.

———. *The Narrative Unity of Luke-Acts: A Literary Interpretation, Volume 2: The Acts of the Apostles*. Minneapolis: Fortress, 1990.

———. *The Shape of Luke's Story: Essays on Luke-Acts*. Eugene, OR: Cascade, 2005.

Taylor, J. "The Community of Goods among the First Christians and among the Essenes." In *Historical Perspectives: From the Hasmoneans to Bar Kokhba in Light of the Dead Sea Scrolls*, edited by D. Goodblatt, A. Pinnick, and D. R. Schwartz, 147–61. Leiden: Brill, 2001.

———. "The Community of Jesus' Disciples." *PIBA* 21 (1998): 25–32.

Thielmann, F. *Theology of the New Testament: A Canonical and Synthetic Approach*. Grand Rapids: Zondervan, 2005.

Thiselton, A. C. *Hermeneutics: An Introduction*. Grand Rapids: Eerdmans, 2009.

Thomas, N. E. "The Church at Antioch: Crossing Racial, Cultural, and Class Barriers." In *Mission in Acts: Ancient Narratives in Contemporary Context*, edited by R. L. Gallagher and P. Hertig, 144–56. Maryknoll, NY: Orbis, 2004.

Thompson, A. J. *One Lord, One People: The Unity of the Church in Acts in Its Literary Setting*. New York: T&T Clark, 2008.

Thompson, R. P. *Keeping the Church in Its Place: The Church as Narrative Character in Acts*. New York: T&T Clark, 2006.

Thornton, T. C. G. "Continuing Steadfast in Prayer." *Expository Times* 83, no. 1 (1971): 23–24.

Tolmie, D. F. *Narratology and Biblical Narratives: A Practical Guide*. Bethesda, MD: International Scholars, 1999.

Travis, S. H. "Form Criticism." In *New Testament Interpretation: Essays on Principles and Methods*, edited by I. H. Marshall, 153–64. Grand Rapids: Eerdmans, 1977.

Trebilco, P. *Self-designations and Group Identity in the New Testament*. Cambridge, UK: Cambridge University Press, 2012.

Treier, D. J. *Introducing Theological Interpretation of Scripture: Recovering a Christian Practice*. Grand Rapids: Baker Academic, 2008.

Tuckett, C. *Reading the New Testament: Methods of Interpretation*. Philadelphia: Fortress, 1987.

Turner, C. H. "Chronology of the New Testament." In *Hastings Dictionary of the Bible*, 1.403–25. New York: Charles Scribner's Sons, 1900.

Turner, M. "The Work of the Holy Spirit in Luke-Acts." *WW* 23, no. 2 (2003): 146–53.

Twelftree, G. H. *People of the Spirit: Exploring Luke's View of the Church*. Grand Rapids: Baker, 2009.

———. "Signs, Wonders, Miracles." In *DPL*, edited by G. F. Hawthorne and R. P. Martin, 875–77. Downers Grove, IL: InterVarsity, 1993.

Tyson, J. B. "Authority in Acts." *Bible Today* 30, no. 5 (1992): 279–83.

———. "From History to Rhetoric and Back: Assessing New Trends in Acts Studies." In *Contextualizing Acts: Lukan Narrative and Greco-Roman Discourse*, edited by T. Penner and V. S. Caroline, 23–42. Atlanta: Society of Biblical Literature, 2003.

———. "The Legacy of F. C. Baur and Recent Studies of Acts." *Forum* 4, no. 1 (Spring 2001): 125–44.

van den Hoek, A. "Widening the Eye of the Needle: Wealth and Poverty in the Works of Clement of Alexandria." In *Wealth and Poverty in Early Church and Society*, edited by S. Holman, 67–75. Grand Rapids: Baker Academic, 2008.

van der Horst, P. W. "Hellenistic Parallels to the Acts of the Apostles (2.1–47)." *Journal for the Study of the New Testament* 24 (1985): 49–60.

————. *Jews and Christians in Their Graeco-Roman Context: Selected Essays on Early Judaism, Samaritinism, Hellenism, and Christianity.* Tübingen: Mohr Siebeck, 2006.

————. "Peter's Shadow: The Religio-Historical Background of Acts v. 15." *NTS* 23, no. 2 (1977): 204–12.

————. "Shadow." In *ABD*. Vol. 5, edited by D. N. Freedman, 1148–50. New York: Doubleday, 1992.

Vanhoozer, K. J. "Introduction: What Is the Theological Interpretation of the Bible?" In *Theological Interpretation of the New Testament*, edited by K. J. Vanhoozer, D. J. Treier, and N. T. Wright, 13–26. Grand Rapids: Baker Academic, 2008.

————. *Is There a Meaning in This Text? The Bible, the Reader, and the Morality of Literary Knowledge.* Grand Rapids: Zondervan, 1998.

Varickasseril, J. "The Lukan Portrait of the Early Church: A Study of the Major Summaries in the Acts of the Apostles." *Mission Today* 7 (2005): 40–50.

————. "Short Summaries in the Acts of the Apostles: Lukan Presentation of Features That Are the Hallmark of the Early Church." *Mission Today* 6, no. 4 (2004): 377–95.

Vaughan, C. *Acts.* Grand Rapids: Zondervan, 1974.

Versnel, H. J. "Miracles." In *OCD*, edited by S. Hornblower and A. Spawforth, 989. New York: Oxford University Press, 1996.

Viola, F. *Reimagining Church: Pursuing the Dream of Organic Christianity.* Colorado Springs: David C. Cook, 2008.

von Baer, H. *Der Heilige Geist in den Lukasschriften.* Stuttgart: W. Kohlhammer, 1926.

Wainwright, G. "Lord's Supper, Love Feast." In *DLNT*, edited by R. P. Martin and P. H. Davids, 686–94. Downers Grove, IL: InterVarsity, 1997.

Wall, R. W. "The Acts of the Apostles." In *NIB*. Vol. 10, edited by L. E. Keck, 3–368. Nashville: Abingdon, 2002.

Walsh, R. "Reconstructing the New Testament Churches: The Place of Acts." In *With Steadfast Purpose: Essays on Acts in Honor of Henry Jackson Flanders*, edited by N. H. Keathley, 309–25. Waco, TX: Baylor University Press, 1990.

Walton, S. "Acts: Many Questions, Many Answers." In *The Face of NTS: A Survey of Recent Research*, edited by S. McKnight and G. R. Osborne, 229–50. Grand Rapids: Baker Academic, 2004.

———. "Acts." In *Theological Interpretation of the New Testament*, edited by K. J. Vanhoozer, D. J. Treier, and N. T. Wright, 74–83. Grand Rapids: Baker Academic, 2005.

———. "Primitive Communism in Acts? Does Acts Present the Community of Goods (Acts 2:44–45; 4:32–35) as Mistaken?" *EvQ* 80, no. 2 (2008): 99–111.

———. "Ὁμοθυμαδόν in Acts: Co-location, Common Action, or 'Of One Heart and Mind'?" In *The New Testament in Its First Century Setting*, edited by P. J. Williams, A. D. Clarke, P. M. Head, and D. Instone-Brewer, 89–105. Grand Rapids: Eerdmans, 2004.

Wansbrough, H. "The Book of Acts and History." *DRev* 113 (1995): 96–103.

Watson, D. F. "The Influence of George Kennedy on Rhetorical Criticism of the New Testament." In *Words Well Spoken: George Kennedy's Rhetoric of the New Testament*, edited by C. C. Black and D. F. Watson, 41–61. Waco, TX: Baylor University Press, 2008.

———. "Paul's Speech to the Ephesian Elders (Acts 20:17–38) Epideictic Rhetoric of Farewell." In *Persuasive Artistry: Studies in New Testament Rhetoric in Honor of George A. Kennedy*, edited by D. F. Watson, 184–208. Sheffield: Sheffield Academic, 1991.

———. *The Rhetoric of the New Testament: A Bibliographic Survey*. Blandford Forum, UK: Deo, 2006.

———. "Why We Need Socio-Rhetorical Criticism and What It Might Look Like." In *Rhetorical Criticism and the Bible*, edited by S. E. Porter and D. L. Stamps, 129–57. New York: Sheffield Academic, 2002.

Watson, F. "Bible, Theology and the University: A Response to Philip Davies." *JSOT* 71 (1996): 3–16.

Wenk, M. *Community-Forming Power: The Socio-Ethical Role of the Spirit in Luke-Acts*. Sheffield: Sheffield Academic, 2000.

Whittaker, M. "Signs and Wonders: The Pagan Background." *SE* 5 (1968): 155–58.

Wiarda, T. *Interpreting Gospel Narratives: Scenes, People, and Theology*. Nashville: B&H Academic, 2010.

Wilder, A. N. *The Bible and the Literary Critic*. Minneapolis: Fortress, 1991.

Williams, C. S. C. *A Commentary on the Acts of the Apostles*. HNTC. New York: Harper & Brothers, 1957.

Winter, B. W. "Acts and Food Shortages." In *The Book of Acts in Its Graeco-Roman Setting*, edited by D. W. J. Gill and C. Gempf, 59–78. Grand Rapids: Eerdmans, 1994.

_____. "Official Proceedings and the Forensic Speeches in Acts 24–26." In *The Book of Acts in Its Ancient Literary Setting*, edited by B. W. Winter and A. D. Clarke, 305–36. Grand Rapids: Eerdmans, 1993.

Witherington, B. *The Acts of the Apostles: A Socio-Rhetorical Commentary*. Grand Rapids: Eerdmans, 1998.

_____. *What's in the Word? Rethinking the Socio-Rhetorical Character of the New Testament*. Waco, TX: Baylor University Press, 2009.

Wooten, C. W. "Dionysius of Halicarnassus and Hermogenes on the Style of Demosthenes." *AJP* 110, no. 4 (1989): 576–88.

Wright, N. T. *The New Testament and the People of God*. Minneapolis: Fortress, 1992.

Yao, S. "Dismantling Social Barriers through Table Fellowship." In *Mission in Acts: Ancient Narratives in Contemporary Context*, edited by R. L. Gallagher and P. Hertig, 29–36. Maryknoll, NY: Orbis, 2004.

Yarbrough, R. W. "Biblical Theology." In *Evangelical Dictionary of Biblical Theology*, edited by W. A. Elwell, 61–66. Grand Rapids: Baker, 1996.

Yarnell III, M. B. "The Person and Work of the Holy Spirit." In *A Theology for the Church*, edited by D. L. Akin, 604–84. Nashville: B&H Academic, 2007.

Zimmerli, W., and H. Conzelmann. "χάρις, ετ αλ." In *TDNT*, edited by G. Kittel and G. Friedrich. Translated and edited by G. W. Bromiley, 9.372–411. Grand Rapids: Eerdmans.

Zimmermann, H. "Die Sammelberichte der Apostelgeschichte." *BZ* 5 (1961): 71–82.

Name Index

Subject Index

A

Ananias and Sapphira   *71, 94, 97, 105, 112, 151*
Anna   *78, 156*
Antioch, Syrian   *121, 123*
Apollos   *125*
apostles
    doctrine   *67*
    hands   *103, 120, 126*
    leadership/authority   *67, 73, 93, 152*
    teaching   *55, 66–67, 122, 124–25, 127–28, 130, 133, 135, 137, 147–49, 161*
Apostles' Creed   *39*
Aristotle   *42, 71, 74, 87*
aspect. *See* imperfect verb form
assimilation of new believers   *147*
authorial intention   *28–29*

B

baptism of repentance   *63–64, 126, 146–47*
Barnabas   *93, 113, 122, 124, 161*
believers, the   *66*
biblical authority   *147–49*
biblical theology   *140–41*
breaking bread   *68–70, 77, 133–34, 137, 150, 166*

C

chiasm   *40, 50*
Christian basilicas   *77*
Christian scholarship   *29*
Christians, first called in Antioch   *123–24*
church
    commitment to   *67, 122, 149, 153*
    God grows   *82–83, 106, 142, 144*

Holy Spirit creates   *1, 62, 83, 92, 124, 146*
    local   *7, 30, 82–83, 99, 135, 147, 157, 163, 166*
church architecture, pre-Constantine   *77*
church life
    in Antioch   *55, 121–25, 161*
    in Ephesus   *125–31*
    in Iconium   *135*
    in Jerusalem   *22, 51, 55, 160*
    in Philippi   *135*
    in Samaria   *119–20, 160–61*
    in Troas   *131–34*
Cicero   *35, 87*
city, love for the   *79–80, 132, 138, 145, 156*
Clement of Alexandria   *97*
Clement of Rome   *13*
commentaries on Acts   *20, 163, 167*
commitments new believers make   *65–66, 147*
communism, Christian   *75, 97, 153*
compositional patterns. *See* narrative technique(s)
Constantine   *77*
Cornelius   *77, 122, 126, 161*
costly membership   *104–5, 138, 159*

D

Dead Sea Scrolls   *96*
defocalization   *43, 45, 47–48, 57*
deliberative rhetoric   *129*
Didache   *70, 73*
diegesis   *42–43*
discourse time   *44–48, 57*
diversity, respect for differences   *160–62*
divine action/sovereignty   *58, 81–82, 111, 122, 124, 130, 143–44, 153, 157*
duration   *44*

Scripture Index

Genesis
1:2   *143*
1:27   *107*
1:28   *58*
4:3   *94*
12:2   *106, 145*
12:7   *93*
15:5   *58*
17:2   *58*
26:4   *58*
26:24   *58*
28:14   *58*
49   *129*

Exodus
4:1–8   *112, 152*
4:21   *112*
4:30   *112, 152*
7:3   *152*
7:3–4   *112*
10:1–2   *112*
11:9   *112*
11:10   *112*
15:11   *112*
18:11   *112*
23:10–11   *92*
24:9–11   *69*
34:10   *112*

Leviticus
19:9–10   *92*
19:18   *80*
23:22   *92, 124*
25:1–43   *92*
25:23   *98*
25:25–27   *93*
25:35   *124*
25:35–38   *92*

Deuteronomy
4:34   *112*
6:5   *88*

6:22   *73, 112*
7:19   *73, 112*
15:1–11   *92*
15:4   *92, 124, 154*
26:8   *112*
28   *37*
29:3   *112*
29:29   *157*
33   *129*
33:3   *93*
34:11   *112*

Joshua
3:5   *112*
14:1–5   *93*
24:1–28   *129*

Judges
6:1–10   *37*
6:13   *112*
6:34   *143*
10:6–16   *37*
13:24   *58*

Ruth
3:4   *93*

1 Samuel
2:21   *58*
2:26   *58*
3:19   *58*
12   *129*
16:13   *143*
18:14   *58*
25:24   *93*

2 Samuel
3:1   *58*

1 Kings
4:20–24   *50*
5:3   *93*

10:23–29   *50*
17:17–24   *134*

2 Kings
2:19–25   *152*
2:43   *134*
4:18–37   *134*
5:15–16   *134*
17:7–23   *37*
20:10   *134*
21:1–15   *37*

1 Chronicles
16:12   *112*

2 Chronicles
7:13–14   *37*
9:22–28   *50*
17:12   *58*
30:12   *88*
35:7   *74*
36:15–16   *44*

Nehemiah
9:10   *73, 112*
9:17   *112*

Psalms
2:2   *83*
4:9   *83*
8:6   *93*
16:8–11   *142*
20:4   *145*
24:1   *98*
33:4   *83*
36:38   *83*
45:5   *93*
47:3   *93*
77:48   *74*
78:43   *112*
105:27   *112*
110:1   *142*
135:9   *73, 112*